UNOBTRUSIVE TESTING
AND LIBRARY REFERENCE SERVICES

by
PETER HERNON
Simmons College

and

CHARLES R. McCLURE
Syracuse University

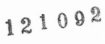

ABLEX PUBLISHING COMPANY
NORWOOD, NEW JERSEY

Library of Congress Cataloging-in-Publication Data

Unobtrusive testing and library reference services.

Bibliography: p.
Includes indexes.
1. Reference services (Libraries) — Evaluation.   I. Hernon, Peter.
II. McClure, Charles R.
Z711.U57   1987   025.5'2   86-28736
ISBN 0-89391-383-9

Ablex Publishing Corporation
355 Chestnut Street
Norwood, New Jersey 07648

LIST OF TABLES

CONTENTS

LIST OF FIGURES

PREFACE

In 1983, the American Library Association published *Improving the Quality of Reference Service for Government Publications*. This book extended unobtrusive testing to a previously unexamined area — the reference service that documents personnel in academic depository libraries provide for factual and bibliographic questions. We tested 17 libraries in the Northeast and Southwest associated with institutions offering, as their highest degrees, the baccalaureuate, the master's, and the doctorate.

Many in the library community have expressed concern about the findings that the general public might experience problems in gaining access to some depository collections and that documents staff members correctly answered a low percentage (37) of test questions and infrequently engaged in referral, either internal or external to the library. In a number of instances documents personnel admitted that they did not know the answer to the question and terminated the interview, without suggesting referral. Further, the interpersonal communications skills of some personnel are limited and library staff tested were abrasive in their dealings with the public.

Since publication of the book, it is still difficult for

> senior policy makers to determine what should constitute rational standards for government publications or a national program for library and information services in this area; nor can front-line practitioners determine where their institution stands in comparison to other depository libraries or to accepted standards (Richardson, Frisch, and Hall, 1980).

The initial study has not lead to generation of a sufficient body of descriptive research in the documents field from which policy and decision making can proceed. However, more unobtrusive testing has been conducted in the general reference area and the commonality of study findings have clear implications for library administrators, the Government Printing Office, and the Joint Committee on Printing, U.S. Congress.

The research reported in this book complements the previous work. Again, library personnel were tested unobtrusively. Chapters 2 and 3 provide a comparative analysis between reference service in two types of libraries. These chapters present results from an unobtrusive test of academic and public library personnel assigned to a depository department/collection and to a general reference department/collection. Further, the 26 libraries were located in three geographical regions of the United States—the Midwest, South, and West. Chapter 4 reports an experimental study intended to provide libraries with a means of self-diagnosis and potential improvement in the quality of their reference services. Thus, this book presents two separate, but interrelated, studies. These studies generally substantiate, and expand, the results from our earlier work.

This book is written to accomplish specific objectives: to

- place unobtrusive testing in the context of reference service evaluation (Chapter 1)
- assess the *correct answer fill rate* as a performance measure and report the findings of two studies (Chapters 3 and 4)
- refine unobtrusive testing as an evaluation methodology (Chapters 2-4)
- explore new applications of unobtrusive testing (Chapters 1, 3, 5, and 6)
- assist library staff in implementing ongoing evaluation of services (Chapter 5)
- discuss the impact of selected findings on larger issues related to library management and library education (Chapters 5 and 6)
- identify additional research areas involving the use of unobtrusive testing (Chapters 3-6)

The book should appeal to the administrators and public service staff of academic and public libraries. It should also interest library school educators—those teaching reference and subject literature courses—because it discusses the quality of reference service, evaluation of that service, and the results of two studies. Further, researchers will be interested in the methodological refinements and applications of unobtrusive testing.

The book does not confine itself to documents librarianship. It examines general reference service in both academic and public libraries. The implications of study findings are viewed in the context of the need for an overall assessment of library goals and objectives. The focus is clearly on library evaluation, the responsibilities of library managers, and educational implications. As the final two chapters emphasize, the level of reference service currently offered in many academic and public libraries presents serious and significant implications to library managers. Indeed, reference service may be in an unrecognized crisis that merits immediate attention and improvement.

The findings and recommendations present a number of challenges to the library community and the government administrators of the depository program. The specifics of these challenges are suggested throughout the book, but a critical challenge for all is to:

- recognize the importance of ongoing research/evaluation of library services
- increase public access to government publications/information
- improve the quality of library reference services
- integrate government information resources into the mainstream of library reference services
- expand upon the research base reported here and incorporate that research base into decision making processes

Only when these are accomplished will academic and public libraries increase the quality of their services and government publications/information be exploited to their full potential as a significant and integral part of a library's collection.

The book raises an important issue. With the U.S. government examining both the cost-benefit and cost-effectiveness of its information resources management activities, what are the implications of distributing thousands of copies of publications to libraries that agree to store them but cannot provide effective access to them or to the holdings of other depository libraries? Clearly, the depository library program does not comprise an effective means of *public access* to government publications published in paper copy and microfiche. One might wonder how depository libraries would perform with test questions seeking electronically distributed/disseminated information as proposed by the Joint Committee on Printing and some librarians, in 1985 and 1986, for distribution to the depository libraries.

To meet the challenges of the present and the future, both library and government administrators must assess the implications of the public approaching libraries and receiving the types of reference service documented in this book and our earlier work (McClure and Hernon, 1983). They must also explore the implications of the experiment (Chapter 4) for continuing education programs, in all phases of reference service.

Ongoing, regular evaluation of library services is essential and library staff must participate in ongoing education and training beyond the Master's in Library Science. If government publications/information are to be mainstreamed with other information services and collections, and to be made accessible to the public at large, if change is to occur and a re-examination of the library profession's underlying service philosophies is to take place, if a national agenda for access to government information is to be established, and if government information services as provided by librarians are to survive and prosper, then much remains to be done.

Addressing the issues and questions posed in this book is a necessary step.

But individual dedication, commitment, and leadership on the part of the library community, in the provision of high quality services, is essential if depository library collections are to be relevant and integral to the information society and meet the public's information needs. By addressing these issues the future can be met, government information services and collections made effective, new challenges met, and librarians can have an important and positive role in the information society of the future.

Peter Hernon
Charles R. McClure
April 1986

ACKNOWLEDGEMENTS

We wish to acknowledge our gratitude to the students who assisted in the collection of data. The participating students from the University of Arizona were Andrea Adams, Darin Frazier, James Hawkins, Clifton Hofmann, Jr., Evan Hofmann, Mina Motamedi, Lillie Nusz, Victoria Pendleton, Martha Renick, Julie Stielstra, and Adela Zubiate-Rodarte. Those who participated from the University of Oklahoma included Kim Granath, Lisa Kammerlocker, Cathy Van Hoy, and Michele McKnelly. Three people from the list merit special recognition. Martha Renick and Adela Zubiate-Rodarte served as proxie supervisors (Chapter 4), and Michele McKnelly participated in the drafting of the slide/script presentation (Chapter 4 and Appendix F).

We wish to acknowledge Pat Kaiser for material contained in parts of Chapter 6. At the time this book was written, she was a research assistant at the School of Library and Information Studies, University of Oklahoma.

The Association of Library and Information Science Education (ALISE) provided a research grant that defrayed a part of the expenses related to the study reported in Chapter 4. We also thank those academic and public library staff who pretested the questions used in the two studies reported in Chapters 3 and 4.

Finally, we acknowledge the support of our families (Elinor, Alison, and Linsay Hernon; and Vicky and Wendy McClure). They endured many discourses about unobtrusive testing, reference services, and the depository library program.

CHAPTER 1

THE ROLE OF UNOBTRUSIVE
TESTING IN THE EVALUATION OF
LIBRARY REFERENCE SERVICES

Evaluation, as used in this book, incorporates the research process, planning, and implementation strategies to change or improve the organization or a specific activity. Ongoing and regular evaluation is not a luxury; rather, it is integral to a dynamic, effective, and efficient organization. Reference service can be evaluated on four criteria:

- *Extensiveness*, or how much of a service is provided. This criterion is a measure of quantity rather than quality. It examines, for example, the number of reference questions asked per capita (see Zweizig and Rodger, 1982, pp. 39–50) or the number of students receiving bibliographic instruction per student population or per class level (e.g., freshman).
- *Effectiveness*, or the extent to which a program or service meets the goals and objectives set by the library. This criterion might also examine the extent to which a service satisfies the demands that users place on it.
- *Cost-effectiveness*, or the operating efficiency of the organization or the meeting of objectives expressed in terms of costs.
- *Cost-benefit*, or determining whether the expense of providing a service or program is justified by the benefits derived from it.

Evaluation can assist library staff in planning and monitoring programs and services, in assessing the impact of those programs or services, and in analyzing their economic efficiency (Rossi and Freeman, 1985).

To conduct an efficiency study, library staff members must be able to determine all costs—direct, indirect, immediate, and long-term. The difference between cost-effectiveness and cost-benefit studies is that in the former a precise monetary value cannot be calculated; cost-benefit requires the assignment of a monetary value to a program, service, or activity.

Regardless of which type of evaluation research is undertaken, library staff must ensure that a study can be replicated and that the validity of the results can

be verified. Evaluation should not be regarded as merely a one-time examination of the effectiveness or efficiency of a particular program or service. Instead,
it is an ongoing, cyclical process whereby programs and services are examined
individually and collectively to monitor interrelationships and to ensure that
stated goals and objectives are being met.

Replication necessitates that accurate and complete records be maintained,
that consistency in findings be available from sample to sample of a target population (reliability), and that data collection instruments, in fact, measure what
they are supposed to measure (internal validity). Reliability and validity must
be addressed when both the research design and methodologies are developed
and modified. Too often insufficient attention is given to these concerns; however, library staff members should give them proper attention if they want to
eliminate intervening variables or extraneous factors and generalize their study
findings (external validity).

In conducting evaluation research, library staff must balance measures of
quantity and quality against local constraints and organizational objectives. At
the same time, they should serve as change agents and enhance the impact that
library services and programs have upon the information gathering public.

Evaluation occurs in the context of planning and existing library goals and
objectives. The purpose is to produce change, discontinue or improve existing
library programs and services, and plan new services and programs. Evaluation requires the support of management and staff who already possess the necessary research skills/competencies. Too often, a dichotomy exists between
pronouncements supporting evaluation and change, and actual practice. Practice frequently emphasizes quantity, presumes that a program or service is effective and efficient, and operates in an organizational climate that does not
fully support decision making based upon the collection of reliable and valid
data. Staff may find it easier to tell managers what they want to hear and to base
decision making on intuition (McClure, 1986). However, factors such as financial stringencies, a questioning or skeptical college/university administration,
or a board of trustees, may necessitate a reassessment of priorities and the for-
mulation of realistic expectations.

The literature on evaluation suggests that numerous facets of library and information science are amenable to evaluation (see, for example, Lancaster,
1977; McClure, 1984; Powell, 1984; Rothstein, 1964; Schrader, 1984; and
Weech, 1974). Such writings link evaluation to management and planning.
Taking managerial action on the results of evaluation, however, is more difficult than some authors might suggest. Implementation and making changes requires a long-term strategy of planning and evaluation, as discussed in Chapter
5 of this book.

Although readers might benefit from an extended discussion of evaluation
and its application in diverse situations, both this chapter and the book adopt a
narrower perspective. They focus on one aspect of evaluating reference

service — the *accuracy* of responses that staff give to questions administered to them. Unobtrusive testing therefore comprises one means by which library managers can assess the existing level of accuracy by which reference staff answer questions and, based upon the insights they gain, can develop intervention strategies that increase that level.

The chapter provides an overview of library reference services amenable to evaluation, input and output measures, and unobtrusive testing. The discussion of unobtrusive testing incorporates an analysis of reviewer comments to *Improving the Quality of Reference Service for Government Publications* (McClure and Hernon, 1983). The analysis examines the content of the reviews and clarifies possible misperceptions about such testing and its use as a research/evaluation methodology. The purpose here is give more attention to unobtrusive testing and help inform the library profession and social science researchers of its strengths and weaknesses.

Chapter 2 discusses the development and implementation of an unobtrusive test of general reference and documents staff in academic and public libraries, while Chapter 3 reports the findings of that study. Chapter 4 views unobtrusive testing in the context of evaluation and a pilot project intended to measure the impact of learning interventions on staff performance. The final two chapters portray study findings in the context of a managerial and educational crisis whereby many academic and public libraries may be supporting ineffective and inefficient reference desk service. Resolution of this crisis requires the full and immediate attention of library managers and the profession as a whole. Further, librarians must become more proficient in evaluating their own services and programs, and in developing strategies that effectively improve the quality of those programs and services.

Unless the profession charts a course leading to better staff performance than that depicted in many of the unobtrusive studies identified in Figure 1-1, the reference staff of many academic and public libraries may continue to be ineffective referral agents and unable to negotiate the range of questions that libraries will receive in the rapidly emerging information age. Including the research reported in this book, approximately 20 studies conducted over two decades have unobtrusively tested the ability of library staff to answer correctly factual and bibliographic questions. Overall, these studies suggest that library staff:

- provide "half right" answers to factual and bibliographic questions; they may answer correctly 50 to 62% of these questions
- spend, on average, no more than five minutes per reference question
- experience problems in conducting reference interviews, in negotiating "typical" questions, and in implementing effective search strategies to resolve the information need

- fail to provide referral to questions when they "don't know" or cannot find an answer

Many of these studies question the capability of staff in meeting information needs related to paper copy sources, ones often held on the shelves of the libraries tested. Studies have yet to be done that evaluate library staff's ability to provide accurate answers to information in other formats. However, one might assure that such studies would not disclose higher accuracy rates than those identified in Figure 1-1.

Figure 1-1   Previous Unobtrusive Evaluations of Reference Service

Year	Author	Library Type	Percentage Correct
1968	Crowley (a)	Public	54
1971	Childers (a)	Public	55
1973	King and Berry (b)	Academic	60
1974	House (c)	Public	40
1975	Peat, Marwick, Mitchell & Co. (d)	Public	40
1978	Childers (e)	Public	47
1978	Ramsden (f)	Public	50
1980	Myers (g,h)	Academic	50
1981	Jirjees (h,i)	Academic	56
1981	Weech and Goldhor (j)	Public	70
1982	McClure and Hernon (k)	Academic	37
1983	Way (l)	Law School	65
1983	Library Research Center (m)	Public	80
1984	Library Research Center (n)	Public	59
1984	Rubenstein (o)*	Public	55
1984	Myers (p)	Academic	56
1984	Van House and Childers (q)	Public (Statewide Reference Referral Network)	74
1985	McClure and Hernon (r)**	Academic and Public	42
1985	Library Research Center (s)	Public	71
1985	The Source (t) and Gers and Seward (u)*	Public	55
1986	Hernon and McClure (v)**	Academic and Public	42
1986	Hernon and McClure (w)***	Academic and Public	62

*This study was reported in three different articles.
**This study was reported as a contracted study, journal article, and chapter of a book.
***This study is based largely on Chapters 2 and 3 of this book.

SOURCES
a.   Terence Crowley and Thomas Childers, *Information Service in Public Libraries: Two Studies* (Metuchen, NJ: Scarecrow Press, 1971).
b.   G. B. King and L. R. Berry, "Evaluation of the University of Minnesota Libraries Reference Department Telephone Information Service, Pilot Study" (Minneapolis: University of Minnesota Library School, 1973), ED 077 517.
c.   David E. House, "Reference Efficiency or Reference Deficiency," Library Association Record, 76 (November 1974): 222–223.

Figure 1-1 *(Continued)*

---

d. Peat, Marwick, Mitchell and Co., "California Public Library Systems: A Comprehensive Review with Guidelines for the Next Decade" (Los Angeles, CA: Peat, Marwick, Mitchell & Co., 1975), ED 105 906.

e. Thomas A. Childers, "The Test of Reference," *Library Journal*, 105 (April 15, 1980): 924–928.

f. M. J. Ramsden, "Performance Measurement of Some Melbourne Public Libraries," Melbourne, Australia: Library Council of Victoria, 1978.

g. Marcia J. Myers, "The Accuracy of Telephone Reference Services in the Southeast: A Case for Quantitative Standards," in *Library Effectiveness: A State of the Art* (Chicago: American Library Association, 1980), pp. 220–231.

h. Marcia J. Myers and Jassim M. Jirjees, *The Accuracy of Telephone Reference/Information Services in Academic Libraries: Two Studies* (Metuchen, NJ: Scarecrow Press, 1983).

i. Jassim M. Jirjees, "The Accuracy of Selected Northeastern College Library Reference/Information Telephone Services in Responding to Factual Inquiries," Ph.D. dissertation, Rutgers University, 1981.

j. Terry L. Weech and Herbert Goldhor, "Obtrusive versus Unobtrusive Evaluation of Reference Service in Five Illinois Public Libraries," *Library Quarterly*, 52 (October 1982): 305–324.

k. Charles R. McClure and Peter Hernon, *Improving the Quality of Reference Service for Government Publications* (Chicago: American Library Association, 1983).

l. Kathy A. Way, "Measurement and Evaluation of Telephone Reference/Information Service in Law School Depository Libraries in the Greater Los Angeles, California, Area," M.L.S. specialization paper, Graduate School of Library and Information Science, University of California at Los Angeles, 1983.

m. Library Research Center, University of Illinois. "An Index of Quality of Illinois Public Library Service," by Danny P. Wallace, in *Illinois Library Statistical Report #10* (Springfield, IL: Illinois State Library, 1983).

n. Library Research Center, University of Illinois, An Index of Quality of Illinois Public Library Service," by Danny P. Wallace, in *Illinois Library Statistical Report #14* (Springfield, IL: Illinois State Library, 1984).

o. Beverly Rubenstein, "Maryland Reference Survey Concludes Our Service Is Worse Than We Thought," *The Crab*, (September 1984), pp. 7–8.

p. Marcia J. Myers, "Check Your Catalog Image," *The Reference Librarian*, 11 (Fall/Winter 1984): 39–47.

q. Nancy A. Van House and Thomas Childers, "Unobtrusive Evaluation of Reference Referral Network: The California Experience," *Library and Information Science Research*, 6 (1984): 305–319.

r. Charles R. McClure and Peter Hernon, "Expanding New Clientele for NTIS Services: An Assessment of NTIS Services Provided through Academic/Public Libraries," Final Report for the National Technical Information Service (Contract 43-TANS-5-70) (August 23, 1985), PB86-106960.

s. Library Research Center, University of Illinois. "An Index of Quality of Illinois Public Library Service," by Loriene Roy, in *Illinois Library Statistical Report* (Springfield, IL: Illinois State Library, 1985).

t. "The Source," *American Libraries*, 11 (May 1985): 348.

u. Ralph Gers and Lillie Seward, "Improving Reference Performance: Results of a Statewide Survey," *Library Journal*, 110 (November 1, 1985): 32–35.

v. Peter Hernon and Charles R. McClure, "The Quality of Academic and Public Library Reference Service Provided for NTIS Products and Services: Unobstrusive Test Results," *Government Information Quarterly*, 3 (1986): 117–132; and Chapter 5 of Charles R. McClure, Peter Hernon, and Gary R. Purcell, *Linking the U.S. National Technical Information Service with Academic and Public Libraries* (Norwood, N.J.: Ablex Pub. Corp., 1986).

w. Peter Hernon and Charles R. McClure, "Unobtrusive Reference Testing: The 55% Rule," *Library Journal*, 111 (April 15, 1986): 37–41.

The findings reported in this book, and elsewhere, should encourage libraries to better integrate and increase the quality of their reference services. With libraries adopting online catalogs and other uses of technology, there must be greater effort to integrate all library resources administratively. Managers must ensure that access to the information their library's contain is not fragmented and that their staff resist the temptation of assuming that online catalogs treat all holdings comprehensively, where, in fact, they do not. Chapter 3 discusses online catalogs in the context of some significant unobtrusive test findings.

In summary, then, the purpose of this book is to both present the findings from two uses of unobtrusive testing and to address issues related to an educational and managerial crisis in the provision of reference service. Throughout the book, the theme is that specific strategies can and must be developed to improve the quality of reference service.

AREAS OF LIBRARY REFERENCE
SERVICE AMENABLE TO EVALUATION

Library staff can evaluate both the *direct* (personal assistance, the effectiveness and efficiency of online search strategies, bibliographic instruction, etc.) and *indirect* (collection development, preparation of guides and other supporting documentation, etc.) aspects of reference service. Both aspects are interrelated. For example, the development of collections containing resources needed by client groups can have a direct impact on the accuracy of the assistance that staff provide. Or the analysis of traffic patterns can influence the location of a reference desk(s), the staffing of that desk, and the placement of reference aids.

Figure 1-2 identifies the range of factors that may have an impact on the quality of a library's reference service. Since these factors may interact with each other, library managers must explore the implications of attacking one factor but not another. For example, the degree and type of bibliographic control that a library provides for its collections relates to the size, type, and complexity of these collections. Technical support such as online services may improve bibliographic access but will necessitate that the staff obtain basic technological skills and a receptivity to using online services. Technical support and bibliographic control are also important for libraries with complex physical organizations and a decentralized placement of materials.

Research has not explored all the facets depicted in the figure and the interrelationships among all the factors. Clearly, management decision making for reference services operates with a knowledge void and managers must often make decisions based on intuition or incomplete data. They ought to obtain as much usable data as possible from evaluation studies. At the same time, they

Figure 1-2   Factors That Impact on the Quality of Reference Service

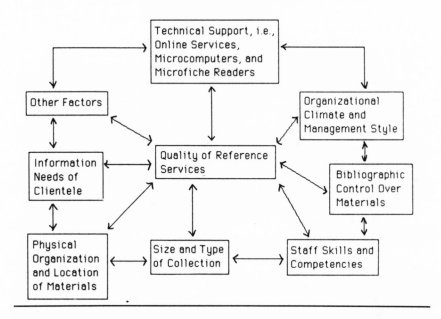

FACTORS THAT IMPACT ON THE QUALITY
OF REFERENCE SERVICE

must probe and challenge presumptions, intuition, and uncritical thinking, as well as reward those able to engage in problem solving.

Figure 1-3 identifies selected aspects of reference service that are amenable to evaluation. Libraries will have to decide which areas of activity have the highest priority and evaluate the effectiveness and/or efficiency of programs and services in priority areas. By focusing on both *inputs* (what goes into the library) and *outputs* (the result or end product of a service activity or that service/ activity received by a user), the figure identifies a broad range of reference activities that potentially might be studied. It also demonstrates an interrelationship between inputs and outputs; there is not always a clear distinction between the two. Staff, especially those servicing reference departments/collections, should be user oriented and examine inputs in relationship to outputs. Clearly, output measures serve as a reminder that the organization has as a primary goal the meeting of current and potential information needs.

The research literature has not examined all the measures depicted in the figure and explored interrelationships. Equally important, research tends to be based on self-reporting assessments that represent a one-time examination of a

Figure 1-3   Example Areas of Reference Service Amenable to Evaluation*

LIBRARY CLIENTELE

A. *Input Measures*
    Characteristics of clientele
    Information needs of clientele
B. *Output Measures*
    Extent of awareness of library services and programs
    Frequency of library use
    Perception of the appropriateness and completeness of the information received
    Perceptions of reference staff—their roles, duties, and functions
    Preferences for types and formats of information
    Reasons for library use and non-use
    Satisfaction with information sources and services
    Sources used to answer questions
    Their hesitancy or willingness to ask questions (e.g., how long must they wait to receive service (are staff available when patrons approach a reference desk)
    Their information gathering patterns and preferences

LIBRARY STAFF

A. *Input Measures*
    Classification
    Departmental organization
    Duties
    Educational background
    Experience
    Financial support
    Range of their work activities (professional versus nonprofessional)
B. *Output Measures*
    Attitudes toward patrons
    Effectiveness and efficiency in answering questions by personnel classification
    Extent of burnout
    Patterns in their search strategies and the information sources consulted
    Sources used to answer questions
    The speed by which staff answer the questions (e.g., the amount of time that a staff member spends in answering questions in relation to the total time spent at the desk)
    Success rate in resolving indirect and faulty information questions and in making appropriate referrals
    Their reference interview skills
    Willingness to assist library users
C. *Combined Input/Output Measures*
    Examine the input measures in the context of whether or not staff correctly answer questions

LIBRARY MANAGEMENT

A. *Input Measures*
    Availability of staff to assist clientele
    Extent of bibliographic control the library provides to source material in its collection
    Composition of public service staff (professional versus support)
    Financial support
    How busy are the staff
    Organizational climate/management style

*This figure is adapted from Powell (1984).

Figure 1-3   *(Continued)*

Staff duties (the range of staff work activities, including how much time is spent on activities other than servicing the public)

Staff training and continuing education opportunities

B.   *Output Measures*

The cost and effectiveness of reference desk service and departmental programs and services

The extent of staff burnout

The extent of the user communities served

The impact of traffic patterns on the staffing of the reference desk and the placement of reference aids

REFERENCE QUESTIONS

A.   *Input Measures*

Information needs of clientele

Number of questions received

Subject of questions

Types of questions asked (e.g., directional and bibliographic)

B.   *Output Measures*

The accuracy of staff in answering questions

Amount of time that staff spend on a transaction

The cost of question answering (e.g., the number of questions fielded in comparison to the salaries for reference staff, or the cost of time devoted to reference transactions)

Librarian response to a question

The number of referrals internal and external to the library

The number of steps staff/users take to answer questions

Reference fill rate — the number of reference transactions completed in proportion to the total number of such transactions

Reference transactions per capita

Search locations

Situational factors, e.g., problems in communication

Type and number of sources staff consult

User perceptions about whether a reference transaction was completed

C.   *Combined Input/Output Measures*

The relationship between questions asked and the use of the catalog

RESOURCES NEEDED TO ANSWER THE QUESTION

A.   *Input Measures*

Budget

Organization and physical location of materials

Quantity and quality of the collection

Types of materials

RECEIPT OF ANSWER

A.   *Input Measures*

Availability of staff to assist clientele

Extent of bibliographic control the library provides to source material in its collection

Composition of public service staff (professional versus support)

Financial support

How busy are the staff

Information needs of clientele

Number of questions received

(Continued)

Figure 1-3   *(Continued)*

Organization and physical location of materials

Organizational climate/management style

Quantity and quality of the collection

Staff duties (the range of staff work activities, including how much time is spent on activities other than servicing the public)

Staff training and continuing education opportunities

Subject of questions

Types of questions asked (e.g., directional and bibliographic)

B.   *Output Measures*

Analysis of search failures

Correct answer fill rate — accuracy of performance and a comparison of the rate to staffing decisions, policies, budget, hours of operation, the amount of time it takes to answer questions, etc.

Enumeration and classification by categories by subject, type of questions, source of question, and search locations

Reasons for poor performance (e.g., lack of subject knowledge or a lack of time)

C.   *Combined Input/Output Measures*

Impact of special subject strengths on the receipt of a correct answer

Size of the library collection in contrast to the receipt of a correct answer

---

particular issue or problem. The studies often depend upon user or staff participation but do not repeatedly collect data over long periods of time.

Compounding these difficulties is that librarians may not be aware of the full range of measures represented in the figure and may not use most of them (or use them in conjunction with each other). Typically so-called evaluation activities focus on the following:

- a count of the reference requests received
- the currentness and "adequacy" of the titles in the reference collection
- ascertaining the information needs of clientele
- development of written policies, goals, and objectives (Bundy and Bridgman, 1984, pp. 164–165)

Libraries may indicate a desire to do more evaluation and to determine the effectiveness and efficiency of programs and services. However, they justify the status quo by stating that " ... at present we can barely keep up with our desk work and the reference collection's maintenance and development" (Ibid., p. 165). Clearly, libraries must reexamine the duties and responsibilities of staff and question the effectiveness of what they are already doing. Libraries need to set priorities and not attempt to do everything — be all things to all people. What is the purpose of staffing the reference desk with individuals who

- answer a maximum of 55% of the factual and bibliographic questions correctly (see Chapters 5 and 6)?

- display discourteous service and fail to negotiate the actual information need (see McClure and Hernon, 1983)?
- respond to questions with "I don't know" and terminate the reference interview without making referral either internal or external to the library?

Should the status quo be maintained in such instances? Are managers aware that stress may result in staff burnout, or an inability to cope with one's work on a daily basis? Further, "burned out" staff may inadvertently make library users into nonusers and severe critics of the library and its stance toward provision of services.

Figure 1-4 identifies some of the facets of reference service explored in the research literature. Yet, a comparison of these selected articles, as well as the previous two figures, to the writings on documents librarianship suggests that documents reference service has received limited attention. The research literature on documents reference service focuses on:

- attitudes of staff toward the servicing and use of government publications (Whitbeck and Hernon, 1977a)
- bibliographic instruction (Whitbeck and Hernon, 1977b; Vertrees and Murfin, 1980)
- the history of that service (Hernon, 1978)
- patterns of use and nonuse of documents collections (Hernon, 1979)
- reference desk service and unobtrusive test results (see Figure 1-1)
- staff use of technology (McClure, 1981; Hernon, McClure, and Purcell, 1985)
- staffing patterns (Hernon, McClure, and Purcell, 1985)
- use of, and access to, technical report literature (McClure, Hernon, and Purcell, 1986)

Clearly, little research has evaluated reference services for government publications/information.

A more complete research base can assist librarians in managing their collections of government publications; enable agencies that administer depository programs to set realistic program goals, objectives, and performance measures; and assist librarians in planning continuing education programs and library school educators in maintaining courses relevant to the current and future needs of the profession. Chapter 6 expands upon these points and encourages the library profession to review and address deficiencies present in academic and public library reference services.

Except for the studies reporting unobtrusive test results, one of the articles on bibliographic instruction, and the book on use of technical report literature, research related to government publications tend to be either historical or survey. Regardless, almost without exception, the research is descriptive; it inter-

Figure 1-4   A Selected List of Representative Studies That Have Investigated General Library Reference Service*

Author(s)	Topical Area	Contribution
Bunge (a)	Obtrusive Testing	Tested the ability of reference staff to answer a prescribed set of questions. Staff members were aware of the test.
Cable (b)	Cost Analysis	A cost analysis of the reference service at one library for all questions taking over 5 minutes.
Ferguson and Taylor (c)	Staff Activities	An activity analysis of the tasks performed by public service staff
Haack, Jones, and Roose (d)	Occupational Burnout	Used a standard inventory to measure burnout
Hallman (e)	Analysis of Reference Questions	Use of a computer-scannable form to record the types of reference questions asked.
Halperin (f)	Desk Staffing	Provides a model for predicting the average number of people waiting in line, the average time spent waiting for service, and the percentage of idle time for any service point.
Halperin and Strazdon (g)	Service Preferences	Uses conjoint analysis to determine student preferences for reference service.
Jestes and Laird (h)	Staff Time	Studied the proportion of the total time that reference desk staff spent with library users and their questions.
Kantor (i)	Availability of Reference Service	Uses a branching diagram to represent the availability of the service. Also explains the "nuisance factor" method for determining availability of service.
Kazlauskas (j)	Study of Body Movement	Reports results of a study of kinesic analysis for public service staff.
Lynch (k)	Reference Interview	Presents results of a study of taped reference interviews in public libraries
Palmour and Gray (l)	Cost Analysis	Identified the amount of time staff spent in answering questions and calculated costs — time spent in comparison to the average salaries of reference staff.
Pizer and Cain (m)	Staff Testing	Tested the ability of staff to verify incomplete and inaccurate bibliographic citations.
Reeves, Howell, and Van Williams (n)	Staff Activities	Based on an evaluation, by a reference staff, of the duties they performed

Figure 1-4   *(Continued)*

Authors(s)	Topical Area	Contribution
		over a three-month period. Staff were interviewed and their duties analyzed.
Spencer (o)	Analysis of Staff Working Time	Samples of reference librarians' working time were taken, using a random alarm device and a checklist. Unit costs of reference questions were then calculated.
Taylor (p)	Analysis of Reference Interview and Question Negotiation	Analysis derived from case study methodology

*For examples of additional studies see Lancaster (1977).

SOURCES

a. Bunge, Charles A. "Professional Education and Reference Efficiency." Ph D dissertation (Urbana, IL: University of Illinois, Graduate School of Library Science, 1967).

b. Cable, Leslie G. "Cost Analysis of Reference Service to Outside Users," *Bulletin of the Medical Library Association,* 68 (April 1980): 247–248.

c. Ferguson, Anthony and John R. Taylor. "What Are You Doing? An Analysis of Activities of Public Service Librarians at a Medium-Sized Research Library," *Journal of Academic Librarianship,* 6 (March 1980): 24–29.

d. Haack, Mary, John W. Jones, and Tina Roose. "Occupational Burnout among Librarians," *Drexel Library Quarterly,* 20 (Spring 1984): 46–72.

e. Hallman, Clark N. "Designing Optical Mark Forms for Reference Statistics," *RQ,* 20 (Spring 1981): 257–264.

f. Halperin, Michael. "Waiting Lines," *RQ,* 16 (Summer 1977): 297–29.

g. Halperin, Michael and Maureen Strazdon. "Measuring Students' Preferences for Reference Service: A Conjoint Analysis," *Library Quarterly,* 50 (April 1980): 208–224.

h. Jestes, E. C. and W. D. Laird, "A Time Study of General Reference Work in a University Library," *Research in Librarianship,* 2 (1968): 9–16.

i. Kantor, P. B. "Analyzing the Availability of Reference Services," in *Library Effectiveness: A State of the Art* (Chicago, IL: American Library Association, 1980), pp. 131–149.

j. Kazlauskas, Edward. "An Exploratory Study: A Kinesic Analysis of Academic Library Public Service Points," *Journal of Academic Librarianship,* 2 (July 1976): 130–134.

k. Lynch, Mary Jo. "Reference Interviews in Public Libraries," *Library Quarterly,* 48 (1978): 119–142.

l. Palmour, V. E. and L. M. Gray. *Costs and Effectiveness of Interlibrary Loan and Reference Activities of Resource Libraries in Illinois* (Springfield, IL: Illinois State Library, 1972).

m. Pizer, I. H. and A. M. Cain. "Objective Tests of Library Performance," *Special Libraries,* 59 (1968): 704–711.

n. Reeves, Edward B., Benia J. Howell, and John Van Willigen. "Before the Looking Glass: A Method to Obtain Self-Evaluation of Roles in Library Reference Service," *RQ,* 17 (Fall 1977): 25–32.

o. Spencer, Carol C. "Random Time Sampling with Self-Observation for Library Cost Studies: Unit Costs of Reference Questions," *Bulletin of the Medical Library Association,* 68 (January 1980): 53–57.

p. Taylor, Robert S. "Question Negotiation and Information Seeking in Libraries," *College & Research Libraries,* 29 (May 1968): 178–194.

prets the historical record, or presents either survey or unobtrusive test results. A body of research in the documents reference area now relates to unobtrusive testing. Including the two studies reported here, five separate studies, since 1983, have conveyed the results of such investigations. In addition, some of the other studies depicted in Figure 1-1 have included documents related questions. Detailed insights into the service that documents and general reference staff in academic and public libraries provide are now emerging. The profession should now examine the implications of the collective findings and pursue additional research based on these results and those from the pilot study reported in Chapter 4.

Viewed from another perspective, the literature on documents librarianship rarely evaluates the effectiveness or efficiency of library programs and services. The writings merely suggest what libraries and their staff are doing, or not doing; they do *not* indicate the extent to which the programs and services meet stated goals and objectives, or the quality of those services.

Both library management and the research literature on government publications would benefit from the sponsorship and reporting of research and evaluation studies that

- examine a wider array of reference problems, e.g., those depicted in Figure 1-4
- employ other methods of data collection, e.g., transactional analysis (examination of logs or records that are automatically generated from each completed transaction, be it for circulation of a title or search of a database)
- use more than one means of data collection
- link their findings to library planning and decision making

The two studies reported in this book accomplish the last two purposes, while expanding the use of unobtrusive testing as a practical methodology for library decision making.

UNOBTRUSIVE TESTING

Overview

Unobtrusive research dates back to the 1960s and the seminal work by Webb et al. (1966). They encouraged researchers to place survey research in proper perspective and to investigate other means of data collection — ones not based entirely on self-reporting. As they discussed (p. vi), researchers can "gain valuable information" from observation and need not ask people to complete a questionnaire.

Unobtrusive research, sometimes called unobtrusive measurement, represents an umbrella term for research based on observation and the use of physical records (see Mullins and Kopelman, 1986). Unobtrusive testing represents one type of such research. It is based on participant observation and assessment of responses to a predetermined set of questions. Since test subjects are unaware of the purpose of the test, the researchers should not encounter abnormal behavior or attitudes during the investigation. At the same time, those administering the test are trained and their data collection should be monitored by the researchers (see Chapter 4). The purpose of the training and observation is, in part, to avoid the effect of a "biased-viewpoint" in scoring subject responses to the test questions (Webb et al., 1966, p. 114).

Clearly, uses of unobtrusive testing must be guided by a realization that the research

- examines the trust relationship that society places in libraries and reference service
- examines the reputation of libraries as information providers
- is based on documented observation

Consequently, researchers have an obligation to adhere to strict practices to guarantee anonymity of the test sites and the personnel actually tested. At the same time, they must ensure that the data are not misused (e.g., used as part of decision making related to promotion or salary increases). Yet they should provide their readers with information upon which to evaluate the study, its strengths and potential weaknesses.

A perusal of the *Chronicle of Higher Education* and other sources in the last couple of years reveals that both the social and health sciences have experienced instances in which researchers apparently manufactured their data or rushed into publication.[1] Conceivably the same could happen with unobtrusive research, including unobtrusive testing. Because of this, Figure 4-2 assumes added significance. It offers the reader and the researchers a checklist of activities to ensure (1) the collection of data and (2) the collection of reliable and valid data. It is important for the reader to know who records the responses of those being observed, what controls are placed on these individuals, the criteria used to develop the test questions, and the host of other issues addressed in Chapters 2 and 4.

Unobtrusive testing provides a means to gather data from the perspective of library users, and it avoids subjective assessments about the quality of reference service. Chapters 3 and 4 present the findings from two unobtrusive tests, while

---

[1] For example, see (Winkler, 1985) and "Scholarly Associations Take New Interest in Writing Codes of Professional Ethics" (1985). These articles address issues such as "How reliable are scholarly books," "How should scholars conduct their disputes," "What is the role of a professional association in setting ethical standards and enforcing them," and "What is the proper punishment for error or malfeasance?" For an excellent discussion of the issues relating to research as intellectual property, see Nelkin (1984).

Chapter 5 explores various uses of unobtrusive research in library and information science.

Unobtrusive testing such as that reported in this book, can relate *outputs* to *inputs*. It can compare the number of correct and incorrect responses to general institutional or organizational variables. Therefore, it can study whether such variables have an impact on the overall accuracy of staff responses. By examining the responses of a library staff to a set of questions, unobtrusive testing views a library as an organization and characterizes the service of the general or documents reference department at a point in time.

Unobtrusive testing must consider factors related to reliability, validity, and utility. The utility factor is especially important for affecting change, since it addresses the following questions (Paisley, 1969, p. A-3):

• What are the findings good for?
• What decisions in the real world can be affected by them?
• How are theories or other knowledge affected by the findings?
• What can be learned from the study, or can the study be dismissed with the comment "so what"?

Utility pertains to applications, impact, and usefulness of the findings. It presupposes that one of the broader purposes for data collection was to affect policy or decision making.

This book, similar to the authors' earlier work (McClure and Hernon, 1983), focuses on the utility criterion. The 1983 book presented the findings of an unobtrusive investigation and then suggested strategies by which the Government Printing Office (GPO) and libraries could examine the quality of service provided in depository libraries and presumably improve the service, where needed.

Williams and Wedig (1984) used the test questions appended to that book. The staff engaged in role playing and examined their ability to answer the questions correctly. Discerning any significant weaknesses in the service provided, management can identify specific problems to address in training sessions and attempt to improve individual staff competencies/skills. For example, unobtrusive studies have demonstrated that library staff have difficulty "in dealing with information that changes more rapidly than the sources used to answer such questions" (Crowley, 1985, p. 61). Information on current affairs provided by standard sources may have recently become either outdated or found to be incorrect. Staff can be alerted to this potential weakness with standard sources and advised to encourage clientele to approach information critically. Staff might also verify the accuracy of answers in other sources, prior to supplying clientele with "the answer."

In this regard, it merits mention that InterAmerica Research Associates, Inc., a management and consulting firm, operated the Consumer Education

Resource Network (CERN). Funded by the U.S. Office of Consumers' Education, Department of Education, it served, during the 1970s and part of the 1980s, as a national network to meet the information needs of consumer educators and to further cooperative efforts among parties interested in consumer education.

CERN's information specialists assisted consumer educators in all phases of an information search, from suggesting ideas about the kinds of materials needed to location of those materials which would meet their needs. These specialists engaged in telephone follow-up in order to determine if the resources had indeed been useful. For them, the accuracy of their answers was a critical component of their service. Therefore, they did not merely look up and report answers from printed sources. They always double-checked the answers from other sources and frequently telephoned a Federal agency or another information provider in the vicinity to determine that they provided the most up-to-date and accurate information (Chen and Hernon, 1982).

Academic and public library staff cannot go to such extremes for each reference query. However, this example should serve as a reminder that libraries should engage in introspection and self-assessment, that other competing information providers exist, that librarians should take care and pride in their service, that they should resist responding with "I don't know" and terminating the reference interview instead of engaging in referral, either internal or external to the library.

In summary, unobtrusive research comprises a well-accepted means for data collection in the social sciences, while unobtrusive testing has been conducted in academic and public libraries for the past two decades. Unobtrusive testing provides a critical means by which these libraries can assess the accuracy of their reference service and explore the effectiveness of learning interventions intended to improve the level of accuracy. Clearly, unobtrusive testing comprises a legitimate means of data collection and it provides insights that cannot easily be obtained otherwise.

The use of unobtrusive testing need not be limited to the one-time asking of a set of questions to the staff of selected libraries. Chapter 4 explores a new use. Further research can expand the practical application of unobtrusive testing to the evaluation of library services. At the same time, libraries and researchers can increase the number of output measures based on *correct answer fill rate,* the percentage of test questions correctly answered. Based upon some of the studies depicted in Figure 1-4, it is possible to calculate the *correct answer fill rate* per capita, per staff salary, or per staff classification (professional or classified staff).

General Criticisms of Such Testing

Plotnick (1985) regards unobtrusive testing as producing a distorted image of reference service. He suggests that such testing ignores that staff are diluged all day long with a wide variety of questions, from diverse user groups. He also suspects that the staff might also be assisting more than one client simultaneously. Under such circumstances, he wonders if other information providers would perform as well; "the questions we do answer correctly are commonly those that other information sources don't begin to answer. Our average: .550; their average: .000!" He suspects that the librarians' average would "skyrocket" if they only asked patrons "Does this answer your question?" He concludes that "with the good skills most reference librarians possess, that caring can make all the difference." "A little positive encouragement" will make all the difference and "half-right" answers will be something of the past.

Such thinking is simplistic and ignores the existing research on the topic. Plotnick apparently assumes that staff are at the reference desk all day, that unobtrusive testing occurs when staff are balancing different requests simultaneously, and that other information providers would have had an inferior score. Further, he assumes that, with a little care there would be dramatic improvement in *correct answer fill rates,* the percentage of correct answers to the test questions. The issue is less one of "positive encouragement" than of staff competencies and their reference skills.

Plotnick also ignores the collective findings of the studies depicted in Figure 1-1. King and Berry (1973), for example, discovered that staff engaged in minimal reference interviewing and provided faulty or inaccurate information. Over half of the questions (57%) in the Gers and Seward study (1985) could have been answered by the *World Almanac*; six additional sources would have raised the percentage to 87. Chapter 4 of this book underscores the complexities of "quick fixes" to *correct answer fill rates.* Chapters 5 and 6 emphasize that improved service depends on the implementation of a formal, ongoing program of planning, evaluation, and continuing education. Both library managers and their staff must be committed to the process.

Some librarians may examine our earlier book (McClure and Hernon, 1983) and compare the *correct answer fill rates* between that study and the ones reported here. They may assume that the higher rates reported in this book invalidate the earlier 37% accuracy rate. Direct comparison between that percentage and the ones given in Chapters 3 and 4 should be made with extreme caution. Any comparison must recognize that:

- the sampling and time frames differ
- the 1983 study examined the service of documents staff in academic depository libraries; Chapter 3 of this book compares two library types and two departments
- different geographical areas were studied
- the 1983 study and the one reported in Chapter 3 drew upon general factual and bibliographic questions, whereas the pilot study (see Chapter 4) explored statistical questions relating to U.S. government publications

The proposed 55% rule suggested in Chapter 5 is offered as a general yardstick and not a precise percentage. Clearly, any comparisons among the studies depicted in Figure 1-1 must take design, methodological, and other considerations into account.

Due to unique and individual characteristics at each library, it is important for managers to conduct their own evaluations and assess the local *correct answer fill rate*. Such insights can be useful in developing and supporting programs that will have a positive impact on the quality of service provided.

Comments Made by Reviewers of the 1983 Study

One method of assessing the current understanding of unobtrusive testing is to examine reviewer comments to *Improving the Quality of Reference Service for Government Publications* (McClure and Hernon, 1983). That book received 14 reviews and was selected by the Reference and Adult Services Division of the American Library Association as one of the 25 best "professional sources" in the past quarter-century.[2] Overall, the reviews were favorable.

As the reviewers commented, the study focused attention on reference service for government publications. Both the GPO and library literature had concentrated on bibliographic control and aspects of collection management. Research had not previously addressed the quality of reference service that depository libraries provided for the publications they received. Reviewers appreciated the book's emphasis on "the process of better integration of documents into general library reference service." The "results are provided in the larger context of a rationale for public access to government information and suggestions for the improvement of documents reference service."

The book explored implications for continuing the depository program as it is currently constituted and questioned the effectiveness of depository reference service. In some cases, reviewers regarded the findings as "a disturbing indictment of the profession" and recommended that the serious deficiencies in the depository program be addressed. "One hopes ... [that] ... documents and reference librarians, will give this book its due and respond creatively to its challenges."

The book was considered controversial because the findings would jolt "the complacency of documents librarians who feel that they do their job well." Some reviewers believed that the study was carefully designed, the procedures

---

[2] The reviews appeared in *American Reference Books Annual* (1984), *Booklist* (October 15, 1983), *Canadian Library Journal* (June 1984), *Government Information Quarterly* (1984), *Government Publications Review* (1984), *Journal of Academic Librarianship* (March 1985), *Journal of Documentation* (June 1984), *Library & Information Science Research* (April-June 1984), *Library Journal* (October 1, 1983), *The Library Quarterly* (July 1984), *Public Documents Highlights* (September 1983), *Public Library Quarterly* (Fall 1984), *RQ* (Winter 1983), and *Wilson Library Bulletin* (January 1984). *RQ* (Fall 1985) reported the book as one of the best 25 professional books written in the past 25 years.

were adequately pretested, and the data were properly analyzed. They found the results "convincing"; other reviewers declared their reservations. Collectively negative reactions focused on unobtrusive testing per se, the research design, implementation of the methodology, data analysis and findings, and the reporting of study findings and their implications. Appendix A summarizes these concerns and responds to a number of reviewer misperceptions and concerns.

One reviewer demonstrated his unfamiliarity with unobtrusive testing and social science research by referring to "unobstructive testing" and commented that testing took place in the "Southeast." It actually occurred in the Southwest. Based on Table 2 of the book (McClure and Hernon, 1983), he averaged all the percentages reported by the unobtrusive studies and derived an exact 52% rate of accuracy. Such a technique is misleading and ignores the methodological and research design considerations of each study.

The same reviewer appears to believe that "unobstructive testing" by students is less valid than if it had been done by library science professors. There is no tangible evidence in the literature to support such a contention. But, perhaps, the most surprising aspect of his review and that of some other reviews is that they all relied on intuition and not the research literature. Disagreements over methodological considerations must go beyond statements such as "I think not" and focus on concrete aspects of the research process.

The purpose of the assessment shown in Appendix A was to identify misperceptions about unobtrusive testing. It was not to attack any reviewers personally or to question their motivation. As the response to reviewer comments illustrates, such testing is subject to misunderstanding. It is hoped that the detailed discussion of reliability and internal validity, as well as the procedures for question administration and proxie supervision, provided in Chapters 2 and 4, will reduce some of the misunderstandings. A key question emerging from the unobtrusive tests conducted over the past 20 years (see Figure 1-1) becomes "How can individual libraries use unobtrusive research for self-diagnosis and improvement?" Chapters 4 and 5 address this question directly.

For some people, unobtrusive testing still comprises a controversial method of data collection. Perhaps if the studies depicted higher rates of accuracy, there might be fewer reservations. One wonders if librarians would object to the methodology if the studies documented that public service staff correctly answered 85–95% of the questions asked!

Limitations

Unobtrusive testing has certain limitations. Unless the researchers develop careful procedures for administration of the test questions, proxies might not provide accurate renditions of the questions or otherwise arouse the suspicions of library staff. Therefore, proxies should be selected with care and trained. As shown in Chapter 4, they should also be supervised.

Unobtrusive testing generally fails to consider local, unique situations within a library that may adversely affect the ability of staff to answer questions. Nonetheless, a good study design and proxie training minimizes these difficulties. By documenting a *correct answer fill rate,* management can ascertain the quality of service at one point in time. Clearly, repeated testing documents performance over time and enables management to examine the long-range effect of learning interventions.

The test questions must be carefully selected so that they are representative of typical questions asked. The questions should be developed according to specific criteria, subjected to a rigorous pretest, and approved by professional reference librarians *before* their use. Reference librarians participating in the pretest can be encouraged to examine the questions that they had received and to indicate those which they believe appropriate for inclusion in the study.

Another possible limitation is the assumption that libraries maintain a "basic reference collection" of publications published by both the Federal government and the private sector. As a precaution, researchers should select questions that can often be answered from more than one source. However, a search of different sources must not yield different answers.

Procedural limitations can be minimized by having the proxies administer the questions to staff who are not preoccupied with other information requests. The proxies should also verify that the sources that will answer the questions were indeed in the reference area.

Because of the unobtrusive nature of the test, clerical staff may answer some of the questions. Thus, this book discusses staff, rather than librarian, responses. Proxies were encouraged to ask questions of individuals who appeared to be professionals, to request a librarian, or to engage the staff member in conversation and attempt to ascertain that person's status. Regardless of whether other than professionals answered questions, unobtrusive testing reflects the type of service that "real-life" clientele might have received. Clerical staff, if they participated, could have referred questions or asked the person to return later when the librarian was on duty.

The results of the studies reported in this book apply only to reference service for certain types of questions. Chapter 3 focuses on questions of a factual and bibliographic nature, while Chapter 4 examines Federal statistical questions. In both instances, the questions were drawn from basic sources distributed through the GPO depository library program.

The results from Chapter 3 can only be generalized to academic and public libraries in three geographical regions. Further, the libraries were drawn from cities displaying certain characteristics. Libraries with characteristics similar to those depicted in Figure 2-5 may be able to draw useful comparisons, insights,

and implications from the study. In the case of Chapter 4, staff from two departments of one library participated. Needless to say, study findings cannot be
generalized to other departments or libraries. Nonetheless, library managers,
library school educators, members of the Government Printing Office and the
Joint Committee on Printing, and professional organizations should be aware
of the possible implications for library programs and services.

The library community should be less interested in the generalizability of the
study findings than in whether the researchers actually measured what they intended (internal validity) (Krathwohl, 1985; Guba and Lincoln, 1981). The
importance of a study is not that the findings may apply to all members of the
depository program in a given state or region, or the nation as a whole. Rather,
the researchers must examine what they set out to study; the findings of
unobtrusive testing should accurately reflect the type of service that real-life
patrons might have received at a point in time.

Other concerns about unobtrusive testing might be that:

• not all the reference staff are tested
• staff are only tested once
• testing does not take place in a wider context, one attempting to diagnose
  staff performance and improvement their *correct answer fill rate*

As reported in Chapter 2, some libraries were tested twice and the two scores
compared. Chapter 4 probed the testing of all professional and classified staff in
two departments, on the basis of a test-retest. And, finally, the two studies reported in this book placed study findings in the context of *correct answer fill rate*.
The final two chapters discuss the utility of this information to library managers
and chart procedures to document the fill rate and to improve staff performance.

Methodological Contributions of the Studies Reported in This Book

Chapter 3 reports on the testing of 26 academic and public libraries from three
geographical regions. Therefore, testing occurred across library types and compared the performance of two departments (general reference and government
documents). The researchers tested all the libraries and then selected some of
the same libraries for retesting. Some of the libraries were therefore tested twice
with the same questions, and test-retest scores were compared. The consistency
of scores suggests a high degree of reliability within those scores.

In the case of one of the public libraries, the researchers selected two questions, which they administered to staff at the main library and half of the
branches. A primary objective was to examine the referral process within a library system. In this instance, they first administered the test questions at the

central library. Later, when they queried the branches, they retested the central library on the same two questions.

The questions used for both Chapters 3 and 4 were pretested. Library staff at other (but similar) institutions reviewed them and offered constructive criticism. Their suggestions led to the revision of the questions. The researchers also reviewed their questions and checked them in reference sources. They also selected a couple of libraries and field tested the questions, prior to their actual use.

As in our other studies, the proxies, the students administering the questions, were trained. For the experiment (Chapter 4), they were also closely supervised by project managers. Figure 4-2 identifies 25 indicators of reliability and validity that the authors employed to ensure the collection of high quality data.

Previously, unobtrusive testing had not been combined with an experimental design, whereby library staff were randomly assigned to one of two intervention groups and individually pretested and posttested. Further, with the emphasis on the utility criterion, the authors have placed the two studies in a management context. Chapters 4, 5, and 6 discuss this framework and its significance. Other unobtrusive research might expand from the examples given in this book. Forthcoming studies should discuss the utility, reliability, internal validity, and perhaps external validity of the data. Similarly, they should link unobtrusive testing to planning, evaluation, and organizational change.

EXPANDING THE ROLE OF UNOBTRUSIVE TESTING

Unobtrusive testing is not an end unto itself. Rather, it comprises a means to a larger end; such testing indicates what proportion of reference questions are answered correctly and shows the necessity of systematic improvement of reference service (Crowley, 1985, p. 63). In this regard, it has clear management and educational implications.

For libraries to improve their services and increase organizational effectiveness, they must have access to high quality data. At the same time, staff need skills and competencies beyond those related to day to day activities. As Swisher and McClure (1984, p. 1) note,

> the prerequisite skills to address ... challenges and opportunities are in areas of producing and understanding action research, making decisions as how best to allocate scarce resources, and planning for increased organizational effectiveness — that is, accomplishment of goals and objectives.

Staff must obtain competencies related to research, planning, and decision making, if a library is to provide effective and efficient programs and services.

Given the seemingly endless array of issues and problems confronting libraries, the staff must prioritize goals and objectives, and select those deemed most important for immediate consideration. *Correct answer fill rate* is basic to reference desk service and requires detailed consideration over time. In addition to determining the number of questions asked (extensiveness), library staff should examine the *accuracy* of their responses and their demeanor in resolving information needs.

In this regard, action-oriented library research becomes increasingly significant. Such research deals with problems concerning library services and operations. Either the staff or outside researchers collect empirical data that address research objectives, hypotheses, or research questions, and have an impact on actual services or operations. Action-oriented research therefore requires the collection of reliable and valid data that have utility — value to decision making.

Research can also generate new knowledge or test theories and knowledge in practice, and modify theory as needed. Such research need not have utility or be useful to local decision making. Unobtrusive testing represents a type of research that can generate knowledge, that can confirm or reject intuition or previous knowledge, or that can demonstrate utility. In so doing, it demonstrates versatility.

Typically, unobtrusive testing in library and information science has been equated with a one-time effort to document the *correct answer fill rate*. Chapter 4 of this book proposes that such testing be used in a new context — to improve staff ability in answering questions. Such a use links unobtrusive testing with teaching and learning processes, effective continuing education, and longitudinal research that gathers and analyzes repeated measures.

That chapter makes another contribution. It encourages the use of unobtrusive testing as but one means of data collection. Different data collection techniques, which are properly sequenced, can build upon each other and permit comparisons among the collective findings.

Consequently this book does not represent a replication of the research reported in *Improving the Quality of Reference Service for Government Publications* (McClure and Hernon, 1983). Rather, it makes a number of methodological contributions to the use of unobtrusive testing. It also combines unobtrusive testing with an experimental design and places study findings in a management and planning context.

The unobtrusive studies conducted over two decades comprise an extensive body of literature, whose results must be viewed collectively. As Webb et al. (1966) suggest,

> once a proposition has been confirmed by two or more independent measurement processes, the uncertainty of its interpretation is greatly reduced. The most persuasive evidence comes through a triangulation of measurement processes. If a proposition can survive the onslaught of a series of ... measures, ... confidence

should be placed in it. Of course, this confidence is increased by minimizing error in each instrument and by a reasonable belief in the different and divergent effects of the sources of error.

Given the substantive body of research, now is the time to point unobtrusive testing in new directions. Chapter 4 suggests one possible direction. Additional directions and roles for the use of unobtrusive testing are likely available and await discovery.

CHAPTER 2

RESEARCH DESIGN AND METHODOLOGY FOR EXPLORING THE *CORRECT ANSWER FILL RATE* IN SELECTED ACADEMIC AND PUBLIC DEPOSITORY LIBRARIES

Unobtrusive testing of reference service is the process of asking reference questions (for which answers have been predetermined) of library staff members who are unaware that they are being evaluated. Figure 1-1 identified the relevant, previous studies, the types of libraries investigated, and the percentage of correct answers each encountered. Basically, these studies have shown that library personnel are not as successful in answering factual and bibliographic questions, posed either in-person or by telephone, as they claim.

Childers, who unobtrusively tested fifty-seven libraries of the Suffolk Cooperative Library System, explored the readiness of library staff to negotiate a question. In several instances, he scored "not on the correctness of the answer they gave, but on their success in arriving at the ultimate step [the actual reference question]" (1980, p. 925). He also followed up on the referral process and "tested the response by any resource agency mentioned by a library" (Ibid). Both of these methodological approaches merit replication, so that a finding of King and Berry (1973) can be further studied; library staff often do not negotiate a question fully and adequately.

Myers discovered that even when academic libraries owned appropriate sources staff members might neither consult nor know how to use them. They might even misinterpret the information contained in a source (1980, p. 229). For this reason, researchers using unobtrusive testing should determine if the libraries tested do, indeed, own the necessary works to answer each question and if these works were actually on the shelves at the time of testing.

McClure and Hernon (1983) have shown that library staff infrequently engage in referral and that when referral does occur, it is most likely internal to the organization. Often when staff members cannot answer a question, they respond with "don't know" or "claim the library does not own the resources necessary to answer the question." In fact, the library probably has the necessary source material on the shelf. Clearly, unobtrusive testing should not limit itself to an examination of the *correct answer fill rate*. It should also probe question negotiation skills and referral capabilities of the staff members tested.

Typically, the studies depicted in the figure have asked general reference staff members a few questions relating to government affairs. These questions, however, have not always been easy to answer. In our 1983 book, we reported on the administration of 20 pretested questions, both by telephone and in-person, to government documents personnel at 17 academic depository libraries in the Northeast and Southwest. Of all the studies employing unobtrusive testing, this one produced the lowest percentage of correct answers. This finding alone suggests the need for further exploration and for drawing upon a larger geographical base. It also suggests that library administrators and educators should examine ways to enhance the ability of staff to answer questions correctly (see Chapters 5 and 6), to encourage the referral of unanswered questions, and to determine the actual information needs of patrons.

In summary, the study incorporates methodological contributions of previous studies. For one question, the researchers scored staff on their ability to negotiate the question correctly (Childers), checked on whether the libraries tested owned the source/information sought and if the title was on the shelf at the time of need (Myers), examined referral capabilities of the staff tested (McClure and Hernon), and the accuracy of any referral suggestions (Childers).

STATEMENT OF THE PROBLEM

The purpose of this study is to extend unobtrusive testing of government documents reference service into two previously unexamined areas — a comparison between two library types and between staff members in two areas of the library. Further, the study adds another dimension; it relates study findings to a performance measure — *correct answer fill rate*.

The study reported in the next chapter differs from our earlier study (McClure and Hernon, 1983) in six ways:

- the sample represents three geographical regions
- both academic and public depository libraries are included
- both government documents staff and general reference personnel received pretested questions
- all questions were administered in-person; telephone questioning was not used

- not all questions specified that a U.S. government publication was sought; the purpose was to see if general reference staff would negotiate and determine the type of information resource sought
- the accuracy of any referral was verified

By combining testing with an experimental design in one particular setting (see Chapter 4), the researchers documented the quality of reference service that they and their proxies received, while exploring strategies for enhancing staff performance.

While the reference process itself is complex, for purposes of this book, it consists of activities which occur between the time a proxy approaches a library staff member with a question and the time when either the question was resolved or the interaction between that staff member and the proxy was discontinued. By emphasizing the perspective of users, the next chapter provides insights into the quality of reference services that two library types, and personnel from both the documents and general reference departments, provide to patrons needing access to U.S. government publications. Further, the chapter illustrates the extent to which academic and public depository libraries encourage or inhibit access to depository publications.

Five primary benefits, it is hoped, emerged from the studies presented in the next two chapters:

- The effectiveness with which both library types provide access to U.S. government publications has been assessed.
- Further recommendations and strategies are offered for improving the effectiveness of depository libraries as providers of government publications and their information content.
- Library school educators teaching a course(s) in government documents, general or advanced reference, or the literature of the social or physical sciences can reassess their approach to teaching effective reference interviews and search strategies.
- The linking of findings to performance measures should appeal to those academic and public libraries adopting or planning to adopt such measures.
- Further methodological refinements for unobtrusive testing can be offered.

OBJECTIVES

The objectives of the study reported in Chapter 3 are to:

- refine and improve the technique of unobtrusive testing of library staff serving depository collections

- identify the accuracy with which staff members from academic and public libraries answer pretested questions of a factual and bibliographic nature
- identify the extent to which staff negotiate reference questions (will they determine that the proxie is, in fact, seeking a government publication)
- identify the factors contributing to the successful and unsuccessful answering of questions by depository library staff in terms of the reasons for incorrect answers, the extent and accuracy of referrals, the difficulty of the questions asked, and the duration of the reference process
- compare the number of correct answers, as well as the reasons for incorrect answers, by library type and department

The purpose for testing general reference staff was threefold: (1) to determine if they associate government publications with the questions, (2) to identify the extent to which they use the reference collection to answer documents related questions, and (3) to study the process by which referrals are made.

These objectives provide direction for the study and underscore the utility of the study for library decision makers. Both documents and general reference staff must first recognize their level of performance before they develop specific strategies to improve such performance. Studying the interaction between the main reference and documents staff may provide possible approaches to increase the effectiveness of the referral process. Finally, study objectives can assist library decision makers to better identify factors that contribute to "successful" and "unsuccessful" reference processes.

HYPOTHESES

Study objectives were translated into formal hypotheses that guided the collection and analysis of data. These hypotheses are:

- There is no statistically significant difference (at the 0.05 level) between *correct answer fill rate* of
  a. academic versus public library documents personnel
  b. academic versus public library general reference personnel
  c. academic library documents and general reference staff members
  d. public library documents versus general reference staff members.
- There is no statistically significant difference between *correct answer fill rate* and
  a. the number of referrals made
  b. the accuracy of those referrals
  c. the ability to negotiate reference questions and determine that a government document was really sought.

Figure 2-1 offers a graphic representation of the first hypothesis and the comparisons between library types and departments.

RESEARCH DESIGN

Depository Library Program

The U.S. Government Printing Office (GPO) administers a depository library program consisting of approximately 1,400 libraries from the 50 states, the District of Columbia, and the possessions of the United States. Participants include academic, public, law school, Federal government, state agency, and special libraries. Over three-fourths of the participating libraries are either academic or public libraries (Hernon, McClure, and Purcell, 1985). Therefore, these two library types comprise an appropriate and important study population.

If a composite profile of the "typical" academic depository library were constructed, it would show that the library gained its depository status after the passage of the 1962 Depository Library Act. This library probably has an annual budget greater than $500,000. The institution itself would offer graduate programs, have an enrollment of 5,000 or less, and employ fewer than 100 faculty members (Ibid., p. 92).

A maximum of one FTE professional, assisted by no more than one FTE per support staff classification, would staff the depository collection. No more than half of the available item numbers would be selected; in fact, the library would probably select 25% or fewer items. The depository holdings would be retained in a separate collection arranged by the Sudocs classification sytem (Ibid.).

The "typical" public library obtained its depository status after the passage of the Depository Library Act of 1962. This library has an annual budget exceeding $1 million and between 100,001 and 400,000 volumes of non-government publications. Similar to the "typical" academic library, it assigns a maximum of one FTE professional, and one FTE per support staff classification, to the depository collection and services. However, unlike its academic library counterpart, the public library classifies its depository collecton by either a combination of methods or the Sudocs system. Either way, government publications typically are kept in a separate collection (Ibid., pp. 96–97).

Another difference between academic and public library depositories relates to the percentage of items selected. The "typical" academic library selects a maximum of 50% of the available items, while the public library counterpart takes a maximum of 25% (Ibid., p. 97).

Selection of Libraries for Testing

As Figure 2-2 demonstrates, the U.S. Bureau of the Census has divided the United States into four geographical regions: the Northeast, Midwest, South,

Figure 2-1   Summary of Possible Relationships to be Studied (A Depiction of the First Hypothesis)*

	Reference Department	Documents Department	Reference Department	Documents Department
Academic Depository Library *Correct Answer Fill Rate*		A	B	
Public Depository Library *Correct Answer Fill Rate*		A	B	

	Reference Department	Documents Department	Reference Department	Documents Department
Academic Depository Library *Correct Answer Fill Rate*	C	C		
Public Depository Library *Correct Answer Fill Rate*			D	D

*The letter in a cell refers to which hypothesis is depicted.

Figure 2-2   Regions and Census Divisions of the United States*

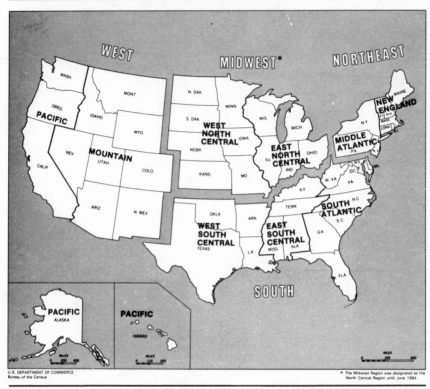

* Source: U.S. Bureau of the Census. Any issue of *Statistical Abstract of the United States* (Washington, D.C.: GPO, annual) contains a similar map.

and West. Since the testing of the libraries selected would be accomplished without outside funding, and since the cost of travel to the Northeast to administer the testing was prohibitive, the researchers omitted libraries in the Northeast from possible inclusion.

The *Statistical Abstract of the United States* (1984) contains a list of cities with a minimum of 100,000 inhabitants based on data derived from the 1980 Census of Population and Housing.[1] Turning to *Government Depository Libraries* (1983), the researchers determined which of these cities had a public depository library and at least one academic depository library. The intent was to reap the maximum benefit from the visit to a city — the testing of two libraries, one academic

---

[1] The researchers selected 100,000 as the minimum because many academic and public libraries with large volume counts and numbers of staff are located in urban setting of 100,000 or more (Hernon, McClure, and Purcell, 1985). The researchers also selected this base to minimize travel expenses and to collect data in the most efficient manner.

and the other public. Figure 2-3 identifies the cities that comprised the study population.

Next, the researchers, using a table of random numbers, selected 8 cities from each geographical region (the West, South, and Midwest). Where a city had more than one academic depository library, they used the same table of random numbers to select which library to test.

The researchers selected two libraries in the West (one academic and the other public) as pretest sites and administered the questions unobtrusively to documents and general reference personnel at these libraries under actual test conditions. The test afforded a final opportunity to review the questions and testing procedures. Since no changes in the questions or in the administration procedures resulted, data from both visits are incorporated into the study findings. As Table 2-1 illustrates, the study sample consists of 10 libraries from the

Figure 2-3   Cities with 100,000 or More Inhabitants and Having Both a Public and at Least One Academic Depository Library*, +

Midwest	South	West
Akron, Ohio	Arlington, Texas	Anchorage, Alaska
Chicago, Illinois	Atlanta, Georgia	Bakersfield, California
Cincinnati, Ohio	Baltimore, Maryland	Boise, Idaho
Cleveland, Ohio	Birmingham, Alabama	Denver, Colorado
Columbus, Ohio	Charlotte, North Carolina	Fresno, California
Dayton, Ohio	Dallas, Texas	Honolulu, Hawaii
Des Moines, Iowa	El Paso, Texas	Long Beach, California
Detroit, Michigan	Fort Worth, Texas	Los Angeles, California
Evansville, Indiana	Houston, Texas	Oakland, California
Flint, Michigan	Jacksonville, Florida	Pasadena, California
Fort Wayne, Indiana	Knoxville, Tennessee	Phoenix, Arizona
Gary, Indiana	Little Rock, Arkansas	Portland, Oregon
Grand Rapids, Michigan	Louisville, Kentucky	Pueblo, Colorado
Indianapolis, Indiana	Memphis, Tennessee	Reno, Nevada
Kansas City, Missouri	Miami, Florida	Riverside, California
Madison, Wisconsin	Mobile, Alabama	Sacramento, California
Milwaukee, Wisconsin	Nashville, Tennessee	San Diego, California
Minneapolis, Minnesota	New Orleans, Louisiana	San Francisco, California
Omaha, Nebraska	Norfolk, Virginia	Seattle, Washington
Peoria, Illinois	Oklahoma City, Oklahoma	Tacoma, Washington
St. Louis, Missouri	Raleigh, North Carolina	Tucson, Arizona
St. Paul, Minnesota	San Antonio, Texas	
Toledo, Ohio	Tampa, Florida	
Youngstown, Ohio	Tulsa, Oklahoma	
	Winston-Salem, North Carolina	

*The academic library does not comprise either a law school or medical library.

+ The list of cities was based upon coverage in *Statistical Abstract of the United States* (Washington, D.C.: GPO, 1984) and *Government Depository Libraries* (Washington, D.C.: GPO, 1983).

Table 2-1   Depiction of Those Libraries Tested*

| | Geographical Region | | | |
	Midwest #	South #	West #	Total
Academic Libraries	4	4	5	13
Public Libraries	4	4	5	13
Total	8	8	10	26

*The actual identity of each library has been withheld.

West, 8 from the South, and 8 from the Midwest. Thirteen academic and 13 public libraries participated in the study.

Ideally the research design should have permitted the inclusion of collection arrangement. However, the published literature does not indicate whether individual depository libraries have separate documents and general reference collections. In some cases, the general reference staff handle all government documents questions. In other instances, libraries are divided into subject divisions, each of which offers reference services. Conceivably, one department might receive all the testing, while in other cases a variety of units might be tested. Collection arrangement, therefore, affects the precision with which the researchers can investigate departmental differences.

Characteristics of Study Sample

As it turned out, 24 of the libraries tested had separate documents and general reference departments/collections. At the remaining 2 libraries (1 academic and the other public), general reference staff received all documents related questions.

Upon completion of the data collection phase, the researchers called each library and obtained the descriptive information depicted in Table 2-2. Both the academic and public libraries tended to have a budget similar in range to those of the so called "typical" depository library. The 26 libraries tended to assign more FTE staff members to the depository collection and services, and to select a larger percentage of item numbers, than did the "typical" academic and public depository. Nevertheless, these slight differences do not affect the generalizability of study findings. The libraries tested did not display any characteristics widely divergent from the general population as described in Hernon, McClure, and Purcell (1985). There is no evidence that the libraries represented any "extreme" cases among members of the GPO depository program.

Further evidence that the libraries tested well represent the academic and public libraries within the depository program (as shown in Hernon, McClure, and Purcell, 1985, Chapters 3 and 4) is that 16 have budgets over $1 million and

Table 2-2   Selected Characteristics of Libraries Tested

	Academic	Public
Volume Count		
Under 500,000	2	3
500,000–1 million	3	3
Over 1 million	8	7
Budget		
Under 500,000	1	—
500,000–1 million	—	1
Over 1 million	12	12
Professional Library Staff		
Under 10	1	1
10–30	4	3
30–50	4	1
50–70	4	1
Over 70	—	7
FTE Staffing		
A. Documents Professional		
Under 1	—	3
1–2	10	6
3–4	1	2
Over 4	2	2
B. Documents Support Staff		
Under 1	3	9
1–2	1	2
3–4	5	2
Over 4	4	—
C. Professional Reference Staff Servicing Documents		
Under 4	1	—
4–8	5	8
9–12	4	2
13–16	1	2
Over 16	2	1
D. General Reference Support Staff Servicing Documents		
Under 1	5	8
1–2	2	—
3–4	3	2
Over 4	3	3
Percentage of Depository Item Numbers Selected		
Fewer than 25%	1	4
26–50%	3	2
51–75%	3	3
Over 75%	6	4

select more than half of the available item numbers. Eight have budgets over $1 million but select fewer than half of the item numbers, while 2 libraries have budgets under $1 million and take fewer than 25 % of the item numbers.

Thirteen libraries had over 1 million volumes and selected more than half of the item numbers. Three had similar volume counts but select less than half, and 8 have under 1 million volumes and receive fewer than 50 % of the items. A comparison of the percentage of item numbers received to the FTE staffing for government documents indicates that 19 (73 %) of the libraries assign a maximum of 2 professionals to the collection. No differences emerged regarding the percentage of items selected; in effect, a library taking fewer than 50 % of the items is as likely to assign the same number of professional staff to the documents collection as a library taking a larger percentage.

Development of Test Questions

The questions were *not* the same as those used in the original study (McClure and Hernon, 1983). However, they called for information primarily from the titles listed in the *Guidelines for the Depository Library System* (1977), as recommended for inclusion in *all* depository collections.

The initial set of test questions was developed according to the following criteria; they

- are similar to those used in the original study
- are answerable, to a large degree, from more than one government document (one generally from the list of titles recommended in the *Guidelines*)
- are answerable with factual information or bibliographic references
- reflect a wide range of document types and time frames
- are answerable from either individual depository collections or are dependent on the referral process

Both researchers reviewed the test questions and had their graduate assistants check the answers and the range of sources that might answer each question. The questions were then submitted to documents and general reference librarians at 3 academic and 2 public libraries for review. These librarians critiqued the test questions and offered suggestions about rewording, as well as questions to add or delete. On the basis of their comments, the list was revised and finalized.

Appendix B reprints the test questions that were used in the study. A total of 15 questions were administered at each library; eight questions were presented unobtrusively to documents personnel in all the libraries, while the general reference staff received another set of questions (7 questions).[2] Appendix C lists

---

[2] Library staff who pretested the test questions certified that the pool was representative of the type likely to be asked at each department and that both sets of questions represented a similar level of difficulty.

additional test questions that were pretested but not utilized in the study.

Special note should be made of two questions administered to general reference staff. Question 14 sought to locate the book *Computer-Based National Information Systems*. The response of a staff member was scored as correct if that person negotiated the question and determined that the proxie sought a government publication. The other question (number 15) dealt with a speech by Glenn English on public policy issues related to electronic information. The proxies were instructed not to volunteer that he is a member of the House of Representatives. Both questions therefore were patterned about Childers' attempt to measure the success of library staff in determining an actual information need.

The study reported in the next chapter presents the findings from administering 15 questions unobtrusively at 26 libraries. In summary, 390 questions were administered over a four month period (March-June, 1985); the proxies administered 192 questions to documents personnel at 24 libraries and 198 questions to general reference staff at 26 libraries. Since 2 libraries had combined their general reference and documents departments/collections, the questions originally intended for documents staff had to be administered to general reference personnel.

Similar to the original study (McClure and Hernon, 1983), the researchers will not reveal the names of the libraries tested. Both this chapter and the next present aggregate data and prevent the identification of individual institutions.

Administration of Test Questions

From March to June 1985, proxies administered the test questions at the libraries selected for testing. These proxies consisted of students enrolled in the documents courses at the School of Library and Information Studies, University of Oklahoma, and the Graduate Library School, University of Arizona. The researchers were also actively engaged in data collection.

To ensure the collection of valid data, the researchers discussed the project with the student "proxies," conducted training sessions, and coordinated and monitored the data collection process. Once the questions had been administered and responses obtained, the proxies completed the "Reference Question Tabulation Sheet," which is reprinted in Appendix D. The researchers discussed the answers with the students to ensure accuracy, consistency, and completeness in data collection. The researchers also double-checked all responses to ensure consistency and completeness in the reporting of responses.

In administering the questions and tabulating the results, the proxies were reminded to follow certain guidelines:

- Ask the question sincerely and accurately, appear to be conducting research or writing a paper in which the information is necessary

- Do not have the "Reference Question Tabulation Sheet" or the list of questions out in the open during administration. Remember the question and complete the tabulation sheet promptly after question administration has been completed
- Attempt to ask the questions during times of the day in which one could expect to find a professional librarian in the documents or general reference area
- Ask for a government documents librarian or whoever is in charge of the government documents, and attempt to ask the 8 questions of these people
- If a library did not have a separate documents department/collection, ask all 15 questions of general reference personnel

The proxies were instructed to use the bottom and the back of the tabulation sheet to add descriptions, comments, notes, or questions regarding each question administration. The researchers reviewed these notes and comments prior to data coding and analysis to ensure that the proxies used consistent tabulation practices.

Many documents departments/collections are understaffed and lack professional staff members to cover the documents reference desk during all hours that the library is open. Thus the proxies varied the hours of their visits, but were encouraged to try to approach professional personnel with a question. If the staff person was obviously a student assistant, they were instructed to return at a later time and ask the question. In those cases in which the proxies were told to return when a reference or documents librarian was on duty, the question was administered at a later time. Even though the testing process may have involved more than professional staff members, it indicates the type of service that we received for our test questions.

Students were reminded that unobtrusive testing requires the collection of data from participants without their knowing the real purpose of the questions. Students were asked not to discuss the project or reveal the study sites. If participating libraries and their staffs realized that they were being investigated, both their behavior and the findings would have been affected.[3] The proxies also were asked not to discuss the project with students in their other classes or with friends, since the information could conceivably have gotten back to the participating libraries and invalidated the findings. Furthermore, the proxies agreed not to disseminate information about a library's scores. All the data are confidential and will not be linked to an individual library.

---

[3] At one test site, the documents staff recognized one of the researchers and the purpose of his questions. Consequently the test findings for that library were disregarded and another area library was selected for participation.

Testing Process

The test questions were of two types: *factual* — that is, the name of an individual or a request for specific statistical or descriptive information — or *bibliographic* — that is, a request for a bibliographic citation, the availability of a publication in the library or through the GPO sales program, or obtaining a Superintendent of Documents classification number (see Appendix B). Pretesting the questions helped to ensure that the questions were representative of those received by academic and public depository libraries. However, testing did not examine all types of conceivable questions.

To place study findings in proper context, a definition of "correct" answer is necessary. For this study, responses from library staff were classified as either "correct" or "incorrect." A correct answer matched one of the answer options specified in Appendix B. The answer, in certain cases, might require the location of a specific factual or statistical information. It might also be the discovery of a bibliographic citation or negotiation of an information need — the need for a U.S. government publication. The answer need not come from a predetermined reference source; public service staff could use whatever reference or referral sources were at their disposal.

An incorrect answer included responses that were wrong or provided inaccurate information, or are characterized as "don't know." If a person at either the documents reference or general reference desk asked the proxy to return when a particular person was available, the proxy did so and did not count the original encounter as administration of the question. In some instances, library staff indicated that a question could not be answered because the necessary reference source was not owned or available on the shelf. The proxies checked not only the accuracy of a response but also whether the library owned a title and if it was indeed on the shelf. If the title was present and if the proxy had not been referred elsewhere, the response was considered incorrect.

Proxies neither suggested sources and places where the answer might be obtained nor encouraged referrals, even when staff members responded with "don't know" and terminated the interview. The proxies were instructed not to argue with personnel or be persistent about obtaining an answer. If staff members indicated that the question was unanswerable or that the "government doesn't publish that type of information," the proxies politely thanked them for their time and left. The response, however, was recorded as incorrect.

Library personnel treated all the questions as legitimate and did not dispute them. If they did not accept a question but encouraged the proxie to return later, testing was postponed. Library personnel might refer a question either internal or external to their department; in such cases, it was noted that referral had been made. However, the correctness of a question was not judged until the proxies had followed through on the referral and received an answer.

When library personnel referred a proxie to a source but did not offer to look for the answer, the proxie would pretend to examine the source for awhile and return to the same person for further guidance in the use of that source. The proxies did not inquire if the person who accepted the question had, in fact, a master's degree in library/information science. They asked questions of personnel who appeared to be full-time professionals rather than student assistants. Those staff members tested were sitting at the reference desk and apparently were not preoccupied with other patrons or telephone questions.

A subjective assessment about which staff members were professional cannot always be correct. It is likely that some paraprofessional personnel participated in answering the questions; therefore, the next chapter reflects reference service that library patrons could have expected from general reference and documents personnel who staffed public service desks when the questions were administered. From comments that test subjects made, the researchers believe that the vast majority of staff members were professional. For example, at one private, baccalaureate institution, once the proxies signed in at the circulation desk, the reference and documents librarians escorted them to their respective departments. The professional staff then negotiated all the test questions.

Limitations

Although the researchers developed clear procedures for administration of the questions, the proxies occasionally may not have provided accurate renditions of the test questions or have otherwise aroused the suspicion of a staff member. Unobtrusive testing does not consider unique situations within a library that may adversely affect the ability of staff members to answer questions. Nonetheless, the researchers believe that the study design and proxie training minimized possible difficulties.

Some librarians may feel uncomfortable about the selection of test questions. These questions were developed according to specific criteria and were subjected to a rigorous pretest and gained the approval of documents and general reference librarians before their use. Some of the questions selected for investigation had actually been asked at the pretest sites. Librarians went through lists of reference questions that they were frequently asked and shared some of those questions that they believed appropriate for inclusion in this study.

Another possible limitation is the assumption that the libraries investigated maintain a "basic reference collection" of publications published by both the government and commercial firms. The researchers believe that if a library serves as a depository, it, in effect, has agreed to maintain a "basic reference collection" necessary to provide at least minimal access to items eligible for depository distribution. Still, as a precaution, the questions could often be answered from two or more sources. The proxies also checked to see if the library actually owned the sources to answer a question and if these sources were currently on the shelf.

Throughout this chapter and the next, "depository library staff" encompasses both professional and paraprofessional staff assigned to the depository collection and the general reference department/collection. The proxies were encouraged to ask the questions of individuals who appeared to be professionals. However, such determinations are not always accurate. Although the researchers think that the results emphasize the quality of reference service provided by professional librarians, paraprofessionals probably answered some questions.

Study results apply only to reference service for questions of a factual and bibliographic nature, covering the U.S. government and paper copy and microfiche publications available through the GPO depository library program. Because of the nature of the study design, the researchers realize that the data are generalizable only to those academic and public depository libraries within the cities represented in Figure 2-3 and those having characteristics similar to those identified in Table 2-2. Other libraries, however, may be able to draw useful insights and implications pertinent to identifying and improving, where necessary, their *correct answer fill rate*.

In summary, the researchers believe that appropriate steps have been taken to minimize the impact of the above-mentioned limitations on the results. Indeed, the study indicates the accuracy with which academic and public library depository staff answered reference questions that called for government publications. Since questions were administered to both general reference and documents personnel, the normal, operating conditions of a library provided the settings in which "real" reference service was provided to proxies who posed as actual library users. Some libraries assign special staff to provide public service for a card catalog. In the instances in which the test libraries did this, testing included general reference, government documents, and card catalog personnel. Clearly, the study represent a cross-section of reference service that the test libraries provided.

RELIABILITY AND VALIDITY

Reliability suggests stability and consistency of measurement — accuracy. One criterion for assessing reliability is the representativeness of the questions about the phenomenon that is being measured: the more representative the questions about the instrument, the higher the instrument's reliability (Witka, 1968, pp. 267–268). On this criterion, the instrument should have high reliability, since the questions were developed according to specific criteria and pretested by practicing academic and public librarians. Both the researchers and the librarians believed that the final set of questions was "representative" of typical questions encountered at the documents and general reference desk.

A second criterion of reliability is accurate and consistent coding; the following actions were taken to increase the reliability of data according to this criterion. First, the proxies followed written procedures for the administration of the questions and completed standardized coding forms for each completed transaction. Second, all proxies attended a training session to assure their understanding of the procedures and definitions on the coding form, as well as to answer any questions about data coding. Also, the researchers reviewed all responses and comments provided by the proxies (often in their presence, in order to elicit additional information) about individual testing situations in an effort to maintain consistency in the coding.

A third criterion for reliability is a coefficient of reliability. There are a number of reliability coefficients, but each coefficient (in general) expresses the ratio of true-score variance (perfect reliability, with no error) to observed-score variance (Kerlinger, 1973, p. 446). Perfect reliability has a coefficient of 1.0, and a coefficient of 0 indicates no reliability. The Kuder-Richardson Formula 20, which assumes different degrees of difficulty on test items, was used to compute the reliability coefficient. This coefficient is computed with knowledge of the mean and the variance of the scores, plus the number of items on the test (Roscoe, 1975, pp. 134–135).

By considering the administration of the 15 questions in each library as 26 different test scores, a coefficient of reliability, based on the Kuder-Richardson formula, can be calculated. The coefficient of reliability was .83, indicating substantial reliability of the responses to individual questions when considered as a group (Nunally, 1967, p. 80).

In August, 1985, the researchers randomly selected two libraries, one academic and the other public, and retested both the general reference and documents staff with the same questions. The coefficient of reliability from the test-retest procedure was .97 for library A and .94 for library B. In November 1985, the researchers selected another city and retested another two libraries. The coefficient of reliability was .91 for library C and .94 for library D. Finally, in December 1985, the researchers selected even another city and retested the two libraries. The coefficient of reliability was .91 for both libraries E and F. These test/retest procedures increase the confidence of the researchers that data collection was, in fact, reliable and accurate.

The validity of data is the extent to which they accurately measure what they purport to measure. The study demonstrated "face validity" because the researchers had a representative collection of test items and "sensible" methods of test construction and administration. They drew upon their past experiences in setting up and administrating large scale unobtrusive testing involving the management of student proxies.

The construct of *correct answer fill rate* has been tested previously and was carefully operationalized (internal validity). The use of this construct and the similarity in findings from the test-retest procedure suggest that the measure, *correct answer fill rate,* demonstrates both internal and construct validity.

Another criterion of validity is the extent to which the study results can be generalized to a population. "Generalizability" is largely dependent on a sampling procedure, the selection of study sites, and the characteristics of participants (in this case, libraries) in the study (Kerlinger, 1973, pp. 456–459). Although the study was limited to 26 libraries, selection was based on carefully developed sampling procedures that permit generalizability to academic and public depository libraries in urban setting with a population of at least 100,000 in the South, West, and Midwest.

The general findings from this study support findings from other unobtrusive tests of reference service (see Figure 1-1). Many of the staff at the libraries tested displayed a limited *correct answer fill rate*; made infrequent referral, either internal or external to the library; failed to negotiate reference questions; conducted ineffective search strategies; and demonstrated limited question negotiation skills. Therefore, it is imperative that the profession develop strategies to improve the effectiveness and efficiency of public service staff in meeting information needs. Other chapters in this book suggest such strategies (as does McClure and Hernon, 1983) and discuss the implications of "half-right" reference service (Crowley, 1985).

CHAPTER 3

QUALITY OF DOCUMENTS REFERENCE SERVICE

This chapter discusses the quality of reference service that the proxies received for the 15 questions that they administered at the 26 academic and public libraries in the Midwest, South, and West.[1] The quality of service is analyzed in terms of the *correct answer fill rate,* the reasons for incorrect answers, the nature of referrals internal and external to the library, the accuracy of those referrals, the difficulty of the questions administered, the duration of the interview and search process, and the interviewing and search skills of library staff. These topics are examined in the context of specific variables, including the type of library, department, budget, volume counts, library staffing patterns, and the percentage of items selected. Nonetheless, the overriding question addressed in this chapter is "Will patrons obtain either the *correct* answer to their questions or referral to a person or source, internal or external to the library, that provides the correct answer?"

OVERALL ACCURACY OF ANSWERS

Personnel from the 26 academic and public libraries correctly answered 241 (61.8%) of the questions (see Figure 3-1). There was no statistically significant difference by type of library—academic versus public (chi square = 1.08, $p > .05$);[2] academic personnel answered correctly 126 questions and their counterparts in public libraries correctly answered 115 questions.

Two of the libraries tested combined general reference and government documents reference services in one department, while the remaining 24 libraries had separate government documents and general reference departments. Of

---

[1] As discussed in the previous chapter, 8 of the questions were asked at the documents department/collection and 7 were first asked at the central reference department/collection.

[2] p stands for probability.

Figure 3-1   Correct Answer Fill Rate for Libraries Tested*

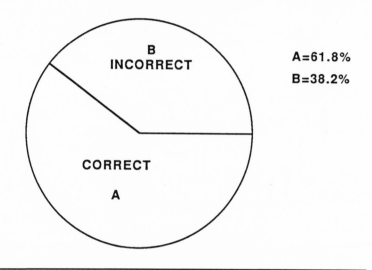

A=61.8%

B=38.2%

* Based on 390 questions asked at both central reference and government document areas in 26 libraries (13 academic and 13 public).

the 192 questions first asked at separate documents departments/collections, 124 resulted in the receipt of a correct answer. For the 198 questions first asked at the general reference departments/collections, 117 questions were correctly answered. Personnel at the two libraries with combined general reference and documents departments successfully answered 18 of the 117 questions. Thus, 64.6% of the questions first asked of personnel in separate documents departments were answered successfully, whereas 59.1% of the questions first asked to general reference personnel were correctly answered. Since only two of the libraries had combined general reference and government documents departments and services, no meaningful comparisons concerning the *correct answer fill rate* can be made to other organizational arrangements.

Figure 3-2 indicates an almost even distribution in the percentage of correct answers given by geographical region. Table 3-1, which summarizes the percentage of correct answers for each question by geographic region, indicates that, collectively, the personnel tested in the Western libraries performed less satisfactorily than their counterparts in the South and Midwest. The difference in performance for Western libraries in both Table 3-1 and Figure 3-1 is explained by the fact that two more libraries were tested in this one region. Therefore, overall Western libraries answered 81 questions correctly but they were administered 30 more questions than libraries in the other two regions.

Figure 3-2   Percentages of Correct Answers by Geographical Region*

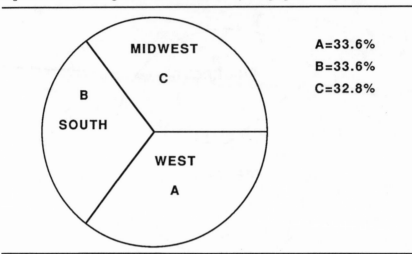

* Total of 241 correct answers (390 questions asked).

Viewing the number of correct answers on an institutional basis indicates that the public service staff of a library successfully negotiated between 4 and 14 questions (see Figure 3-3). The mean *correct answer fill rate* was 9.7 correct answers for academic libraries and 8.9 for public libraries. Only public libraries answered correctly 6 or fewer questions, while both of the libraries that successfully negotiated 12 or more questions were academic.

All the libraries owned a source that would have answered each question. They might not own some of the titles requested but they had sources that provided the bibliographic citation or other pertinent information for locating and obtaining the title elsewhere. For example, each library possessed the *Monthly Catalog of United States Government Publications* [hereafter cited as the *Monthly Catalog*] or Poore's *A Descriptive Catalogue of the Government Publications of the United States* (1885). However, staff members might not be familiar with Poore's bibliography and how to use it.

Library personnel only checked the OCLC database[3] for only 4 (1%) questions — twice for question 6 (the FAA publication issued in the mid-1970s) and twice for question 13 (seeking Salaman and Hettinger's *Policy Implications of Information Technology*). Staff from the general reference and documents department each consulted the OCLC database twice. Viewed from another perspective, all these staff members were associated with academic libraries. Personnel

---

[3] OCLC is a national bibliographic utility that OCLC Inc. operates from Columbus, Ohio. Since July 1976, the Government Printing Office has used it to generate MARC records and to produce the *Monthly Catalog*.

Table 3-1 Summary of Correct Answers by Region

Question Number	Question	Questions Answered Correctly, South		Questions Answered Correctly, Midwest		Questions Answered Correctly, West		Questions Answered Correctly, All	
		No.	%	No.	%	No.	%	No.	%
A.	**Asked at Documents Department/Collection**								
1	Imprisonment of Free Black Seaman	6	7.5	5	6.2	5	6.2	16	6.6
2	Seeking Document on Microcomputers	6	7.5	7	8.8	8	9.9	21	8.7
3	High School Dropouts	8	10.0	7	8.8	7	8.6	22	9.1
4	Production of Bituminous Coal	8	10.0	6	7.5	8	9.9	22	9.1
5	Name of Administrator, Agricultural Marketing Service	8	10.0	8	10.0	9	11.1	25	10.4
6	Seeking FAA Publication	1	1.2	2	2.5	3	3.7	6	2.5
7	USDA Regulations on Lemons	5	6.2	6	7.5	6	7.4	17	7.1
8	Task Force on Food Assistance	4	5.0	6	7.5	3	3.7	13	5.4
B.	**Asked at General Reference Department/Collection**								
9	Act Creating Office of Science and Technology Policy	7	8.8	8	10.0	9	11.1	24	10.0
10	Summary Statistics on the Speed of Vehicles	6	7.5	4	5.0	—	—	10	4.1
11	Office of the Historian	6	7.5	4	5.0	6	7.4	16	6.6
12	1980 Law on Patents for University Inventions	7	8.8	7	8.8	8	9.9	22	9.1
13	Seeking Policy Implications of Information Technology	2	2.5	2	2.5	2	2.5	6	2.5
14	Seeking the Book Computer-Based National Information Systems	2	2.5	2	2.5	2	2.5	6	2.5
15	English's Speech on Electronic Information	4	5.0	6	7.5	5	6.2	15	6.2
	Average		66.7%		66.7%		54.0%		61.8%

Figure 3-3   Number of Libraries Answering Questions Correctly

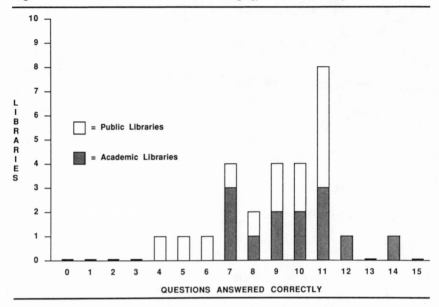

from the public libraries did not consult OCLC or another other bibliographic utility.

Two of these 4 questions where OCLC was used were answered correctly. In one case where an incorrect answer was given, the staff member read the wrong record. In the other instance (question 2: the price of the document on microcomputers), the person located the correct entry on the *Publications Reference File* (PRF) but read the price for the preceding record. Carelessness can contribute to the provision of an incorrect answer.

The most frequent reason for an incorrect answer was that library staff gave wrong data (96 cases, 64.4% of the instances). In an additional 30 cases (20.1%), staff responded with "don't know" and terminated the search, without suggesting any referral. In the remaining 23 cases (15.4%), they claimed that the library did not own a source that would answer the question, when, in fact, they did and that source was on the shelf at that time. No significant differences among these reasons occurred on a regional basis, or by type of library; predominantly incorrect answers resulted from the staff supplying wrong information.

The only difference on a departmental basis (general reference versus government documents) was that general reference staff were most likely to claim that the library did not own a title (20 of the 23 cases). Staff responses to question 13 (seeking the Salaman and Hettinger publication) largely account for this departmental difference. Typically, general reference staff indicated that if the title was not represented in the general library catalog, the library did not own it.

ANALYSIS OF QUESTIONS ANSWERED

Some questions had a much greater likelihood of being answered correctly than did others (see Table 3-1). The questions were ranked, within each region, from "most frequently answered correctly" to "most frequently answered incorrectly." Table 3-2 ranks the questions by percentage of correct answers. (When two or more questions had the same percentage of correct answers, they were ranked the same.)

None of the questions were correctly answered by all 26 libraries. All the Southern libraries correctly negotiated questions

- 3: the number of high school dropouts
- 4: total production of bituminous coal for 1868
- 5: the name of the administrator, Agricultural Marketing Service, and his mailing address

Midwestern libraries successfully answered questions

- 5: administrator of the Agricultural Marketing Service
- 9: text of the law creating the Office of Science and Technology Policy

In contrast, the libraries in the West taken collectively could not answer any of the questions totally correctly. In fact, as will be discussed, these libraries were more likely to find the test questions to be harder. None of the Western libraries successfully answered question 10 (summary statistics on the percentage of vehicles exceeding the 55 m.p.h. speed limit), whereas two-thirds of the Southern, and half of the Midwestern, libraries correctly answered the question.

A comparison was made between the top three ranks (easiest) for each region and the bottom ranks (most difficult) to identify possible agreement about the degree of difficulty for specific questions. To be identified as easiest or most difficult, all three regions had to agree on the general ranking of the question; otherwise, questions were not labeled as either "easiest" or "most difficult."

Six questions were the most likely to receive a correct response. Questions 9 (the text of the act creating the Office of Science and Technology Policy) and 12 (the law providing universities and small businesses with the right to obtain patents for inventions) were asked of general reference staff and, as will be noted subsequently, were often referred to the documents department/collection. The other 4 questions were asked at the documents department/collection. Number 2 asked for the cost of a publication (one on micro-

Table 3-2 Ranking of Questions by Percentage of Correct Answers

	South		Midwest		West	
Rank	Question Number	Brief Description	Question Number	Brief Description	Question Number	Brief Description
1	3	Number of High School Dropouts	5	Administrator, Agricultural Marketing Service	5	Administrator, Agricultural Marketing Service
	4	Production of Bituminous Coal	9	Law Creating the Office of Science and Technology Policy	9	Law Creating the Office of Science and Technology Policy
	5	Administrator, Agricultural Marketing Service				
2	9	Law Creating the Office of Science and Technology Policy	2	Cost of Microcomputer Book	2	Cost of Microcomputer Book
	12	Law Covering Patents for Inventions	3	Number of High School Dropouts	4	Production of Bituminous Coal
			12	Law Covering Patents for Inventions	12	Law Covering Patents for Inventions
3	1	Imprisonment of Free Black Seamen	4	Production of Bituminous Coal	3	Number of High School Dropouts
	2	Cost of Microcomputer Book	7	USDA Regulations on Lemons		
	10	Number of Vehicles That Speed	8	Task Force on Food Assistance		
	11	Office of the Historian	15	English's Speech		
4	7	USDA Regulations on Lemons	1	Imprisonment of Free Black Seamen	11	Office of the Historian
5	8	Task Force on Food Assistance	10	Number of Vehicles That Speed	7	USDA Regulations on Lemons
	15	English's Speech	11	Office of the Historian		
6	13	Salaman and Hettinger Work on Information Technology	6	The FAA Publication Issued in Mid-1970s	1	Imprisonment of Free Black Seamen
	14	The Work on Computer Systems	13	Salaman and Hettinger Work on Information Technology	15	English's Speech
			14	The Work on Computer Systems		
7	6	The FAA Publication Issues in Mid-1970s			6	The FAA Publication Issued in the Mid-1970s
					8	Task Force on Food Assistance
8					13	Salaman and Hettinger Work on Information Technology
					14	The Work on Computer Systems
9					10	Number of Vehicles That Speed

computers),[4] while number 5 required the name of an administrator (Agricultural Marketing Service) and his office address. The remaining two questions called for brief statistical data; number 3 needed the number of high school dropouts and number 4 required the total production of bituminous coal for 1868.

Three questions were the hardest for staff to answer correctly; each was successfully negotiated in 23.1% of the test situations (6 of 26). Number 6, which was administered to documents personnel, called for a publication of the Federal Aviation Administration issued in the mid-1970s. In contrast, questions 13 and 14 were asked of the general reference staff, in particular those servicing the online, microfiche, or card catalog. Number 13 requested R. K. Salaman and E. C. Hettinger's *Policy Implications of Information Technology*, while number 14, which sought *Computer-Based National Information Systems* was scored as correct if the staff negotiated the question and identified the title as a government publication.

Undoubtedly staff associate certain types of questions with government publications. A request for a public law suggests the *Statutes at Large* or similar sources, while the need for basic statistical data signifies a search of either *Statistical Abstract of the United States,* for current information, or *Historical Statistics of the United States,* for retrospective data. On the other hand, a correct answer for question 6 necessitates a search of the *Monthly Catalog* for 1982, a microform service that combines records for multiple years of the *Monthly Catalog* in one place, or a detailed shelflist that indicates individual holdings. Some of the libraries tested subscribed to the "GPO Monthly Catalog Subscription Service" of Auto-Graphics, Inc. (Monterey, California). This service represents a consolidated and self-contained version of the *Monthly Catalog* from mid 1976 to the present.[5]

The titles mentioned in both questions 13 and 14 appear to be commercially issued and not government publications. Therefore, staff members frequently did not think of a government as the likely publisher. They concentrated their search on the general library's catalog or a source such as *Books in Print* (Bowker).

DURATION OF REFERENCE INTERVIEW AND SEARCH

For purposes of this section, the interview and search process (I&S) encompasses all those activities from the time that the question was asked until a resolution to the question was provided and the I&S terminated. The resolution

---

[4] Question 2 was easy to answer, in part, because the correct answer was available in either the *Monthly Catalog* or the *PRF*. Nonetheless, staff at 5 libraries could not successfully negotiate the question.

[5] For a discussion of this service, see *Government Information Quarterly,* 1 (1984): 339–342. For a comparison of the Auto-Graphics service to similar packages, see *Government Information Quarterly, 4* (1987), No. 1.

could have been either a correct or an incorrect answer. The study did not collect separate data on the duration of each component of I&S: the reference interview, question negotiation, and the search process.

Over one-fourth of the questions (27.9%) received a maximum of 1 minute of I&S, while 81.5% generated no more than 5 minutes of I&S. At the other end of the spectrum, 4 questions (1.2%) benefited from 26 to 36 minutes of staff attention. Staff members provided two-thirds of the correct answers within 3 minutes of I&S and 89.3% within 5 minutes. An analysis of the relationship between correct answer and I&S of 5 minutes and less, versus 6 or more minutes, was not statistically significant at the .05 level (chi square = 1.82, $p > .05$). I&S lasting longer than 5 minutes does not guarantee that a question is more likely to receive a correct answer. In fact, library personnel did not often spend more than 5 minutes on I&S, even if they did not appear to be busy answering the questions of other library clientele.

Table 3-3 lists the average duration of I&S by question and region, as well as whether the question was answered correctly or incorrectly. Regardless of the

Table 3-3   Average Duration of Interview and Search Process by Question and Region

Question	Average Time (Minutes)		
	South	Midwest	West
A. Asked at Documents Department/Collection			
1. Imprisonment of Free Black Seamen			
Correct Answer	4	11	5
Incorrect Answer	2	2	5
2. Cost of Microcomputer Book			
Correct Answer	2	2	2
Incorrect Answer	1	2	2
3. Number of High School Dropouts			
Correct Answer	4	5	4
Incorrect Answer	—	2	6
4. Production of Bituminous Coal			
Correct Answer	6	9	4
Incorrect Answer	—	8	3
5. Administrator, Agricultural Marketing Service			
Correct Answer	2	2	3
Incorrect Answer	—	—	1
6. FAA Publication Issued in Mid-1970s			
Correct Answer	10	7	5
Incorrect Answer	2	6	3
7. USDA Regulations on Lemons			
Correct Answer	2	3	3
Incorrect Answer	2	6	2

Table 3-3   Average Duration of Interview and Search Process by Question and Region

Question	South	Midwest	West
	Average Time (Minutes)		
8. Task Force on Food Assistance			
Correct Answer	6	5	5
Incorrect Answer	6	5	5
B. Asked at Documents General Reference Department/Collection			
9. Law Creating the U.S. Office of Science and Technology Policy			
Correct Answer	3	4	3
Incorrect Answer	3	—	3
10. Percentage of Vehicles That Speed			
Correct Answer	4	—	7
Incorrect Answer	4	6	6
11. Office of the Historian			
Correct Answer	6	7	2
Incorrect Answer	3	1	5
12. Law Covering Patents for Inventions			
Correct Answer	6	7	7
Incorrect Answer	16	6	3
13. Salaman and Hettinger Work on Information Technology			
Correct Answer	5	1	2
Incorrect Answer	2	2	1
14. Book on Computer Information Systems			
Correct Answer	5	1	1
Incorrect Answer	2	1	1
15. English's Speech			
Correct Answer	5	6	3
Incorrect Answer	2	1	4
ALL QUESTIONS			
Correct Answer	5	5	4
Incorrect Answer	3	3	5

question, the time spent on I&S by library staff members in each region is similar. When one compares the I&S time in terms of the resulting answers being either correct or incorrect, however, significant differences emerge among the regions. As listed at the bottom of the table, the average duration for I&S in the South and Midwest was identical; it was 5 minutes for a correct answer and 3 minutes for an incorrect response. Staff members in the West answered questions correctly, on average, in 4 minutes but incorrectly in 5 minutes. In short, staff members in the South and West spent more I&S time to obtain a correct answer than an incorrect one; those in the West spent more time to obtain an incorrect answer than a correct one!

An examination of Table 3-3 indicates that library personnel in the Midwest spent the most time obtaining a correct answer for question 1 (the imprisonment of free Black seamen), while Southern staff members spent the most time answering question 6 (the FAA publication issued in the mid-1970s) correctly. Midwestern personnel spent the most time answering question 4 (the total production of bituminous coal) either correctly or incorrectly. Library staff in the West spent the most time obtaining an incorrect answer to question 3 (the number of high school dropouts), while personnel in the Midwest spent the most time answering question 7 (USDA regulations on lemons) incorrectly. Southern library staff spent the most time answering question 12 (the law covering patents for inventions) incorrectly and questions 13 (Salaman and Hettinger's work on information technology) and 14 (the work on computer information systems) correctly. They were less willing to rush to judgment concerning whether their libraries owned the publications specified in questions 13 and 14.

The duration of I&S did not differ significantly by either library type (chi square = 1.10, $p > ,05$) or department (chi square = .046, $p > ,.05$). Neither library type nor department reflected greater efficiency in answering the test questions.

Another point of interest is to determine the average time necessary to obtain a correct answer for the questions identified as easiest versus those identified as most difficult. On average, staff members took 4 minutes to answer the easiest questions correctly and 4.1 minutes to answer the difficult questions correctly. The combined I&S for the more difficult questions is misleading. Questions 13 and 14 were asked of the staff servicing the library's general catalog. Question 14 was scored as correct if they determined that the proxie was seeking a government publication, while question 13 sought a particular title. Obviously many library staff spent minimal time with both questions. Considering question 6 (the FAA publication issued in the mid-1970s) by itself, the combined I&S necessary to produce a correct answer, regardless of region, was 7.3 minutes.

As shown in Figure 3-4, staff from the Southern libraries peaked with the number of their correct answers at 2 minutes of I&S; their performance fell off dramatically the longer time. The correct answer rate for Midwestern personnel increased up to 3 minutes before dropping off, while Western personnel achieved their largest number of correct answers with minimal I&S—1 minute. Regardless of region, the success rate of library personnel decreased the longer that I&S lasted.

Figure 3-5 presents the "flip-side" of the previous figure and examines I&S for *incorrect* answers. Personnel from the Western libraries gave the most incorrect answers immediately upon contact with the proxie. Staff from the other two regions also provided a large proportion of incorrect answers within the first minute of I&S; however, they showed a sharp increase in the number of incorrect answers at the third minute of I&S. Both Figures 3-4 and 3-5 indicate

Figure 3-4   Correct Answers by Interview/Search Duration and Region

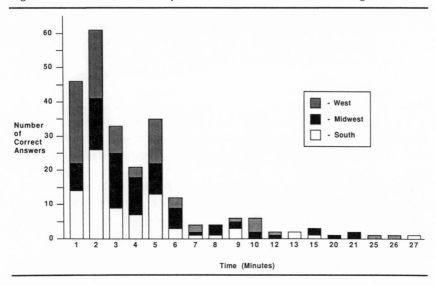

Figure 3-5   Incorrect Answers by Interview/Search Duration and Region

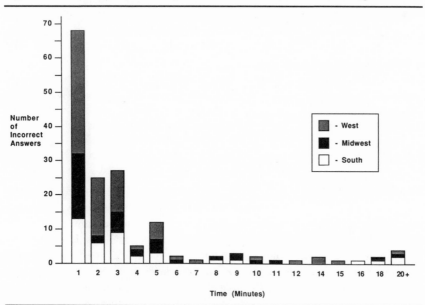

that the proxies received little I&S beyond 7 minutes. When they did, the answer was as likely to be incorrect as correct.

Both figures also indicate that, whether or not they are correctly answering questions, library staff members spend similar amounts of I&S time on questions. Staff in the Southern libraries answered 77 (64.2%) of the questions, either correctly or incorrectly, within 3 minutes of I&S. Their counterparts in the Midwest answered 66 (55%) questions in the same time frame, while personnel in Western libraries handled 108 (72%) of the questions within 3 minutes. Overall, approximately two-thirds of the 390 questions (251 or 64.4%) were answered within 3 minutes. These findings suggest that staff might have an "internal clock" that affects the amount of time that they are willing to spend on I&S.

The findings in this section regarding duration of the I&S process for library staff members participating in this study must be seen in the context of numerous additional variables that the study did not explore. Additional factors include:

• the competency of the staff members and their knowledge of the reference interview, question negotiation, and search strategies
• their workload at the time the questions were asked
• the number of patrons they were also serving at the same time
• the sophistication of the user in presenting the question and providing follow-up information
• the theory of reference practiced and adherence to a specific policy regarding the amount of time to spend on questions at each participating library
• staffing patterns and the use of nonprofessional personnel to provide reference assistance
• the location of government publications within the library

Nonetheless, the I&S process is an important factor in overall staff accuracy in answering questions.

FIRST CONTACT ANSWER

Another aspect of the overall quality of reference service is termed "first contact answers." A first contact answer is a specific answer to the proxy, whether it was correct or incorrect. Referrals that received an answer (any answer) resulting from the first contact also comprise first contact answers. If a proxy was asked to return at a later time or given a response of "don't know" and the reference interview was terminated, the answer was not a first contact answer.

Data were collected on this variable because the researchers wanted to determine the degree to which proxies did not obtain any specific answer to the questions that they asked. Such data might indicate the frustration encountered by patrons who attempt to obtain answers to their questions. Overall, 92.3% of the questions received a first contact answer. Table 3-4 suggests that the percentage of first contact answers was similar for 11 questions; it ranged between 92 and 100%. For the remaining 4 questions, the percentage of first contact answers ranged from 73 to 88.

In no instance when library staff members responded that they "did not know" did they refer proxies to another member of the staff or another information provider. This finding is surprising since the depository library program supposedly encourages referral to regional and other selective depository libraries (Hernon, McClure, and Purcell, 1985).

REFERRAL SERVICES

When libraries provide information and referral services, they are "facilitating the link between a person with a need and the service, activity, information, or advice outside the library which can meet the need" (Childers, 1979, p. 2036). Referral is either "internal" — to another area of the library or member of the library staff — or "external" — to other information providers such as another depository (selective or regional), GPO bookstore, or specific government agency. A central question becomes: How frequently do documents and general reference staff from both academic and public libraries engage in referral, either of an "internal" or "external" nature? This section of the chapter addresses

Table 3-4   Percentage of First Contact Answers for Each Question

Question Number	Question Description	Percentage of First Contact Answers
A. Asked at Documents Department/Collection		
1	Imprisonment of Free Black Seamen	92
2	Cost of Microcomputer Book	96
3	Number of High School Dropouts	100
4	Production of Bituminous Coal	96
5	Administrator, Agricultural Marketing Service	100
6	FAA Publication Issues in Mid-1970s	73
7	USDA Regulations on Lemons	96
8	Task Force on Food Assistance	92
B. Asked at Reference Department/Collection		
9	Law Creating the Office of Science and Technology Policy	92
10	Percentage of Vehicles That Speed	96
11	Office of the Historian	88
12	Law Covering Patents for Inventions	100
13	Salaman and Hettinger Work on Information Technology	81
14	Work on Computer Information Systems	85
15	English's Speech	92

this question and suggests the extent to which library staff encourage library clientele to use interlibrary loan services and view the depository library program as an interlocking network of member libraries cooperating to provide the public with effective and efficient access to publications that the government has made publicly available.

Of the 241 correctly answered questions, 51 involved referral activity; therefore 190 correctly answered questions did not receive any referral. With the inclusion of the 51 questions, referral service was suggested in a total of 66 instances (16.9% of 390 test situations). Predominantly referral was internal — either from the general reference department/collection to the documents department/collection (50 or 75.7%) or another department within the library (8 or 12.1%). In the remaining instances (12.2%), referral was to either another depository library (4 or 6.1%) or a government agency (4 or 6.1%). Interestingly, library staff never specified the name, address, and telephone number of another library to consult.

For question 13 (seeking Salaman and Hettinger's work on information technology), internal referral was to the interlibrary loan department. In one instance, when the proxie indicated that he needed the publication "very soon," the member of the reference department could think of no alternative search location and terminated the reference interview with "don't know." Yet the publication was on the shelf in the depository collection. In the other instance, the proxie went to the interlibrary loan department, where the librarian located the title in the OCLC database and recorded the Sudocs number. She encouraged the proxie to check the library's own depository collection before resorting to interlibrary loan. The publication was discovered in the collection, and the library received a correct score.

Question 13 was correctly answered in 6 libraries and received 7 referrals, two of which were to the documents collection. It is perhaps surprising that the proxies did not receive more referrals to interlibrary loan or more staff did not check the OCLC database. Staff members, on the whole, gave minimal attention to helping the proxies with either questions 13 or 14.

In one case (question 11: Office of the Historian, State Department), a staff member from a public library actually called the Federal Information Center (General Services Administration) and obtained the requested information.

In 17 instances, referral service produced an incorrect answer, primarily the wrong answer (14 or 82.3%). Twice staff responded that they did not know and terminated the reference interview. In the final instance, they claimed that the library did not own the source material necessary to answer the question, when, in fact, they did.

Table 3-5 identifies referral patterns for individual questions. Including question 14, which was scored on the ability of staff to identify that a government publication was sought, 7 questions did not receive any referrals. All of these questions, except number 14, were administered to the documents per-

Table 3-5   Referral Location for Individual Questions

Question Number	Description of Question	Number of Referrals	Referral Location			
			Documents Department	Another Department	Government Agency	Another Depository
A.	**Asked at Documents Department/Collection**					
1	Imprisonment of Free Black Seamen	3		1		2
2	Cost of Microcomputer Book	—				
3	Number of High School Dropouts	—				
4	Production of Bituminous Coal	—				
5	Administrator, Agricultural Marketing Service	—				
6	FAA Publication Issued in Mid-1970s	1			1	
7	USDA Regulations on Lemons	—				
8	Task Force on Food Assistance	—				
B.	**Asked at the General Reference Department/Collection**					
9	Law Creating the Office of Science and Technology Policy	14	13	1		
10	Percentage of Vehicles That Speed	11	9	1		
11	Office of the Historian	6	2	1	3	
12	Law Covering Patents for Inventions	14	14			
13	Salaman and Hettinger Work on Information Technology	7	2	4		1
14	Work on Computer Information Systems	—				
15	English's Speech	10	10			
	Total:	66	50	8	4	4

sonnel. Since two libraries had combined documents and reference departments and the staffs of these libraries made two of the referrals for question 1
(imprisonment of free Black seamen), personnel from separate documents departments made only two referrals.

Questions 9 and 12 sought a public law and were clearly associated with the
specialized holdings of a depository collection. Once library personnel negotiated that Glenn English is a member of the House of Representatives, they
referred the proxies to the depository collection for access to his speech (question 15). Question 10 (the percentage of vehicles that speed) was also clearly associated as a documents related question. Together these four questions
accounted for 49 or 74.2% of all the referrals.

Surprisingly, question 11, which sought the name of the historian of the Office of Historian, State Department, generated 6 referrals, three internal to the
library and three external. The staff of academic and public libraries were
equally as likely to engage in referral. Reference personnel made referrals to the
government documents department/collection but documents staff accounted
for only 2 referrals and did not associate the questions with other holdings of the
library or the external environment.

A final general observation is in order. Staff members made half of the referrals (33) within 3 minutes of I&S and another 39.4% (26) between 4 and 9 minutes of I&S. Only 10.6% of the referrals (7) occurred with longer periods of
I&S.

Assumptions Tested

It might be assumed that whenever staff members do not provide a first contact answer, they are more willing to make a referral. Such an assumption,
however, is rejected. Those library personnel tested infrequently provided referral service, from either a first contact answer or a follow-up request. Some
variation occurs when the data are analyzed on the basis of geographical region.
Staff members from Southern libraries were most likely to provide referral (26
or 39.4% of the referrals). Midwestern library staff offered 21 (31.8%) referrals
and Western library personnel made the remaining 19 (28.8%) referrals.

Documents personnel typically view the assistance they provide in isolation
from the expertise of their co-workers and other referral options. If they cannot
answer a question or if they are unwilling to do so, they do not suggest other
ways for addressing the information need. In effect, it is the responsibility of the
patron to identify other avenues for information gathering. The other assumptions in this section support this conclusion.

Library staff members generally gave some response to patron queries. This
response, however, might not be the correct answer or an attempt to lead
patrons to proper sources, within or outside the library, for resolving the infor-

mation need. Another assumption is that in virtually all instances where the library staff member responded to a reference question by stating "I don't know," a referral was forthcoming. However, this assumption is not supported from the findings of the study. In all but 1 instance where library personnel responded that they did not know (96.7% of the situations), there was no referral activity to another person on the staff or information provider (e.g., another depository library or a government agency). Thus, in effect, staff members told the proxies that they did not know the answer, could not think of any place else to search, and terminated the reference interview.

One might assume that the longer the duration of the reference interview and search process, the chance for referral increases. This assumption is also rejected. There were only 66 instances of referral, and 46, or 69.7%, of them came within the first 5 minutes of the search process. Extending the search process another five minutes added another 13 referrals (19.7%). Data analysis on the basis of geographical region does not alter this finding.

Over 70% (72.7%) of the referrals (48 of the 66) came from staff members associated with libraries selecting more than 50 percent of the available item numbers. Nonetheless, 41 (85.4%) of these referrals were from general reference personnel to the documents department/collection. The remaining 7 referrals were directed to other departments in the library. For whatever reason(s), all the external referrals came from personnel at libraries selecting fewer than half of the available item numbers.

The number of documents staff members does not influence the willingness to engage in referral. Some 63.3% (42) of the referrals came from libraries that employed a maximum of 2 FTE documents librarians. Still, the overwhelming majority of questions asked of these same libraries (243 of the 285, 85.3%) did not result in referral of any kind. An increase in the chance of referral is also not related to the number of FTE paraprofessional. Although the majority of referrals came from libraries that employed 3 or more FTE documents paraprofessionals (40 of the 66, or 60.6%), the referrals were typically from the general reference to documents department/collection.

An examination of referral patterns on the basis of FTE general reference professional and support staff did not disclose any significant patterns. The willingness to engage in referral does not appear to be attributable to general staffing patterns.

The final assumption to be examined is that personnel who are assigned to manage separate documents collections actively and regularly engage in referral activity when they are unable to answer a reference question. A presumed advantage of separate documents collections is that specially trained personnel are available to assist in meeting information needs. This assumption concerning separate collections is rejected. Staff members in separate collections infrequently suggested referral; documents personnel in separate collections made only 2 referrals (3% of the 66 referrals).

INSTITUTIONAL VARIABLES

A number of institutional variables were examined to identify possible relationships to the quality of reference service, including: the number of library
volumes held, the size of the library budget, the percentage of item numbers selected, and staffing patterns (the number of FTE library professionals, FTE
documents professionals and paraprofessionals, and FTE general reference
professionals and paraprofessionals). These variables were selected for investigation because they were used in our previous investigation (McClure and
Hernon, 1983) and were seen as possible factors that might impact on the overall quality of the reference service provided.

The central issue to be addressed in this section of the chapter is to what degree the above-mentioned institutional variables affect the quality of government documents reference services, remembering that "quality" is measured in
terms of *correct answer fill rate*. To address this issue, the remainder of this section
examines the relationship between the institutional variables and *correct answer
fill rate*. Table 3-6 summarizes the major findings for each of these variables.

Undoubtedly the staff members themselves, their ability to conduct a reference interview, and to implement sound search strategies also impact upon reference service. Although such factors comprise a secondary consideration of
this investigation, a caution of Myers (1979, p. 287) merits remembering:

> It has not been established that patrons really care about the accuracy of the re-
> sponse; they may be more concerned with the librarian's attitude. It should be
> pointed out that patrons do continue to use our less than perfect reference/
> information services. Perhaps they know the librarian performs better than they
> [patrons] would in both accuracy and search time.

Research into the information-gathering patterns of the general public has also
found that accuracy is but one criterion that is viewed as important in the resolution of an information need. Depending on the information seeker and his or
her specific need, criteria such as the understandability of the answer, up-to-
dateness of the response, and the cost in time and money in gathering the necessary information may be equally as important. The information-gathering
public may be willing to settle for some tradeoffs for the speedy resolution of an
information need (Chen and Hernon, 1982).

The level of data analysis is on questions, rather than on the institutional
characteristics. The institutional analysis is therefore limited due to the reduced
sample size which occurs when there is shifting from a question to an institutional level. Further, data were not gathered on the individuals who responded
to the test questions (e.g., whether they were professional staff members and
the number of years of library experience). Nonetheless, the study indicates the
type of reference service that the researchers and their proxies experienced at
the 26 libraries for the 390 questions that they administered.

Table 3-6   Summary of Answers by Institutional Variables

A. Library Volumes

Answer	Under 500,000	500,000-1 million	Over 1 million
Correct	43	51	147
Incorrect	32	39	78

B. Library Budget

Answer	Under 500,000	500,000-1 million	Over 1 million
Correct	7	10	224
Incorrect	8	5	136

C. Professional Library Staff

Answer	Under 20	20-43	49-74	136-358
Correct	37	91	63	50
Incorrect	23	44	57	25

D. FTE Documents Professionals

Answer	Under 1	1-2	3-4	Over 4
Correct	24	144	28	45
Incorrect	21	96	17	15

E. FTE Documents Paraprofessionals

Answer	Under 1	1-2	3-4	Over 4
Correct	104	26	67	44
Incorrect	76	19	38	16

F. FTE General Reference Professionals

Answer	8 and Under	10-42
Correct	135	106
Incorrect	75	74

G. FTE General Reference Paraprofessionals

Answer	Under 1	1-2	3-4	Over 4
Correct	115	17	51	58
Incorrect	80	13	24	32

H. Percentage of Item Numbers Selected

Answer	Less than 25%	25-50%	51-75%	Over 75%
Correct	32	49	62	98
Incorrect	43	26	28	52

The data were analyzed on the basis of library type. Since no statistically significant differences emerged between library type and any institutional variable, the subsequent presentation of these variables focuses collectively on the 26 libraries, without distinguishing between academic and public libraries.

Number of Library Volumes

Volume counts ranged from under 500,000 to well over 1 million. Fifteen libraries (57.7%) held more than 1 million volumes, while 6 (23.1%) had between 500,000 and 1 million volumes and 5 (19.2%) had fewer than 500,000. There was no statistically significant difference between whether or not a correct answer was received and the number of volumes held (chi square = 2.82, $p > .05$).

Library Budgets

Only two of the libraries tested had annual budgets under $1 million. There was no statistically significant difference between whether or not a correct answer was received and the total library budget (chi square = 1.63, $p > .05$).

Staffing

There was no statistically significant difference between library type and the number of reference librarians (chi square = .000, $> .05$), FTE documents librarians (chi square = 1.28, $> .05$), and general reference FTE paraprofessionals (chi square = .764, $> .05$). Ten of the academic and 10 of the public libraries each employed 10 or fewer reference librarians. Three academic and 3 public libraries had 11 or more reference librarians. Ten academic libraries had a maximum of 2 FTE documents librarians, while 3 had 3 or more. On the other hand, 9 public libraries had a maximum of 2 documents librarians and 4 assigned 3 or more.

There was a statistically significant difference between library type and the number of FTE documents support staff (chi square = 7.72, $p < .05$). The academic libraries tested tended to assign more paraprofessionals to the documents collection. Eleven of the 13 public libraries employ a maximum of 2 FTE documents paraprofessionals, while 9 of the 13 academic libraries have 3 or more FTE documents paraprofessionals.

FTE Library Professionals. The number of professional staff employed by the libraries ranged from 4 to 358. Five libraries (19.2%) have 20 or fewer professional personnel; 15 (57.7%) have a maximum of 54 librarians. Over three-fourths of the libraries (21 or 80.8%) have between 4 and 74 librarians. No statistically significant difference emerged between the number of professional staff and whether or not a correct answer was received (chi square = 32.36, $p > .05$).

FTE Documents Professionals. Nineteen (73.1%) of the libraries assign a maximum of 2 FTE librarians to service the depository collection. Three libraries (11.5%) have between 3 and 4 documents librarians and the remaining 4 libraries (15.4%) employ more than 4 documents librarians. There was no statistically significant difference between the number of documents librarians and whether or not a correct answer was received (chi square = 6.12, $p > .05$).

FTE Documents Support Staff. Fifteen of the libraries (57.7%) have a maximum of 2 FTE documents support staff, and the other 11 libraries (42.3%) assign more support staff. The largest proportion of libraries (12 or 46.2%) have less than 1 FTE support staff, followed by 7 libraries (26.9%) using 3-4 FTE support staff. Five libraries (15.4%) assign more than 4 FTE. There was no statistically significant difference between FTE support staff classification and whether or not a correct answer was received (chi square = 5.1, $p > .05$).

FTE General Reference Professionals. Half of the libraries have a maximum of 8 FTE reference libraries who service the documents collection. The other libraries assign between 10 and 42 FTE reference librarians to assist in servicing the depository collection. There was no statistically significant difference between the number of FTE reference librarians and whether or not a correct answer was received (chi square = 1.18, $p > .05$).

FTE General Reference Support Staff. Half of the libraries assign less than 1 FTE general reference support staff to service the depository collection. Two libraries use between 1 and 2 FTEs, 5 assign 3 to 4, and 6 use more than 4. There was no statistically significant difference between the number of support staff and whether or not a correct answer was received (chi square = 2.48, $p > .05$).

Percentage of Item Numbers Selected

Sixteen (61.5%) of the libraries tested take 50% or fewer item numbers. In fact, 10 (38.5%) take more than 75%. Five libraries select between 26 and 50% of the item numbers and 5 receive less than the 25% recommended in the *Guidelines for the Depository Library System* (1977).

Libraries receiving less than half of the item numbers accounted for one-third of the correct answers (81 or 33.6%). There was a statistically significant difference between the percentage selected and whether or not a correct answer was received (chi square = 14.73, $p < .05$). However, the data were skewed; as it turned out, libraries receiving more than half of the item numbers were more likely to be represented in the study sample.

Impact of Institutional Variables on the Receipt of Correct Answers for Individual Questions

The distribution of correct responses per question indicates that neither the number of staff (professional and support staff for general reference and documents departments, and professionals in the entire library system) explain performance. The receipt of a correct answer is also not attributed to the percentage of items selected or the library's budget or volume count. Performance on a question is obviously related to individual interests and ability to resolve information needs.

Library Budgets. Since 24 of the libraries tested had budgets over $1 million, data are skewed; comparisons between those libraries with budgets greater and less than $1 million cannot be made. Libraries with budgets over $1 million were most likely to answer questions 5 (the administrator of the Agricultural Marketing Service) and 4 (the production of bituminous coal) correctly. They found questions 13 and 14 most difficult.

Number of Volumes Held. All the libraries holding fewer than 500,000 volumes correctly answered questions 3 (the high school dropout rate) and 5 (administrator of the Agricultural Marketing Service). However, these same libraries all missed question 13 (Salaman and Hettinger's work on information technology). Only 2 libraries with fewer than 1 million volumes correctly answered question 1 (imprisonment of free Black seamen); the other 9 libraries neither located the title in their collection nor identified the Serial Set and documents number from sources within their collection.

Percentage of Items Selected. None of the libraries selecting a maximum of 25% missed question 5 (the administrator of the Agricultural Marketing Service). All the libraries receiving 26–50% had a perfect score for 6 questions and those taking 51–75% did not miss 4 questions. In contrast, the libraries selecting more than 75% did not have a perfect score for any questions. Libraries taking 26–50% had their greatest success with questions 13 (Salaman and Hettinger's work on information technology) and 14 (the work on computer information systems); they accounted for half of the correct answers to these questions.

Staffing. Reference personnel performed the best with questions 9 and 12, which called for public laws. They typically equated these questions with government publications and referred the proxies to the documents department/collection. In contrast, they performed the worst with questions 13 and 14.

Documents personnel found question 6 (the FAA publication of the mid-1970s) most difficult. Libraries with fewer than 1 FTE support staff servicing the documents reference desk provided 4 of the 6 correct answers to this question.

Summary

Institutional characteristics of the 26 libraries were compared to the profile of academic and public depository libraries reported in Hernon, McClure, and Purcell (1985). Although the researchers did not select the test sites based on individual institutional characteristics, they can attest that the test sites did not represent any extreme cases and that the libraries were representative of the sampling frame discussed in the previous chapter.

When the correct answer index, the percentage of correct answers arrayed on an ordinal scale, is correlated to the institutional variables, no statistical significance of .05 or less is discovered by use of either the Kendall tau or the Spearman rho tests.[6] This finding provides further evidence that the institutional variables examined do not explain performance levels.

The analysis also confirms findings of previous studies that have found a statistically significant relationship between certain institutional variables themselves. Table 3-7 reports those institutional variables found to have statistical significance in this study. In brief, when the institutional variables are compared to the responses of the persons tested, no statistical significance emerged. Staff performance, therefore, is not related to the institutional variables examined; however, significant relationships are found among various institutional variables themselves.

As a final check on the nonsignificance of the relationship between the institutional variables and the receipt of a correct answer, the researchers performed an analysis of variance.[7] In addition to the institutional variables, they also examined the receipt of a first contact answer, the length of the reference interview, and the time of day that the question was administered. Together, these variables accounted for 48% of the variance related to correct answers. In other words, other factors are potentially more important in explaining *correct answer fill rates* than those investigated in this study. Such findings add evidence to the proposition that the major factor may be the competency and attitude of individual staff members. The investigation of various personal and professional traits on the receipt of a correct answer merits additional analysis.

PROXIE OBSERVATIONS

The researchers instructed the proxies to maintain a log of each transaction and to prepare a written summary of their experiences upon completion of the project. This section draws upon their observations and those of the researchers

---

[6] Both Kendall's tau and Spearman's rho are nonparametric correlations in which assumptions are not made concerning the distribution of cases on the variables. These correlations indicate whether two rankings of the same cases are similar. Kendall coefficients are more meaningful when numerous cases are classified into a few categories and the ranking of data produces a large number of tied ranks. Spearman's rho is preferred when the ratio of cases to categories is smaller and there are few ties at each ranking (Siegel, 1956).

[7] Analysis of variance permits a comparison of a number of samples at the same time in order to determine if they came from populations identical in their means. Analysis of variance also enables researchers to draw inferences about the differences between populations and the factors that produce those differences (Chase, 1976, pp. 177–191).

Table 3-7 Significant Relationships among Institutional Variables

	Library Volumes	Library Budget	Percentage of Items Selected	Library Professionals	Documents Librarians	Documents Paraprofessionals	Reference Librarians	Reference Paraprofessionals
Library Volumes	—	.001	.001	.001	.01	.007	.001	.01
Library Budget		—	.001	.001	.005	.001	.001	.01
Percentage of Item Numbers Selected			—	.001	.007	.002	.008	.009
Library Professionals				—	.005	.003	.005	.009
Documents Librarians					—	.002	.001	.025
Documents Paraprofessionals						—	.008	.032
Reference Librarians							—	.023
Reference Paraprofessionals								—

A. Kendall Tau

	Library Volumes	Library Budget	Percentage of Items Selected	Library Professionals	Documents Librarians	Documents Paraprofessionals	Reference Librarians	Reference Paraprofessionals
Library Volumes	—	.001	.001	.001	.001	.025	.001	.003
Library Budget		—	.001	.001	.001	.004	.001	.003
Percentage of Item Numbers Selected			—	.001	.005	.002	.029	.005
Library Professionals				—	.005	.05	.01	.001
Documents Librarians					—	.001	.02	.01
Documents Paraprofessionals						—	.001	.025
Reference Librarians							—	.041
Reference Paraprofessionals								—

B. Spearman's Rho

as they also participated in data collection. It recounts some general observations and staff responses to selected questions.

General Observations

The reference interview skills of some of the librarians tested were surprisingly poor. They failed to negotiate the fact that question 14 (seeking the work on computer information systems) referred to a government publication. In some instances, they did not put the proxie at ease and conducted the reference interview in a "cold and distant manner" as if they "did not care whether they helped resolve the information need."

For example, imagine asking question 15 (English's speech) to the social sciences librarian and then he abruptly asks "Where do you think the speech would be published?" Every response of his began with "Where or what do you think?" "If this had not been a test situation, I would have walked away and tried to find the answer on my own."

Another proxie reported that when she approached the general reference desk, the librarian was busy cleaning a clock. The proxie waited at the desk for two minutes before the librarian stopped her work and acknowledged the proxie's presence. In response to question 3 (the number of high school dropouts), the librarian pointed to the shelving that contained *Statistical Abstract of the United States*. When the proxie claimed that she was not familiar with that source, the librarian accompanied her and helped her find the source. Throughout the entire reference interview and search process, the librarian never stopped cleaning the clock!

A large public library assigns reference librarians to handle questions about the holdings in the card catalog. One of the proxies approached the card catalog desk and waited 5 minutes while the librarian helped another patron. Finally the librarian, who was approximately 10 feet away from the proxie, looked up from the book that he was holding and shouted "Do you have a question?" The proxie paused for a moment and the librarian becoming impatient said "Well, what is it!" The proxie asked question 13 (Salaman and Hettinger's work on information technology) and the librarian responded that the card catalog was a comprehensive list of that library's holdings. He then looked back at his book and terminated the reference interview.

In some cases, staff members refused to leave the reference desk (although other patrons were not present) and merely pointed to the location of a title. The proxies had to bring the title to the reference desk. In four cases, the staff member interrupted the reference interview with the proxie and answered the telephone. That person then negotiated and answered the telephone question, before returning to the proxie and resuming the reference interview.

And, finally, on three occasions, general reference staff told the proxies "I hate to send you to government documents, but there is no alternative." If the patrons had not been a proxie who had to follow through on referral, one can imagine the impact that such a statement might have.

Specific Questions

Frequently, staff searching for the answer to question 6 (the FAA publication issued in the mid-1970s) consulted the *Monthly Catalog,* for 1975–1977, or the *Cumulative Title Index to United States Public Documents, 1789–1976* (Carrollton Press). They assumed that the year of publication and index coverage was identical or similar. They did not realize that the GPO may not receive a title until some years after publication and that the title must then be cataloged and entered into the *Monthly Catalog.* Some documents librarians tested were "surprised" that they could not find the document in the *Monthly Catalog* for the mid-1970s because this index "provides comprehensive access to all government publications soon after their publication."

The excellent service of one librarian merits recounting. The documents librarian checked the *Monthly Catalog* for 1971 through 1981 but did not locate the FAA publication. If she had just searched one more year (1982), she would have found it. At any rate, she then checked OCLC, located the title, recorded the Sudocs number, and checked the shelf where she found the publication.

Half of the libraries where the staff correctly answered the question had the "GPO Monthly Catalog Subscription Service" of Auto-Graphics, Inc. This rollfiche service includes all the entries for the *Monthly Catalog* from 1976 to the present. Consequently, the staff could promptly locate the complete citation for the FAA publication. However, a different experience occurred with question 2 (the price of the microcomputer book) at one of these libraries. The documents staff member asked a colleague if she was familiar with the title. She replied that she was not. Then both of them tried to get the proxie to accept another work on microcomputers ("we have many books on computers"). When the proxie insisted on the one title, they checked the Auto-Graphics service but failed to discover the title. Terminating the reference interview and search process, they claimed that "for it to be a government publication, it would have to be included on this service." Clearly, some public service personnel are becoming dependent on this service.

At two of the libraries tested, one of the proxies monitored the use of the service for a two hour period. He noticed that the staff tended to use it prior to consulting the paper copy of the *Monthly Catalog* or other documents indexes. In one instance (a public library), the machine broke down and the newly hired documents librarian had to negotiate the depository collection without access to the service. She did not realize that coverage between the service and the *Monthly Catalog* was identical. Instead, she searched the *PRF* for any index related question and did not realize that this microfiche index only pertains to the sales program of the Superintendent of Documents.

A typical response to questions 13 (Salaman and Hettinger's work on information technology) and 14 (the work on computer information systems) was "if it's not in the catalog under the author or title, we don't have it." This seemed especially true of those libraries having microfiche or online catalogs. The reference staff tended to treat these sources as comprehensive listings for the entire library's holdings. However, these libraries had not placed all their government publications into the catalog.

In some instances, the reference staff member might also check *Books in Print*. Unable to locate it there, that person assumed that the publication had only recently been published. One librarian explained that so much is published on technology that we can only selectively acquire the material. "We attempt to purchase those materials that do not become quickly obsolete. Obviously the book that you are seeking is already obsolete."

At two of the libraries tested, staff members obtained a correct answer for question 14. The staff had did not negotiate the question; rather, they discovered the title in their general catalog (online or microfiche).

For question 15 (English's speech), general reference personnel might consult the *New York Times Index, Speech Index, Reader's Guide to Periodical Literature, Magazine Index,* or *Vital Speeches of the Day*. After exhausting this pool of resources, they might either claim that the speech was not published and terminate the interview, or negotiate the fact that the person was a member of the House of Representatives. If they determined that Mr. English was a member of Congress, referral to the depository collection resulted.

HYPOTHESES

As mentioned in the previous chapter, specific hypotheses guided data collection. This section reports on the findings for each hypothesis tested.

There is no statistically significant difference (at the 0.05 level) between the correct answer fill rate **and**

    a. Academic versus Public Library Documents Personnel. This hypothesis is not rejected; no statistically significant difference emerged (chi square = 1.28, $p > .05$). Academic documents personnel themselves correctly answered 83 questions, while their counterparts in public libraries successfully negotiated 79 questions. Academic library staff only answered 4 more questions than did public library staff.

    b. Academic versus Public Library General Reference Personnel. No statistically significant difference merged (chi square = 1.02, $p > .05$). General reference personnel in academic libraries correctly answered 33 questions and public library reference personnel successfully negotiated 28 questions. Again, the performance for the two departments was almost identical.

c. Academic Library Documents and General Reference Staff Members. A statistically significant difference emerged (chi square = 26.2, $p < .05$). Documents staff correctly answered 83 questions and general reference personnel answered 33 questions. It merits reemphasizing, however, that reference staff made numerous referrals to the documents collection/department and that reference personnel received 7 questions and documents staff had 8 questions. These differences may account for the statistical significance. The findings cannot, in themselves, suggest that the personnel of one department are more competent than those of another department.

d. Public Library Documents versus General Reference Staff Members. Similar to the previous hypothesis, a statistically significant difference emerged (chi square = 35.0, $p < .05$). General reference personnel correctly answered 28 questions and their counterparts in the documents department/collection negotiated 79 questions. The same qualification identified in the previous hypothesis also apply here.

There is no statistically significant difference between the correct answer fill rate and

a. The Number of Referrals Made. As already reported, no statistically significant difference emerged. Only 66 of the 390 questions (16.9%) received referral. Fifty-one of these 66 questions resulted in the receipt of a correct answer. Viewed another way, of the 149 questions incorrectly answered, only 15 (10.1%) received any referral. Clearly, library staff infrequently engage in referral, either internal or external to the library.

b. The Accuracy of Those Referrals. Again, as already shown, no statistically significant difference emerged. Referral service, when provided, often results in the receipt of a correct answer. However, tempering this conclusion is the fact that staff made few referrals and the overall *correct answer fill rate* was just over 60%.

c. The Ability to Negotiate Reference Questions and Determine That a Government Document Was Really Sought. This hypothesis was not tested for statistical significance. Only questions 14 (seeking the work on computer information systems) and 15 (English's speech) tested the negotiation skills of library staff. Both questions were administered to reference personnel. The findings clearly illustrate that staff members often failed to negotiate the question either at all or to a large degree.

The section on proxie observations notes instances where both documents and general reference personnel conducted less than satisfactory question negotiation and reference interview skills. It would seem that there is a correlation between the *correct answer fill rate* and staff interview and search skills.

TESTING A PUBLIC LIBRARY SYSTEM

Although all the testing at the 26 libraries occurred at the main library — the one housing the depository collection — many users of a public library consult a branch and not the central building (McClure, Hernon, and Purcell, 1986). Therefore, an important question becomes "How would public service personnel at the branches perform on the test questions and would they refer questions to central reference and government documents personnel?" In particular, the researchers wondered if branch staff would

- refer question 13 (Salaman and Hettinger's work on information technology) to the main library
- negotiate that question 14 (the work on computer information systems) dealt with a government publication and refer to the depository collection housed in the main library

They also questioned if referral would result in the receipt of a correct answer.

These two questions were selected for the test because neither is clearly linked to a U.S. government publication and because the previously reported testing had shown both questions to be difficult to answer. The researchers believed that library patrons might call a branch library and inquire about the availability of a title. They might not realize that the title was, in fact, a government publication, and that the library may not have a record of all its holdings in one place. At the same time, it is important to identify the extent of staff awareness of information resources; do they associate titles merely with monographs and the general catalog's holdings?

The researchers selected one of the 13 public libraries originally tested and known to own both titles in the depository collection. They also knew that neither title was represented in the library's general catalog. During December 1985, they revisited the city in which the library was located and randomly selected half of the 24 branch libraries. They then telephoned each library twice — once for question 13 and again for question 14.

None of the branch libraries owned the Salamon and Hettinger work. For question 14, personnel from 7 libraries inquired if the caller knew the name of the author and the publication date. Staff from two of these libraries asked one additional question — "Is it a textbook?" They then checked the general catalog to determine if the branch had the title.

Regardless of question, 7 branch libraries made referral to the central library — the general reference department (4 referrals), the business library (2 referrals), and the science/technology department (2 referrals). Both the general reference and business reference staff merely checked the general catalog, claimed that the library did not own the title, and terminated the interview. The science/technology department also services the government documents collection. Yet for question 13, the documents librarian suspected that the work was privately issued and claimed that she could only search for it if she knew where the paper was presented (the name and date of the conference). For question 14, another documents librarian merely suggested that the researcher try "a more specialized library."

In summary, the researchers did not receive a correct answer to either question. Question 14 generated few attempts at question negotiation; library personnel accepted the question at face value and concluded the reference interview within 2 minutes. Five branches did not engage in any referral; they merely stated that the branch did not own the title sought.

This pilot project suggests that a client of a branch library might receive referral to the central library but that referral may not result in the receipt of a correct answer. Library staff associated titles with the general monograph collection but not other information resources, e.g., government publications.

The extent of staff dependency on a general catalog provides a rationale for such catalog to represent a comprehensive record of the holdings of a library. Clearly, staff need to become familiar with the diverse range of a library's collections and explore more search options. They need to develop their referral skills and to better assist patrons in resolving information needs.

SUMMARY

This chapter describes the results of an unobtrusive test of the quality of reference service as measured by the *correct answer fill rate,* in a sample of academic and public libraries from three geographical regions. Overall, 62% of the questions were answered correctly and 38% were answered incorrectly. Similar to other unobtrusive studies on library reference services, the findings suggest that the most important factors affecting the quality of reference services are individually based, i.e., the attitude and competencies of individual staff members.

Figure 3-6 summarizes study findings and conclusions. The overall *correct answer fill rate* falls within the higher end of the "typical" range of scores found in other unobtrusive library studies (see Figure 1-1). Chapters 5 and 6 will discuss these scores and their implications in greater detail.

Generally, library patrons themselves must identify and consult alternative information sources and providers when library staff cannot provide a correct

Figure 3-6   Summary of Findings and Conclusions

Overall

1. Participants in the study answered 62% of the questions correctly and 38% of the questions incorrrectly.
2. There was no statistically significant relationship between the *correct answer fill rate* and type of library or geographical region, although Western libraries did not perform as well as their counterparts in the other regions.
3. The most frequent reason for an incorrect answer was that library staff gave wrong data (96 cases, 64% of the instances). In an additional 30 cases (20.1%) staff responded with "don't know" and terminated the search without suggesting any referral. In the remaining 23 cases (15.4%), they claimed that the library did not own a source that would answer the question, when, in fact, it did own such a source.
4. Patrons have a greater probability of obtaining a correct answer from the documents department than from general reference.
5. Overall, 92% of all the questions received a first contact answer.
6. The institutional variables examined were not statistically significant when related to *correct answer fill rate.*

Use of Information Technologies

7. Only 4 of all the questions (3%) were checked via OCLC or another bibliographic utility; academic library staff did all the checking.

Awareness of Government Publications

8. Titles that "appear" to be commercially issued frequently were not considered as government publications, and thus were not located.

Duration of Search and Interview

9. Average duration for an interview and search was approximately 3 to 5 minutes, regardless of the question. No statistically significant differences emerged by library type (academic or public) or department (documents or central reference).
10. The probability for obtaining a correct answer peaks in each library between 1 to 5 minutes, and increased interview and search time after that peak time will not increase the probability of obtaining a correct answer.
11. The highest probability for obtaining a correct answer occurs during the first few minutes after contact with library staff.
12. Approximately two-thirds of the 390 questions were answered (correctly or incorrectly) within 3 minutes after contact with library staff.

Referral

13. In no instance when library staff members indicated that they "did not know" the answer did they also refer the proxies to another member of the staff or another information provider.
14. When referral occurred, 75.7% were internal (within the library) and only 12% were to another depository library.
15. The number of reference and documents staff members does not influence their willingness to engage in referral.
16. Over 70% of the referrals came from libraries selecting more than half of the item numbers; however, 84.5% of these referrals were from the general reference to the documents department/collection.
17. Patrons have the responsibility for finding alternative information providers; reference and documents personnel do not offer suggestions for alternative information sources and providers.

Figure 3-6 *(Continued)*

Overall Conclusion

18. The major factors that appear to affect *correct answer fill rate* are individually based, i.e., the competency and attitude of the staff member in terms of search skills, question negotiation, and knowledge and use of basic reference sources.

---

answer. In instances when staff responded with "don't know," no referral was attempted. When referral occurred, it was generally internal to the library — from the general reference to the documents department/collection. Indeed, the findings suggest that the depository library program does not comprise an interlocking network!

An examination of selected instructional variables uncovered no statistically significant relationships with *correct answer fill rate*. Such is *not* to say that available library resources, in terms of these variables, do not have an impact on the quality of documents reference service. Rather, there is a large amount of variance in *correct answer fill rate* that is, as yet, unexplained by such institutional variables. Much of this variance, or explanation of the *correct answer fill rates*, is probably the result of the attitudes, skills, and competencies of individual staff members.

The library profession must seriously reconsider the role and importance of reference services within the larger context of library services. When staff members typically answer a maximum of 62% factual and bibliographic questions correctly, spend, on average, 3 to 5 minutes per reference question, are unable to exploit available information technologies for public services, and fail to provide referrals to questions when they "don't know" the answer, *correct answer fill rates* of 50 to 62% should not be surprising. The final two chapters discuss the implications of these findings in terms of "acceptable" levels of performance and the overall quality of reference services that "should" be provided.

CHAPTER 4

AN EXPERIMENTAL APPROACH TO UNOBTRUSIVE TESTING[1]

Unobtrusive testing documents the responses of reference personnel to questions certified as similar to those libraries might actually receive. Nonetheless, such testing does not comprise a regular method for the evaluation of library and information service performance (Schrader, 1984, p. 208).[2] The studies identified in Figure 1-1 have not linked unobtrusive testing to an experimental design for diagnosing and, if deemed appropriate, improving the *correct answer fill rate* of the staff of one library.

The pilot study reported in this chapter addresses this research void and attempts to deal "with the many and seemingly endless sources of error in reference work" (Crowley, 1985, p. 67). The study is also significant because the library administration and the staff of both the central reference and government documents departments consented to participate in an experimental approach using unobtrusive testing. By employing proper safeguards (to be discussed later), the researchers avoided "the ethical issues of disguised observation and the probable negative reaction of librarians who would be subjected" to such observation (Young, 1985, p. 71). Neither the researchers nor the departmental chairs intended to use test data as part of an individual's performance evaluation.

McClure (1984) encourages libraries and fellow researchers to explore unobtrusive testing for assessing the *correct answer fill rate* and measuring the impact of different interventions on the rate of accuracy. Olson (1984) supports the use of unobtrusive testing as one means of evaluation of reference personnel in medium-sized academic libraries. She recommends that such testing occur over a semester or longer, that proxies not be known to the personnel tested,

---

[1] This chapter is based upon our paper "Unobtrusive Testing of Library Reference Services: An Experimental Approach," which was the 1986 recipient of the Library Research Round Table's (American Library Association) Research Competition Award. The research for this chapter was partially supported by a 1985 grant from the Association of Library and Information Science Education (ALISE).

[2] Chapters 1 and 5 suggest background readings on the evaluation of library reference services and the uses of unobtrusive testing.

and that each librarian receive 10 questions during the evaluation period. Aside from possible ethical problems inherent in using such testing for personnel evaluation, "one must also consider the costs involved in planning, developing the test instruments, evaluating results, recruiting proxies who are strangers to the librarians, and implementing [the testing] in such a way that the librarian is unaware of being tested" (Young, 1985, p. 71). In addition,

> the latter difficulty would be particularly acute over an entire semester, even in medium-sized libraries where more than a few reference librarians were practicing. If they become aware that they are being tested, the validity of the results is questionable (Ibid.).

A number of important issues and research design factors must be considered in an unobtrusive study that employs an experimental approach.

In addition to reporting the results of the investigation, the pilot study discussed in this chapter extends the base for refining and improving unobtrusive testing methodologies. Methodological advancements in researching library/ information services are essential for better understanding and assessing the uses and impacts of those services. Combining unobtrusive and experimental designs offers researchers a potentially powerful approach to investigate the reference and referral process.

STUDY OBJECTIVES

The authors' earlier studies (see Figure 1-1) stressed the development of the unobtrusive measure, *correct answer fill rate,* and the assessment of library staffs' knowledge of particular information services and products. Thus, the objectives for this particular project, viewed within that larger context, were to:

A. *Primary*:

- explore the feasibility of libraries using unobtrusive testing procedures as a practical means for self-diagnosing their *correct answer fill rate,* a performance measure examining the extent to which factual and bibliographic questions are correctly answered (practical is defined in the hypotheses section)

B. *Secondary*:

- explore methods by which libraries can improve their *correct answer fill rate*
- examine interventions which are not too costly or time-consuming for individual libraries to employ
- employ and compare two interventions in terms of:
  a. cost
  b. development/implementation time

c. accomplishment of learning objectives

d. the ease of data collection and interpretation

- develop learning objectives related to knowledge and use of government statistical sources

- test the extent to which the intervention strategies accomplish these learning objectives

Addressing both the primary and secondary objectives should ultimately enhance the sophistication of the research designs used to assess the quality of reference services and assist in the development of strategies to improve those services.

HYPOTHESES AND RESEARCH QUESTIONS

To guide the direction of the study, both hypotheses and research questions were developed. They were based, in part, on the results from the researchers' previous findings as reported in Figure 1-1.

Hypotheses:

- *Correct answer fill rate* for both groups will improve as a result of the intervention (the group mean from the posttest will be compared to the group mean from the pretest).

- There is no statistically significant difference in learning outcomes between the two interventions. The group mean from the two posttests will be compared.

- There is no statistically significant difference between *correct answer fill rate* for the pretest and posttest and the amount of time spent in answering the question.

Research Questions:

- Will the participants' impressions about the value of an intervention strategy (as measured through the exit questionnaire and subsequent staff debriefing) match the presumed difference between group mean scores on the pretest and posttest?

- Will unobtrusive testing prove to be both an effective and efficient means for determining *correct answer fill rate*? This question will be examined in terms of its "practicality":

a. The cost and time required to set up and administer the procedure

b. the insights that it offers into *correct answer fill rate*

c. the level of sophistication required to set up and administer the study

d. the ease of data collection and interpretation

Data addressing these hypotheses and research questions enable the researchers to accomplish the study objectives and offer recommendations about the appropriateness of unobtrusive testing as a means for improving the quality of library reference service.

PARTICIPANTS

In January 1985, the researchers approached a library about participation in the project. They promised that the name of the library and the performance of individual staff members would not be divulged. The only descriptive characteristics of the library that can be revealed are that the library had separate general reference and documents departments located on different floors of the main library.

The next month, the chairs of the government documents and central reference departments for that library, with the concurrence of the central administration, agreed to participate in the pilot study, as long as the staff members themselves agreed. That same month, the professional and classified personnel from both departments agreed to participate in an unspecified intervention strategy and to be tested unobtrusively. At no time were they informed about the specifics of the project; for example, they did not know the nature of the questions, who would administer the questions, and when testing might occur. In administering the study, the researchers dealt directly with the departmental chairs and not other members of either department.

In total, 21 staff members including the two departmental chairs, participated in the study. As will be discussed subsequently, the two departmental chairs comprised one internal validity check. Table 4-1 depicts the number of participants by department and classification.

STUDY CONCEPTUALIZATION

Figure 4-1 offers a graphic conceptualization of the study. The professional and classified staff of the two departments were randomly assigned to one of two interventions and the chair of each department certified that the two groups

Table 4-1   Study Participants

Department	Professional	Career Support Staff	Total
Government Documents	2	5	7
Central Reference	11	3	14
Total	13	8	21

Figure 4-1   Conceptualization of Pilot Study

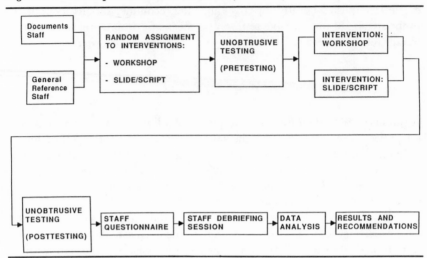

were indeed similar in terms of experience and knowledge of government publications. Next, participants were pretested unobtrusively; department chairs supplied written descriptions of each participant so that the researchers could identify the group to which he/she was assigned. After completion of both intervention strategies, participants in both groups were posttested unobtrusively and the study objectives, hypotheses, and research questions assessed.

Upon completion of the posttest, participants received a questionnaire to elicit written comments on the value of the intervention in which they participated, as well as suggestions for improving the intervention (see Appendix E). As a final means of assessment, the researchers made an oral presentation on the study and discussed participants' observations, concerns, and recommendations.

RESEARCH DESIGN

The research design combined unobtrusive testing with an experimental approach. As Table 4-1 and Figure 4-1 illustrate, each participant was randomly assigned to one of the two groups based on whether he/she was: (1) in the government documents or central reference department, and (2) professional or classified personnel. As a result, both groups contained a similar proportion of staff, as shown in the table and figure, and, as already noted, departmental chairs certified that both experimental groups contained staff members of similar experience and knowledge of government publications.

Although 21 library staff members participated in the study, the numbers are still small for the purposes of extensive statistical comparisons. Consequently the researchers employed two contrasting groups, but not a control group, and distinguished between primary and secondary objectives. Similarly, many libraries will not have a sufficient number of public service personnel to permit the use of a control and experimental groups.[3]

Contrasting Interventions

Both interventions focus on knowledge about, and the use of, statistical data disseminated by the Federal government. The purpose of an intervention was to increase *awareness* of basic source material. Similar designs could lead to investigations of interventions covering topics such as specialized statistical data, the process of legislative bill tracing, administrative law, basic government indexes and other reference aids, and various uses and applications of online database searching for U.S. government publications.

Questions requiring the use of statistical publications were chosen for investigation because these publications comprise one of the most important types of government publications and because many library users seek such publications (Hernon, 1979).

The specific learning objectives for the interventions were to:

- increase library staff members' awareness of *basic* U.S. government statistical publications
- demonstrate procedures for the effective use of *basic* U.S. government statistical sources
- discuss the strengths and weaknesses among a selection of *basic* U.S. government statistical publications
- improve the ability of general reference and documents personnel to answer questions requiring the use of U.S. government statistical sources
- further sensitize general reference staff to U.S. government publications within their collection and the depository collection
- improve the ability of the main reference staff to answer U.S. government statistical questions directly rather than to refer these questions to the documents department/collection

Based on these learning objectives, two intervention strategies were used:

- *Workshop*: A four hour workshop was given to those 10 staff member from the two departments randomly assigned to this intervention. The workshop,

---

[3] It merits mention that a control group is not an essential element for a pilot study. A full-scale study, however, should use one. For a useful discussion of control groups, see Tuckman (1978).

conducted by the two researchers, offered an overview of *basic* U.S. statistical sources, their strengths, weaknesses, and utility.

- *Slide/script presentation*: The 11 reference and documents personnel randomly assigned to this intervention viewed a slide presentation, with an accompanying script, that reviewed selected *basic* statistical sources of the Federal government. These library staff members examined the slide/script presentation at their convenience during a specified one week period.

The researchers carefully planned the contents and organization of the workshop. They obtained user guides to selected publications and developed instructional handouts for distribution to the participants. They also set an informal environment for the workshop so that both the researchers and participants could discuss the sources and search strategies informally.

The researchers developed the slide/script presentation over a four month period prior to initiation of the intervention. This presentation consisted of 108 slides and a 37-page script that presented more than 30 government statistical sources. The researchers selected each source for its:

- broad range of subject content
- general ease of use
- recognition as a "key" reference source
- appropriateness for use at both a main reference desk and a government documents department

The text for the script was keyed to the slides and emphasized significant and unique aspects of each title. Appendix F reprints the bibliographic script that accompanied the slide presentation.

Both interventions covered the same reference titles. The researchers then used these sources to develop their pool of unobtrusive reference questions.

UNOBTRUSIVE TEST QUESTIONS

During the spring of 1985, 60 questions related to Federal statistical sources were developed according to whether they:[4]

- were answered from *basic* reference titles which the Federal government issued

---

[4] If the researchers merely administered their test questions to whoever is staffing the documents or central reference desk at a particular time, they could not determine the *correct answer fill rate* for each of the 21 participants. Since the researchers intend to test each participant, they needed a large pool of possible test questions from which to select the actual pretest and posttest questions.

- were answered with a fact, date, or bibliographic citation
- involved a maximum of a two step search process, assuming the staff member was efficient in the search process that he/she used

Once developed by both the researchers and their graduate assistants, the 60 questions were submitted to a jury consisting of the documents and reference staffs of three libraries similar to that being tested. The jury was instructed to clarify question phraseology where necessary, identify the range of sources in their collections that would answer the questions, and certify that the questions were similar to those that "real-life" clientele might ask.

The librarians were encouraged to substitute questions that they considered more appropriate for general testing and to rate the questions on a 5-point Likert scale representing the degree of question difficulty:

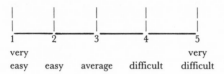

Question difficulty was based on four criteria:

- the length of time to answer the question most efficiently
- presumed familiarity with the required source
- ease in using the required source
- clarity of primary topic in the question

Any question that the jury challenged was eliminated from use. The remaining questions were assessed as reflecting a similar level of difficulty and served as the pool of pretest and posttest questions. One purpose of conducting the study was to examine the use of the test questions, field test them, and certify that, in fact, they all had the same level of difficulty. Certification of the level of difficulty enables the researchers to document that any variations between pretest and posttest scores are not likely to be attributed to the test questions themselves and the differences in their level of difficulty.

Based on jury comments, the initial 60 questions were reduced by 10, with 6 additional questions suggested as possibly more difficult. Consequently the researchers had 44 questions from which to conduct the pretesting and posttesting (see Appendix G). From this pool of 44 questions, the researchers, using a table of random numbers, selected 3 pretest and 3 posttest questions for each participant. Therefore 63 questions were administered in the pretest and another 63 in the posttest. The administration of 126 questions generated sufficient cases per cell for data analysis at the group level. The researchers wanted to determine whether they could conduct unobtrusive testing without arousing staff suspi-

cions and calling attention to the proxies and the actual experiment. They believed that the use of more than 3 questions per unobtrusive test, especially for
the posttest, might jeopardize the integrity of the pilot study.

As an alternative approach, the researchers might have asked each participant the same questions in both the pretest and posttest. However, they rejected this approach; given the small number of participants involved, and the
likelihood that if some questions were referred within a department or from the
central reference to the documents department, staff members might remember questions and possibly associate them with the experimental project.

TESTING PROCEDURES

Two library school students served as proxie supervisors. They recommended
seven of their non-library school friends to serve as proxies and, along with
these proxies, participated in the training session that the researchers conducted. The session covered the purpose of the project, guidelines for data collection (Appendix H), the identification of participants, the assignment of
questions to a proxie, the asking of questions and recording of the outcome, and
the time frame for completion of pretesting and posttesting. Proxies were instructed to test the accuracy of all referrals and provide a detailed written description of each question administration. If they received answers other than
the predetermined correct ones, they were to record the answer and the source
from which it was obtained. The researchers then would verify the accuracy or
inaccuracy of the answer.

The proxies used the same reference transaction tabulation sheet that the researchers had used successfully in their previous unobtrusive studies and Chapter 3 (see Appendix D). Individual proxies were assigned to one of the two
supervisors who then monitored data collection, assisted the proxies in locating
the staff members that they were to test, and verified that, indeed, the proxies
asked the questions of each test participant.

Proxies did not test the same participants in both the pretest and posttest. In
the pretest, the proxies asked three questions of the same person, but not at the
same time. They were instructed to revisit that person at different times. In the
posttest, the proxies never asked more than two questions of the same staff
member. In many cases, they only asked one question, the purpose being to
minimize staff recognition of both the proxies and the test questions.

DATA COLLECTION AND ANALYSIS

The planning for the experiment, including pretesting the test questions and
deciding on the content of the interventions, was finalized during the summer
of 1985. In mid-September, participants were unobtrusively pretested and the

workshop was conducted the end of that month. During the first week of October, those staff members selected received the slide presentation and accompanying script. During the latter part of that month, all 21 individuals were unobtrusively posttested. In early November, 1985, the participants completed the exit questionnaire and received a formal presentation on the study from the researchers.

For purposes of hypothesis testing, the level of statistical significance was set at .05 and the researchers used the t-test for matched pairs, and the chi square test for independence (*StatPac — Statistical Analysis Package Manual,* 1985, pp. 82–89, 92–97). The researchers also generated frequency counts and percentages. However, it merits mention that not all of the objectives, hypotheses, and research questions lend themselves to statistical analysis.

QUALITY OF THE DATA

Prior to implementing the study, the researchers carefully considered a number of techniques to ensure the generation of high quality data. The precautions that they took are grouped under four criteria:

- reliability
- validity
- participants' unawareness of unobtrusive testing
- utility

Methodological refinements within each criterion were built into the study. At the same time, the combined use of an unobtrusive and experimental design provides researchers with increased opportunities to collect high quality data and to include various "checks" throughout the study to ensure the generation of such data.

Figure 4-2 summarizes the steps taken to collect reliable and valid data. Reliability suggests stability and consistency of measurement — accuracy. One criterion for assessing reliability is the representativeness of the questions about the phenomenon being measured: the more representative the questions about the instrument, the higher the instrument's reliability (Witka, 1968, pp. 267–268). On this criterion, the instrument should have high reliability since the questions were based on specific criteria and pretested by practicing documents and reference librarians. The final set of questions was accepted by both the researchers and the librarians as "representative" of typical questions encountered at a general reference and documents desk.

A second criterion of reliability is accurate and consistent coding, and the following actions were taken to increase reliability of data according to this criterion. First, written procedures and standardized coding forms were used by

Figure 4-2   Precautions to Ensure Reliability and Validity

Reliability	Validity
1. Use of pretested questions of a similar level of difficulty and developed with specific criteria in mind	1. The random assignment of participants to an intervention; the groups were similar
2. The training of proxies	2. The pretesting of questions and certification that they are appropriate
3. Supplying proxies with written instructions and a recording log used in previous studies	3. Staff unable to identify proxies and test situations
4. Review of the completed logs to ensure consistency in reporting	4. The time period between pretesting and posttesting was insufficient for maturation to affect the outcome
5. Researchers monitored data entry	5. The same learning objectives guided both interventions
6. Researchers monitored data gathering and scoring of answers	6. All professional and classified personnel in both departments were tested
7. The randomized assignment of questions to participants	7. *Correct answer fill rate* comprises a construct — construct validity
8. An identical method of data collection was used for both the pretest and posttest	8. A representative collection of test items and "sensible" methods of test construction and administration — face validity
9. Departmental chairs aware of the project were tested and only able to spot 1 of 12 test situations	9. The researchers did not use any methods of data collection that might influence posttest scores; both the questionnaire and the debriefing session were done two weeks after completion of the posttest
10. Minimal recognition of the test situations and questions occurred at the staff debriefing session	10. Minimal number of test questions administered in the pretest and posttest, minimizing the possibility of staff associating test questions with the study
11. The computation of a coefficient of reliability — .63 (test-retest reliability)	11. Except for the department chairs, the participants were unaware of the study design and timing of the unobtrusive testing
12. The use of proxie supervisors to monitor data collection	12. The use of test questions of the same level of difficulty
	13. During the data collection and the conducting of the two interventions, departmental chairs did not schedule any workshops or seminars that might have influenced posttest outcomes

all proxies for administering the questions and coding the responses of library personnel. Second, all proxies went through a training session to assure their understanding of the procedures and definitions regarding data coding. Also, wherever questions emerged during the actual testing, the proxies had immediate feedback from the two supervisors. The researchers reviewed the proxies' written responses and comments about the testing process in an effort to maintain consistency in coding.

A third criterion for reliability is a coefficient of reliability. There are a number of reliability coefficients, but each coefficient, in general, expresses the ratio of true-score variance (perfect reliability, with no error) to observed-score variance (Kerlinger, 1973, p. 446). Perfect reliability has a coefficient of 1.0 and a coefficient of 0 indicates no reliability.

Test-retest reliability involves the administration of a test to the same group of people on two separate occasions and the correlation of the paired scores. Since library personnel participated in both a pretest and posttest, the researchers determined the test-retest reliability to be .63. Nunally (1967, p. 80) suggests that instruments with a reliability coefficient of .50 to .60 have moderate reliability and suffice for purposes of measurement, especially for pilot investigations. A test-retest coefficient assumes that the characteristic being measured by the test is stable over time and that there is no practice or memory effect. A memory effect may inflate the reliability estimate (Carmines and Zeller, 1979, pp. 37–40).

Validity is the extent to which the researchers measure what they purport to measure: "one validates not the measuring instrument itself but the measuring instrument in relation to the purposes for which it is being tested" (Ibid, p. 17). Our purpose was to measure the *correct answer fill rate,* which is operationally defined as the percentage of correct answers for all the questions asked.

"Face validity," a conceptual criterion of validity, simply requires a representative collection of test items and "sensible" methods of test construction and administration. If the general literature on the methodology (unobtrusive testing) finds it to be appropriate and if users of the test and people knowledgeable about the topic agree that the method and the instrument are sound and well administered — as in this study — the measure has face validity (Nunally, 1967, p. 80).

In the experimental design, staff members were randomly assigned to an intervention. By maintaining a short time frame between the administration of the pretest and posttest, the researchers minimized the internal validity threat of maturation. The chairs of both departments cooperated in seeing that no outside interventions might have influenced posttest outcomes. For example, they did not have departmental personnel engage in continuing education or training sessions that might have affected their performance on the posttest.

As will be noted subsequently, only in a couple of instances had the library staff associated the proxies with the test questions and the experiment. Since the departmental chairs were aware of the project and the other staff members had only very general knowledge about the study, the research team studied the *correct answer fill rate,* without widespread staff knowledge of the actual test situations.

is pragmatic and seeks to increase the degree to which the data can be used to make decisions and affect policy, i.e., that the results of the study have a likely prospect of effecting change in the library and increasing organizational effectiveness (Swisher and McClure, 1984, pp. 94–95).

The utility of a study is based, largely, on its objectives, hypotheses, and research questions. The researchers believe that the data might have practical value to library decision makers in terms of:

- reviewing the usefulness of unobtrusive testing as a self-diagnostic to identify the continuing education needs of library personnel
- assessing the degree to which unobtrusive testing measures increased staff competencies from educational interventions, i.e., workshops and slide/script presentations
- determining whether increased staff awareness of a topic affects their performance or competency for that same area

In short, the study attempts to consider the practical usefulness of unobtrusive testing in terms of continuing education interventions in a library context (see Chapters 5 and 6). The identification of these decision areas as a basis for the development of the objectives, hypotheses, and research questions; the nature of the intervention strategies; and the data collection instruments all increase the overall utility of the study and its findings.

The above discussion suggests *indicators* that the study obtained reliable and valid data, within the limitations, definitions, and assumptions previously defined. As Blalock (1982) has noted, social science research is difficult (at best) due to the constant fear of omitting variables unknowingly, having measures confounded by other variables' affecting the study, and the measurement problems associated with human behavior. His advice is to identify assumptions and limitations clearly, and to distinguish generalizations from speculations. Given Blalock's admonitions, the researchers conducted a pilot study and used appropriate data analysis techniques.

GENERAL FINDINGS

Summary Correct Responses

The *correct answer fill rate* for the pretest was 63.5% (40 of 63 questions answered correctly), while for the posttest, it was 52.4% (33 questions answered correctly). As shown in Figure 4-3, combining the pretest and posttest scores produces an overall *correct answer fill rate* of 57.9% (73 of 126 questions answered correctly).

Test results suggest that 4 of the 44 questions may have been harder or easier to answer than the others. These questions are

Figure 4-3   Overall Correct Answer Fill Rate

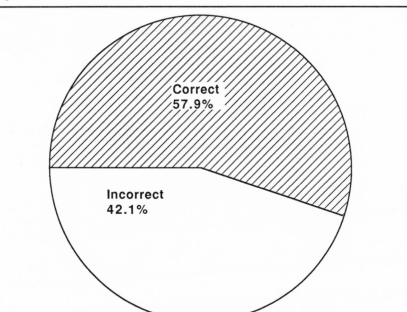

- Number 2: "How many calves were slaughtered in the U.S. for the years 1980–1982," which was answered correctly in all 4 instances.
- Number 6: "What percentage of people in Pima County (Arizona) used public transportation and car-pools in 1980," which was answered incorrectly in all 5 instances.
- Number 15: "How many passports were issued to women in 1981 and 1982," which was answered correctly in all 4 instances.
- Number 33: "Do more men or women receive baccalaureate and master's degrees in clinical social work," which was answered correctly in all 4 instances.

The remaining questions were used at least two times and no clear patterns emerged; they were as likely to be answered correctly as incorrectly.

Except in one instance where a staff member during the pretest responded with "don't know" and terminated the search, all occurances of an incorrect answer are attributable to the receipt of wrong information.[5]

---

[5] This is a significant improvement over our earlier study (McClure and Hernon, 1983, p. 36) where 53% of the incorrect answers were "don't know." Chapter 3 also notes a large number of "don't know" responses.

Referral

Of the 84 questions administered to personnel at the central reference desk, 49 or 58.3% were referred. Yet for two-thirds of the questions (66.7%, 56 of the 84 questions), the reference collection contained a title that would have answered the question; in each instance, the work was on the shelf at the time of the search. Documents staff members referred 4.8% (2 of 42) of the questions that they received; in both instances referral was directed to another person in the department.

During the pretest phase, 24 or 38.1% of the questions were referred either internally or externally to a department. For the posttest, 27 or 42.9% of the questions were referred. For neither the pretest nor the posttest was there a statistically significant relationship between whether or not referral was made and a correct answer was received (pretest, chi square $= .01$, $p > .05$; posttest, chi square $= 3.44$, $p > .05$). Table 4-2, which highlights the referral locations, indicates that the majority of referrals were to the documents department. Reference personnel made most of the referrals, whereas documents personnel attempted to find an answer, either correct or incorrect. Documents reference staff made both of the referrals within the same department.

Any time that reference or documents personnel received any of the following six questions, they automatically referred it either internal or external to their department:

• Number 1: "How much dry milk (nonfat) did the U.S. export to the Sudan in 1981 and 1982?" Two general reference staff members referred the question to government documents, although the reference collection contains *Agricultural Statistics*.
• Number 8: "How much, in wages, was paid to U.S. government civilian workers during each year of the Eisenhower administration?" In both instances, reference personnel referred the question to documents.

Table 4-2   Referral Locations

	Pretest		Posttest		Combined	
Location	No.	%	No.	%	No.	%
Another person in same department	1	4.2	1	3.7	2	3.9
Documents department	21	87.5	24	88.9	45	88.2
Another department of library	—	—	2	7.4	2	3.9
Branch library	2	8.3	—	—	2	3.9
TOTAL	24	100.0	27	100.0	51	99.9*

*Percentages rounded to nearest tenth.

- Number 9: "How much, in wages, was paid to military workers during the Eisenhower administration?" Although *Historical Statistics of the United States* contains the answer, reference personnel automatically referred the question to the documents collection.
- Number 10: "How many cases of gonorrhea were reported in the U.S. in 1970 as compared to 1929?" This question could also be answered from *Historical Statistics of the United States.* Two members of the reference staff referred the question to documents, while 1 documents member referred the question to another member of the same department.
- Number 12: "How much property tax did state and local governments collect in 1980 through 1983?" Reference personnel either referred this question to documents or special collections. The latter referral resulted in an incorrect answer.
- Number 14: "How many units of blood were voluntarily donated to the Red Cross in 1981 as compared to 1983?" Reference personnel either referred the question to documents or the serials department. The latter referral resulted in an incorrect answer.

A most interesting finding is that the above list contains all 3 questions from *Historical Statistics of the United States.*

Amount of Time to Answer Questions

Table 4-3 reports the amount of time that the proxies and the staff members spent on the information request together and with the proxies following the recommendations of the staff tested. By collapsing percentage columns into quartiles, it is evident that:

- in the first (up to 25% of the questions), the staff and proxies spent a maximum of 4 minutes
- in the second (25%–50% of the questions), they spent between 5 and 6 minutes
- in the third (50%–75% of the questions), they spent between either 7 and 12 minutes (pretest), or 7 and 14 minutes (posttest)
- in the fourth (the remaining questions), they spent more than 12 (pretest) or 14 (posttest) minutes

Neither the variables of department nor whether a correct answer was received had a statistically significant impact on the interview and search process, for either the pretest or posttest. Therefore, for participants as a whole or by department, the longer that they spent in negotiating a reference question was as likely to result in the receipt of an incorrect answer as a correct one.

Table 4-3   Amount of Time Spent on Answering
the Test Questions

	Pretest		Posttest		Combined	
Minutes	#	%	#	%	#	%
1	2	3.2	6	10.0	8	6.5
2	8	12.7	1	1.7	9	7.3
3	4	6.3	6	10.0	10	8.1
4	3	4.8	2	3.3	5	4.1
5	10	15.9	14	23.3	24	19.5
6	5	7.9	1	1.7	6	4.9
7	2	3.2	1	1.7	3	2.4
8	3	4.8	2	3.3	5	4.1
9	–	–	2	3.3	2	1.6
10	10	15.9	9	15.0	19	15.4
12	1	1.6	–	–	1	0.8
13	4	6.3	–	–	4	3.3
14	–	–	1	1.7	1	0.8
15	3	4.8	6	10.0	9	7.3
20	3	4.8	4	6.7	7	5.7
22	–	–	1	1.7	1	0.8
25	–	–	1	1.7	1	0.8
30	4	6.3	–	–	4	3.3
35	1	1.6	1	1.7	2	1.6
46	–	–	1	1.7	1	0.8
60	–	–	1	1.7	1	0.8
TOTAL	63	100.0	60*	100.0	123*	99.9**

*In three cases, the proxies did not record the length
of search time.
**Percentages were rounded to the nearest tenth.

The receipt of a correct or incorrect answer, the willingness of a staff member to engage in referral, or the referral location were not affected by the type of intervention that the 21 participants received.

Interpersonal Skills of the Staff Tested

The proxies only reported one staff member as "unfriendly"; the authors' previous research (see Figure 1-1) disclosed higher incidents of discourteous service. The other studies also identified more incidents where staff members responded with "don't know" and terminated the search. The pilot project probed one area — Federal statistical data — and showed the extent of staff reliance on the *American Statistics Index*. To be expected, documents personnel rely on it quite extensively, while general reference staff might forget that the title was in their collection and refer proxies to the copy in the documents department.

HYPOTHESES

Correct answer fill rate for both groups will improve as a result of the intervention.   This hypothesis is not accepted. As already noted, the *correct answer fill rate* for the pretest was 63.5% and, for the posttest, 52.4%. In both instances, the number of correct responses was similar to that found in the overwhelming majority of studies depicted in Figure 1-1, between 50 and 65%.

A t-test for matched pairs was computed for the correct answers of all participants on both the pretest and the posttest, regardless of the intervention to which they were assigned. The mean score for the pretest was 1.37 and 1.48 for the posttest, for a difference of 0.11; there is no statistically significant difference between the two (t-statistic of 1.261). Excluding the possible impact of an intervention, the mean scores for the pretest and posttest are similar.

There is no statistically significant difference in learning outcomes between the two interventions.   This null hypothesis is not rejected; staff members assigned to either the workshop or slide/script presentation answered the same number of pretest questions correctly (20). On the posttest, workshop participants correctly answered 18 questions and members of the other group answered 15 questions.

Using the t-test for matched pairs, the pretest and posttest scores of workshop participants can be computed and compared statistically. The same is true for participants in the other intervention. Workshop participants had a pretest mean of 1.32 and a posttest mean of 1.43, for a difference of -0.100; the t-statistic was 0.787. There was no statistically significant difference in the pretest and posttest mean scores for workshop participants.

Personnel assigned to the slide/script presentation had a pretest mean score of 1.39 and a posttest mean score of 1.55, for a difference of -0.152; the t-statistic was 1.229. There was also no statistically significant difference in the pretest and posttest mean scores for participants in this intervention.

In summary, neither intervention had a measurable impact on improving posttest performance. In fact, as will be discussed subsequently, library staff regarded both interventions as providing them with information that they already knew.

There is no statistically significant difference between the correct answer fill rate for the pretest and posttest and the amount of time spent in answering the question.   This null hypothesis is not rejected; there was not a statistically significant relationship between the amount of time spent on answering the question and whether the question was answered correctly. By using the chi square test of association, no statistically significant differences emerged by department, for either the pretest (chi square $= 4.32, p > .05$) or the posttest (chi square $= 1.26, p > ,05$).

RESEARCH QUESTIONS

Will the participants' impressions about the value of an intervention strategy (as measured through the exit questionnaire and subsequent staff debriefing) match the presumed difference between group mean scores on the pretest and posttest?   No difference emerged between the pretest and the posttest scores. An examination of completed exit questionnaires also did not disclose differences by either intervention or department. Over 70% of the participants believed that neither the slide presentation nor the workshop

• increased their awareness of *basic* U.S. government statistical publications
• showed them ways to use *basic* U.S. government statistical sources more effectively
• increased their awareness of the strengths and weakness among a selection of *basic* U.S. government statistical publications
• increased their ability to answer questions related to U.S. government statistical sources

Twelve (85.7%) of the general reference staff did not think that the instructional unit that they had received had directly improved their ability to answer *basic* U.S. government statistical questions. However, some suggested that the unit had reminded them to "think documents" and refer questions to the documents collection.

Four (57.1%) of the documents staff suspected that the instructional unit in which they participated might have improved the ability of general reference staff to answer *basic* U.S. government statistical questions directly rather than to refer such questions to them.

Given these findings, it would seem that the interventions had a successful component. They reminded some general reference personnel about government publications and encouraged them to refer questions.

Most of the suggestions for improving the instructional unit were aimed at the slide/script presentation. Staff members requested:

• more description of a title
• more examples showing how to use a source
• a discussion of the types of questions that a title could answer
• improving the legibility of some slides
• the deletion of irrelevant slides
• placing the reference to a slide at the beginning or conclusion of a section, and not in the middle of the text; it was hard to view the slides in a darkened room, while still following a written text
• more coverage of access points to a source
• less presentation of information; some felt overwhelmed by the amount of information presented

Comments directed to the workshop involved the presentation of fewer titles, less coverage of "basic titles as we already know these," and the need to gain hands on experience for the titles discussed. Participants wanted more examples and opportunities to simulate reference transactions.

Only 8 of the participants (38.1%) professed interest in the development of similar instructional units for other aspects of U.S. government information. They were most likely to suggest:

- conducting legislative histories
- gaining access to report literature
- using more complex statistical sources
- conducting online searching of government documents databases

Yet only 5 participants (23.8%) believed that library personnel at other institutions would benefit from access to an instructional unit such as the one that they had received. The participants in the slide/script presentation made clear that their negative reaction was based on the script in its present form. If the script could be improved, they might reconsider their negative evaluation. Participants also emphasized that the instructional units had not improved their effectiveness in dealing with sources and some of them resented that they had not been involved in the planning of the interventions and that they were not given an opportunity to select which intervention to attend.

During the debriefing session, central reference and documents personnel echoed their beliefs that neither intervention had increased their awareness of sources or improved their effectiveness and efficiency in handling reference questions. Participants in this session seemed to divide into two camps: those accepting unobtrusive testing as one means of self-diagnosis versus those who questioned the use of such testing.

During the 90 minute debriefing session, staff members raised questions about:

- the proxies, their training and question asking techniques
- the test questions, their development and similarity to the type that "we actually receive"
- the scoring of an answer as either correct or incorrect
- the immediate value of the interventions to them
- methods by which individual performance can be diagnosed and improved

One participant suggested that the findings "indicate that we are friendly but incompetent," while another wanted to dismiss the "exercise" for asking "Jeopardy-like [the game] questions." Two reference librarians announced that "whenever we suspected that a question was one of yours, we referred it." Yet, as discovered during the debriefing session, they often incorrectly associated tual reference questions with those used for this project.[6] Further, the staff was not informed of the time period when testing occurred.

Conceivably, the staff members were trying to rationalize the *correct answer fill rate* of their department and perhaps even their own scores. Obviously, they had expected higher *correct answer fill rates* than those that emerged. Perhaps some of the negative reaction to the testing might be explained on this basis. They mentioned that the posttesting coincided with a library skills exercise in which freshman English students worked with statistical sources and were expected to complete the assignment without any library staff assistance. One proxie reported that he had been asked if he was enrolled in the freshman course. Once he responded in the negative, the staff member proceeded to assist him.

The library and its staff displayed great courage in permitting the use of unobtrusive testing for a research project. They welcomed and supported the project, despite some reservations from a few participants. Both departmental chairs were supportive. The documents chair was concerned about the occasional referral to inappropriate library departments. She was not that concerned about the low rate of referral within her department. As she explained, "since I was not present that much during the posttesting, the classified staff could not refer questions to me." She suspected that these people would have made frequent referrals to her.

Three members of the reference department contacted the researchers for summaries of the reference transactions in which they participated. They believed that by studying the search processes, they might be able to improve their own reference service.

Will unobtrusive testing prove to be both an effective and efficient means for determining correct answer fill rate? This question will be examined in terms of its "practicality":

a. The cost and time required to set up and administer the procedure.   The findings for the question suggest that the costs and time factors identified in Table 4-4 are not excessive for large and well-funded libraries. A number of practical benefits can be derived from studies that assist library decision makers in a number of different areas (see Chapters 5 and 6).

A library replicating the experiment would not necessarily have identical costs. The staff can benefit from the conceptual base provided in this chapter and might have different costs, e.g., the hiring of a consultant team, the freeing of some staff to develop and implement the testing procedures, or the use of a "prepackaged intervention." We were fortunate to have the cooperation and

---

[6] During the debriefing session, a couple of reference librarians claimed that they associated some reference questions with the project. However, further discussion revealed that they were generally incorrect. For example, they mistakenly thought that one of the test questions had been "How many people have lived since creation?"

Table 4-4   The Costs and Amount of Time Involved

Expenses	Amount	Time	Hours
Payment of proxies ($15 per proxie for pretest; $20 per proxie for posttest	$245	Proxie training, supervision, and discussions	15
Slide production	$150	Development of interventions	40
Assistant for script production	$100	Proxie testing	20
Xeroxing (workbook and resources for workshop)	$45	Conducting workshop	4
Coding, data input, and analysis	— *	Coding, data input, and analysis	10
Travel	$250	Conceptualization of study and controlling for possible reliability and internal validity issues	50
Lodging, food, and transportation	$350	Development of questions and pre-testing	30
Refreshments for workshop	$35		
Communication between research-ers	$50		
Wordprocessing	$250		
Total:	$1,475		169

*No costs were incurred because the researchers performed these tasks themselves, with computer hardware and software already within their departments.

support of two outstanding administrators, the chairs of both departments, who, among other things, arranged the room accommodations for the workshop and a secure location for the slides and the other equipment that slide/script participants needed.

b. The insights that it offers into the correct answer fill rate *and the use of unobtrusive testing.*   Although the pilot project found that the interventions did not affect the *correct answer fill rate,* it did demonstrate that staff, on the whole, may accept the use of unobtrusive testing and that such testing can be implemented on a large scale, without arousing staff suspicions. While in some instances, interventions can focus on increasing staff awareness of certain titles in their collection; they should also increase staff competencies.

Other researchers can build from the methodology and research design reported in this study and explore additional refinements to enhance the *correct answer fill rate* and the study benefits, while minimizing costs such as those identified in Table 4-4.

c. The level of sophistication required to set up and administer the study. The development of the study and the preparation of the interventions was complex and time-consuming. At the present time, replication of the experiment may be beyond the research expertise of many library staff members and the budgets of some libraries. For the immediate future, researcher need to continue to refine the methodology and make it easier for libraries to replicate the study and therein improve the quality of their reference services.

While it is possible to simplify unobtrusive methodologies, such is typically done at the expense of study reliability, validity, and utility, as well as arousing staff awareness that unobtrusive testing is occurring. The complexity of using the methodology is largely associated with developing the procedures necessary to ensure the collection of quality data and in linking the testing to an experimental approach testing all participants. The research may also have to accommodate unique factors in a library.

   d. The ease of data collection and interpretation.   Data collection was very complex. Although one of the researchers, each week for the entire semester, received the desk schedules of both departments for distribution to the proxies, staff members might not be at the reference desk at the time specified. They might be ill or trade time slots with their colleagues so that they can attend special meetings, etc.

   Two library school students managed the proxies and coordinated data collection. They provided encouragement to the proxies when it became difficult to track down the actual desk schedules of some staff members.

   The departmental chairs provided written descriptions of the library personnel to be tested. With these descriptions, the project supervisors visited the library and identified individual staff members. They then identified participants for the proxies. To simplify the identification of so many people, the supervisors strongly urged that subsequent testing rely on photographs of participants. The pilot project did not involve the photographing of staff members, because this method might have aroused their curiosity or suspicion.

   Another aspect of data collection relates to data coding and entry into the microcomputer for analysis. This phase of the study went smoothly. All data were entered into StatPac (*StatPac — Statistical Analysis Package Manual*, 1985), a user friendly statistical analysis software program. Without much training, personnel unskilled with statistics and computer manipulation of data can become proficient with StatPac, or similar data analysis software. The administration of data collection and data analysis calls for both time and expertise regarding research methodology and research design. Such skills are essential for in-house use of unobtrusive testing.

METHODOLOGICAL REFINEMENTS

One objective of the study was to refine and enhance the use of unobtrusive testing for assessing and improving the quality of library reference services. Based on study findings, a number of recommendations may assist researchers and library staff wishing to engage in such testing.

   Study objectives based on utility criteria. Conducting unobtrusive testing simply as a means to determine *correct answer fill rate* begs the larger utility question of "How can a library use findings from unobtrusive testing to improve the quality of its reference service and increase, overall, the effectiveness of that service?" At the time that study objectives are developed, careful consideration should be given to the use of the data for library decision making and identifying "actionable" variables, i.e., those that lend themselves to change and improvement. Future unobtrusive tests might focus on study objectives more closely related to utility-based criteria.

Focused versus non-focused reference questions. By using questions from U.S. government statistical sources, study questions were focused, in terms of publisher (the Government Printing Office) and type of sources (statistical). At present, there is no clear indication of the appropriateness of conducting unobtrusive testing, or measuring *correct answer fill rate,* on either a narrow (focused) or a broader, more generalized (unfocused) area. Thus, researchers and library staff wishing to use unobtrusive testing should determine, as part of the study objectives, the specific *type* of reference area to test and the degree to which they will focus on that area.

Representativeness of test questions. Although the test questions were developed according to specific criteria and pretested, some of them might not have been similar to the "typical" type of questions that the library tested actually receives. One approach to resolve this problem is to have one of the staff members *not* to participate in the answering of test questions but, rather, to serve as a validity check on the appropriateness and level of difficulty of the questions. Such an approach will reduce subsequent staff criticism that the questions were not "typical" of the types that they receive and that those used do not comprise a valid indicator of their reference answering skills.

Administration of test questions. This study, as have most other unobtrusive studies, used student proxies to administer the test questions. Alternative types of proxies, e.g., department heads (Williams and Wedig, 1984) merit exploration.

Library school students who have served as proxies have found the experience worthwhile because it demonstrates "real-life" reference service. Reference staff might benefit from participation in the asking of unobtrusive questions. Such an approach allows them to role play as a client and, in some cases, to regain a user perspective to information gathering. As participants, they will also observe effective and ineffective reference negotiation techniques and skills.

Intervention development. The study design emphasized methodological more than staff learning objectives. Actual interventions should be based on the particular characteristics/constraints found in a library. A broad range of reference-related interventions to improve the quality of reference services has been proposed elsewhere (McClure and Hernon, 1983, pp. 111–160) and can be "matched" to the actual needs of the staff. Future interventions should positively affect staff behaviors and increase their competencies.

SUMMARY

The pilot project represents the first application of unobtrusive testing, in the context of an experiment, for library reference service in which participants were randomly assigned to an intervention. Although no statistically significant differences emerged between pretest and posttest scores, or between learning outcomes from the two interventions, the project documents that unobtrusive testing methodologies and companion research designs merit further analysis and exploration.

The study is also important for its attempt to develop research designs and methods of data collection that improve the reliability and validity of unobtrusive testing. Although unobtrusive testing has been used in evaluating library reference services for some time, inadequate attention has been given to methodological factors that will improve unobtrusive testing techniques. As shown in Figure 4-2, a number of safeguards can, and should, be taken to ensure the receipt of accurate findings from unobtrusive testing.

Figure 4-4 summarizes the major findings related to the hypotheses and research questions. It identifies the climate in which unobtrusive testing can oc-

Figure 4-4   Summary of Findings Related to the Hypotheses and Research Questions

1. Overall, there was no statistically significant difference between the pretest and posttest *correct answer fill rates.*
2. Participation in either the workshop or slide/script presentation made no statistically significant difference on the group's *correct answer fill rate.*
3. The interventions had no statistically significant affect on the amount of time spent in answering the questions.
4. The participants' impression of the interventions being of limited value appears to match the finding of no statistically significant difference (or change) in *correct answer fill rate* before versus after the interventions.
5. The practicality of unobtrusive testing as an effective and efficient means for determining *correct answer fill rate* can be viewed in five contexts:
   a. The costs and time required for conducting unobtrusive testing appear to be appropriate for the information received and its overall value for decision making in large libraries.
   b. A number of insights regarding the quality of reference services can be realized by the use of unobtrusive testing and computing a *correct answer fill rate.* Yet this performance measure must be viewed in a subject context for a specific time period. "The *correct answer fill rate* for Federal statistical sources during September and October 1985 was . . ."
   c. Staff members will accept the use of unobtrusive testing and such testing can be implemented on a large scale without arousing staff suspicions.
   d. Developing unobtrusive testing designs requires the participation of individuals in-house or external, with advanced research skills; libraries without such skills in-house and/or unable to obtain external assistance should not use unobtrusive testing techniques.
   e. Data collection and analysis for unobtrusive testing requires the participation of individuals in-house or external, with advanced research skills; libraries without such in-house research skills and/or unable to obtain external assistance should not use unobtrusive testing techniques.

Figure 4-5   Summary of General Findings*

1. The *correct answer fill rate* for both the pretest and posttest of government documents and general reference personnel was 57.9%, about what Figure 1-1 has suggested as "typical."

2. Except in one instance where a staff member responded with "don't know," all occurances of an incorrect answer were attributable to the supplying of wrong information.

3. Central reference staff referred 58.3% of all questions asked, despite the fact that 66% of all the questions that they received were answerable from sources within the general reference collection.

4. Central reference staff made 88% of their referrals to the government documents department.

5. There was not a statistically significant relationship between the amount of time spent on answering a question and whether the question was answered correctly. Also the testing of this relationship by department did not indicate a statistically significant difference.

6. No statistically significant difference was identified for the *correct answer fill rate* of the reference and the documents staff between the pretest and the posttest.

7. Unlike other unobtrusive investigations, this one found only one instance in which a staff member may have been unfriendly.

---

*The findings based upon a comparison by department should be tempered by the fact that, due to referrals, the general reference staff actually answered fewer questions than did the documents staff.

cur and encourages further research combining unobtrusive testing with an experimental approach. Libraries need to determine the extent to which continuing education and other learning interventions affect the *correct answer fill rate* of their staff members.

Figure 4-5 highlights the general findings of the experimental study in light of findings from previous unobtrusive testing. The *correct answer fill rates* were similar to those found in other studies, and staff members make infrequent referral external to the library (McClure and Hernon, 1983). Further, the study raises important issues about the utility of "one-shot" interventions as a means of increasing reference staff effectiveness. The concluding chapter of the book will discuss these issues.

Readers should not necessarily characterize the reference service that this library provides as "inferior" or "adequate." The test questions only probed one area — Federal statistical sources — and for over a four week period. Nonetheless, findings from both the studies reported in this chapter and Chapter 3 provide a base from which researchers can explore additional intervention strategies and library decision makers can assess the implications of the preliminary findings on the quality of service that their reference staff provides.

CHAPTER 5

MANAGERIAL USES OF UNOBTRUSIVE REFERENCE TESTING: LINKING EVALUATION TO PRACTICE

Unobtrusive testing is a valid, reliable, and practical means of assessing the *quality* of one type of reference activity, i.e., the accuracy with which library staff answer factual and bibliographic questions. More importantly, the methodology assesses reference services from the vantage of the patron. A key concern, however, is that library staff recognize the importance of obtaining this assessment, and develop managerial strategies to act upon the results of their assessment.

Unobtrusive testing of reference services is not an end unto itself but a means toward improving the *quality* of library services. For unobtrusive testing to be effective, library staff must wish to ascertain the quality of services that they currently provide and take action based on that knowledge. Unobtrusive testing occurs within a larger context of library evaluation and the development of managerial strategies to improve library services. In short, the information that results from the unobtrusive testing must be incorporated into library decision making and planning processes.

The library profession frequently is "shocked" to learn the *correct answer fill rates* that have emerged from the various tests depicted in Figure 1-1. After overcoming their initial shock, library staff typically, display skepticism about the studies and rationalize the score, e.g., either testing occurred on a non-typical day at the library or the researchers used invalid research methodologies. Yet, informally, in a number of instances, library staff have asked us if their library was one of those tested in the various unobtrusive studies we have conducted. They suspected that their staff would have performed similar to the libraries tested.

Most library staff have not determined their *correct answer fill rate*. This passivity to self-assessment and blind faith that *their* services are fine, and of high quality, represent a critical managerial problem. *Correct answer fill rates* that hover around 55% should be of much concern to reference staff. Yet, that managers rarely determine what the rates are in their particular library and develop specific strategies to improve the quality is of equal concern.

Previous chapters in this book have concentrated on the use of unobtrusive testing to determine the *correct answer fill rate* and have shown that, in addition, unobtrusive testing provides insights into:

- the interviewing skills of staff
- the effectiveness and efficiency of search strategies
- the referral skills of staff
- the demeanor and communication skills of staff

Yet these insights represent only a portion of the possible uses for which unobtrusive evaluation techniques could be used in a library setting.

Increased use of unobtrusive testing of reference services is necessary because it:

- provides an excellent means to "see" the library and its services from the viewpoint of the patron
- reinforces the importance of regular self-assessment and ongoing library evaluation
- provides empirical data from which decisions and managerial strategies can be based

But *taking action* on the results of unobtrusive testing is the critical link in improving the quality of library reference services. A reassessment of library management's commitment to reference services and the effectiveness with which those services are offered must be made. Such a reassessment must be conducted in a context that links research related to library management and unobtrusive testing directly to specific strategies for improving the quality of library information services. Currently, existing knowledge from library management, unobtrusive testing, and evaluation research is poorly incorporated in the day-to-day management of library reference services.

This chapter discusses managerial responsibilities regarding the uses of unobtrusive testing and improving the quality of reference services, provides an overview of an evaluation system that can be formalized in the library setting and that can encourage ongoing self-assessment, and identifies additional types of unobtrusive testing that may be useful in a public services context.

In a previous book, the authors specified strategies by which reference staff might improve the quality of their services (McClure and Hernon, 1983, pp. 111–160). The final chapter of this book discusses the educational implications from such testing and the need to develop ongoing post-MLS educational programs. Ultimately, however, the responsibility for ensuring that patrons' information needs are met belongs to library management.

The underlying theme of this chapter is that sufficient knowledge exists about library management strategies, unobtrusive testing of reference services, and evaluation methodologies to develop methods whereby the quality of reference services can be reviewed and improved on a regular basis. Indeed, such methods must be implemented if academic and public libraries are to meet successfully their primary mission of meeting patrons' information needs. Library management must assume responsibility for the provision of quality information services.

MANAGERIAL RESPONSIBILITIES

There are numerous specific skills required by library managers if they are to offer leadership regarding the provision of high quality reference services. Katz and Fraley (1982) review a number of these skills and managerial activities. But some of the most important components affecting the provision of quality reference services are attitudinal and knowledge-based. To encourage high quality reference services, special attention should be given to these managerial activities. Library managers, both at the organizational and departmental levels, must provide leadership in each of the areas discussed in this section.

Supportive Organizational Climate

Organizational climate is a psychologically based method of describing how peoples' value systems coexist with those of the organization. This climate reflects the internal environment of an organization; it is experienced by its members, influences their behavior, and can be described in terms of values held by organizational members (Tagiuri and Litwin, 1968). A number of factors may combine to produce an organizational climate, including management style, interpersonal skills, physical facilities, and other resources. Depending on the interaction of such factors, the organizational climate may support and encourage high staff performance and productivity.

Recent research suggests that supportive library organizational climates tend to be those with high scores on the following characteristics (McClure and Samuels, 1985):

- *innovation*: the degree to which a library is ready to pursue innovative practices, policies, and services
- *support*: the degree to which a library maintains mutually supporting relationships between different work groups within that library
- *democratic governance*: the extent to which library staff feel that they have the opportunity to participate in library decision making (*not* the degree to which they actually participate — an important distinction)
- *esprit*: the level of morale and shared purpose among library staff.

Managers must develop supportive organizational climates in their library if they intend to promote overall library effectiveness.

Methodologies have been developed by which the organizational climate of academic and public libraries can be measured on the above characteristics (McClure and Samuels, 1985; and Samuels and McClure, 1983). Figure 5-1 describes the organizational climates at two public libraries as reported in these studies. The libraries are relatively similar in terms of collection size, staff size, and number of branches. The measures along the left margin of each table represent the Z-score of the library on a particular scale as compared to the scores from all libraries on that particular scale.[1] Library A demonstrates supportive organizational climate characteristics, while Library B does not.

After obtaining the findings reported in the figure, investigators conducted structured observation unobtrusively at these two libraries. Over a four hour period, on two different days, they monitored staff activities at the library's main reference desk. Generally, staff at Library A, with a supportive organizational climate (see Figure 5-1):

- spent 3 to 5 minutes longer per reference interview than did Library B
- more frequently left the immediate area of the reference desk with patrons to demonstrate the use, or show the location, of a reference source
- demonstrated better interpersonal skills, non-verbal communication skills, and knowledge of basic reference sources
- showed greater empathy for the needs of the user and used more sophisticated question negotiation skills

Generalizations from these two unobtrusive observations must be made with care since *correct answer fill rates* for each library were not obtained. Nonetheless, the quality of reference services at the library with a supportive organizational climate appears to be substantially better than at the library with a non-supportive organizational climate.

While additional research is necessary there appears to be a link between supportive organizational climates and the quality of reference service. Library managers have a responsibility to:

- understand psychologically based indicators of organizational behavior
- recognize the importance of management styles, organizational climates, and other managerial considerations as factors that affect the quality of staff performance
- develop management strategies to enhance organizational climates and improve the managerial setting in which staff work on a daily basis

---

[1] Z scores compare the mean of all scores. They provide a method for the standardization and comparison of results on different scales or measures.

Figure 5-1   Z-Scores for Two Libraries

	Information Acquisition	Information Dissemination	Democratic Governance	Support	Innovation	Esprit
LIBRARY A						
Highest Score	2.38	2.21	1.64	1.51	1.80	1.40
	1.29	1.91	1.46	1.37	.99	1.37
	.85	1.42	1.01	1.16	.88	.94
	.84	.52	.85	/1.12	.85	.85
	.62	.38	.75	.28	.75	82
	.40	.29	.68	.15	.61	.72
	.32	.20	.64	− .05	.33	.64
	.26	.12	.49	− .07	.21	.61
	.22	− .26	.11	− .22	.10	.25
	.08	− .39	− .09	− .31	− .02	− .18
	− .41	− .47	− .29	− .35	− .22	− .38
	− .77	− .60	− .60	− .40	− .86	− .40
	− .81	− .62	− .76	− .46	− .88	− .50
	− .84	− .68	− .78	− .59	− 1.00	− .59
	− .85	− .78	− .79	− 1.82	− 1.14	− .80
	− .95	− .95	− 1.20	− 2.11	− 1.38	− 1.01
Lowest Score	− .97	− .96	− 1.30		− 1.91	− 1.79
	− 1.67	− 1.35	− 1.82			− 1.94

However, many library managers are unaware of their library's organizational climate in terms of *measureable* criteria and fail to recognize the impact of such climate conditions on the provision of high quality reference services.

Emphasizing the Importance of Quality

A primary responsibility for library managers is to increase staff awareness of issues related to the *quality* of reference services as opposed to the quantity of such services. Many library reference departments stress quantity of services rather than quality. For example, recording the number or types of reference questions asked and online searches performed encourages the mentality that "how much" is done may be of greater importance than "how well" activities are accomplished.

Figure 5-1   *(Continued)*

	Information Acquisition	Information Dissemination	Democratic Governance	Support	Innovation	Esprit
LIBRARY B						
Highest Score	2.38	2.21	1.64	1.51	1.80	1.40
	1.29	1.91	1.46	1.37	.99	1.37
	.85	1.42	1.01	1.16	.88	.94
	.84	.52	.85	1.12	.85	.85
	.62	.38	.75	.28	.75	.82
	.40	.29	.68	.15	.61	.72
	.32	.20	.64	− .05	.33	.64
	.26	.12	.49	− .07	.21	.61
	.22	− .26	.11	− .22	.10	.25
	.08	− .39	− .09	− .31	− .02	− .18
	− .41	− .47	− .29	− .35	− .22	− .38
	− .77	− .60	− .60	− .40	− .86	− .40
	− .81	− .62	− .76	− .46	− .88	− .50
	− .84	− .68	− .78	− .59	− 1.00	− .59
	− .85	− .78	− .79	− 1.82	− 1.14	− .80
	− .95	− .95	− 1.20	− 2.11	− 1.38	− 1.01
Lowest Score	− .97	− .96	− 1.30		− 1.91	− 1.79
	− 1.67	− 1.35	− 1.82			− 1.94

The day-to-day pressures on reference staff may also contribute to an overemphasis on quantity of services. Results presented in Chapter 3 of this book confirm earlier research findings (McClure and Hernon, 1983) that reference staff have "internal clocks," which typically conclude a reference transaction after 3 to 5 minutes. While such may occur as a result of inadequate staffing or other reasons, the effect is to "get on to the next patron" or some other activity. Since only few reference departments will ever have "adequate" staff or other resources, priorities will have to be decided between provision of *quantity* versus *quality* reference service.

Library management must be committed to excellence and instill that commitment into the reference staff. Attributes which Peters and Waterman identify as contributing to organizational excellence include (1982, pp. 13–16):

- *a bias for action*: getting on with it, trying alternatives and not being paralyzed into doing nothing about a clearly identified problem

- *staying close to the customer*: organizations must learn from the people they serve and incorporate that knowledge into daily activities
- *autonomy and entrepreneurship*: encouragement of risk taking, innovation, and trying new ideas
- *productivity through people*: the single most important resource in any organization is its staff; they must be treated with respect and concern
- *hands-on knowledge*: managers must have first hand information and knowledge about what is happening in their organizations; they must also be visible to employees
- *stick to the knitting*: stress the provision of services and products which the organization knows best and has the appropriate resources to provide
- *simple form — lean staff*: organization structures must be uncomplicated, clear lines of authority are needed, and the organization should not be "top heavy" with managers
- *simultaneous loose-tight properties*: allowing both autonomy for the individual on the "front line" within a firm management framework or policies and clearly defined responsibilities displaying a decentralized style

This distillation of attributes that foster excellence encompasses both *attitudes* and specific skills. If reference staff observe poor attitudes in library managers and a lack of concern related to quality services, they are also receiving a message about the level of quality managers will accept. In short, library managers need to promote the attitude that excellence and high quality services are primary commitments of the organization.

Encouraging Measurement and Evaluation

Developing supportive organizational climates and emphasizing the importance of quality reference services is essential, but not sufficient. Ultimately, there is the need to assess the quality of the reference services that the library staff provide. Library managers cannot automatically assume that "surely *our* library provides high quality services." If formal evaluations have not been done, then such statements are assumptions. Without empirical evidence describing the level of quality provided, it is difficult to develop effective managerial strategies to *improve* reference services.

The concept of measurement is the process by which numbers are assigned to describe or represent some object or phenomenon in a standardized manner (Kaplan, 1964, pp. 171–213). While measurement may lead to evaluation and evaluation usually requires measurement, the two processes are not the same. Evaluation, as used in this book, includes the measurement process and adds components of the research process, planning, and implementation strategies to change or improve the organization or a specific activity (see the next section of this chapter).

Apparently, academic public service librarians do not believe that formal evaluations of the quality of reference services are of much utility. Rather, they maintain that (McClure, 1986):

- intuitive assessment of performance is as accurate as formal means of evaluation
- there are few rewards and benefits for librarians who do engage in formal assessments of the quality of reference services
- resulting data that assessed the quality of reference services are not likely to be reliable or valid
- even when such data are produced they are rarely incorporated into library decision making and planning

A key implication of these findings is that library managers do not encourage the use of evaluation methodologies, are unfamiliar with the use of various performance measures (such as *correct answer fill rate*), and set an example for their staff that does not encourage the use of such techniques.

This study also identified little librarian interest in the use of unobtrusive testing (McClure, 1986). In addition, a citation analysis of Crowley and Childers' (1971) seminal work on unobtrusive testing concluded that "unobtrusive procedures have not yet become a component of the standard methods for evaluating library and information service performance" (Schrader, 1984, p. 208). Without greater basic knowledge of qualitative research methodologies, including unobtrusive techniques, library reference services cannot be meaningfully evaluated and strategies implemented for their improvement. Worse, reference service will continue as it is, typically unevaluated and providing "half-right" reference service (Crowley, 1985).

The larger issue here is that library managers must develop a positive attitude toward the importance of utilizing empirical data in decision making and planning. They must know how to conduct evaluation research and employ research techniques such as unobtrusive testing in order to describe existing levels of library services empirically. Minimally, library managers should be able to:

- identify reference service areas requiring study
- state research problems and questions
- develop appropriate methodologies to answer the research questions
- collect reliable and valid data
- analyze and report the results
- implement strategies to improve the quality of reference services

If library managers cannot perform these basic procedures, re-tooling or gaining basic evaluation competencies is in order.

In short, library managers must promote the importance of formal evaluations of reference processes, state their commitment to obtaining reliable and valid data, and demonstrate that such data, once obtained, will be integrated directly into day-to-day decision making regarding reference services. They must radiate a commitment to and support for the provision of *quality* reference services, strive to develop a supportive organizational climate, and use management techniques that encourage library staff to *want* to provide high quality services. Knowledge of basic evaluation and research skills is an essential component for success in meeting these responsibilities.

ESTABLISHING FORMAL EVALUATION SYSTEMS

If reference services are to be improved, they must be evaluated on a regular basis and produce longitudinal data. The following discussion provides an overview for instituting an ongoing *program* of regular evaluation. As suggested earlier in this chapter, evaluation without resulting action, or an implementation stage, is of little usefulness in improving library services. Most libraries have neither the time nor the resources to engage in an evaluation process if the results cannot be translated *directly* into policy decisions to improve library services or operations.

Space does not permit an in-depth review of the literature that describes methodologies for assessing *quality*-based criteria for reference services. The classic work by Webb et al. (1966) on *Unobtrusive Measures* is basic, introductory reading. However, recent works by Nachmias and Nachmias (1981, pp. 243–266), Jick (1983), Miles and Huberman (1984), and Rossi and Freeman (1985) augment reference evaluation techniques discussed by Lancaster (1977, pp. 73–139), Katz and Fraley (1984), McClure (1984), and Powell (1984).

Thus, the following overview of a formalized evaluation process serves as an introduction on how such a process can be developed in a library setting. It is based on the following assumptions:

* many staff, and if appropriate, some library clientele are involved in the process
* the evaluation process emphasizes areas where services are actionable, i.e., where change can be accomplished
* the inclusion of performance measures, quality standards, or criteria for success is essential in the evaluation process
* the process must be closely linked to organizational goals and service objectives
* the process should be practical and feasible such that it can be applied straightforwardly and with relative ease

Throughout the entire process, the evaluations must be based on basic knowledge of research techniques in the social and behavioral sciences.

Figure 5-2 summarizes three broad phases of the overall evaluation process:

- Phase I: *Preparation*: the library makes certain that organizational goals and quantifiable objectives are established, staff are adequately trained to conduct evaluations, potential uses for evaluation are identified, and the library staff have a basic understanding of the issues, topics, and techniques related to that evaluation.
- Phase II: *Evaluation Research*: Here, the specific evaluation research questions, performance measures, research designs, and methodologies are developed and implemented to investigate the effectiveness/efficiency of the services and activities under consideration.
- Phase III: *Organizational Development:* The final phase is one in which the library assesses the results of the evaluation process and makes value judgements concerning which services or activities to modify, how to modify them,

Figure 5-2   The Evaluation Process

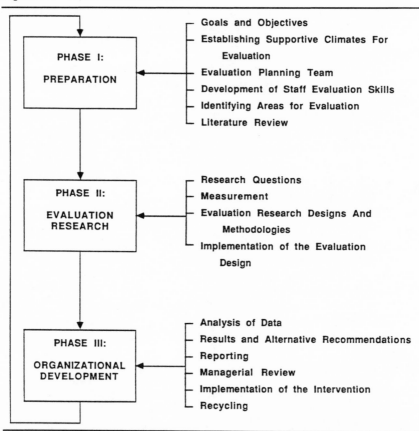

and how to implement strategies to change those services or activities and improve organizational performance.

Each of these three phases is important; successful evaluation depends on the ability of library management to orchestrate the components of each phase carefully with other phases and to improve the quality of services.

Phase I: Preparation

The objectives of the preparation phase of the evaluation process are to establish an organizational setting that encourages successful evaluation, and to make certain that the staff understand the basic components of the evaluation process. Factors discussed earlier in this chapter must be considered as well. Successful evaluations *do not* begin with data collection; rather, they establish a mission statement, organizational goals and objectives, and reference service policy statements (Edgar and Herrick, 1982), as well as identify and review areas for possible evaluation. Preparing for successful evaluation is critical for the success of the process and may, in fact, require a number of months before the library can move into Phase II.

Goals and Objectives. Simply stated, the effectiveness of reference services cannot be determined without the setting of goals and measureable objectives since, by definition, effectiveness is the degree to which objectives are accomplished. Establishment of specific reference and related service objectives is dependent on the organization's larger statement of goals and its mission. Objectives force the establishment of *priorities* — which services are most important. Since the library cannot provide all services for all types of clientele, priorities are essential. Failure to establish service priorities is a primary cause for the provision of poor quality services.

Although goals and objectives for reference service should be cast in the larger context of the library's mission and organizational planning, evaluation can proceed with only the articulation of reference service goals and objectives. It may be necessary for library management to develop a process for specifying objectives and policies, obtaining input from the reference staff during the process, and producing a *written* statement summarizing these objectives and policies. Such a written statement sets the context for evaluation and provides a basis for making value judgements about which services are appropriate for that particular library and the level of quality that will be acceptable. Riggs (1984, pp. 29–36), Donald (1976), and Palmour et al. (1980, pp. 57–69) can assist library staff in the stating of goals and objectives.

Establishing Supportive Climate for Evaluation. As discussed earlier in this chapter, it is important for library management to develop supportive organizational climates, promote the importance of ongoing evaluation, and demonstrate a positive attitude that stresses the library's concern for the provision of high quality information services. While some management skills rely on certain interpersonal and individual competencies, a number of skills require training and knowledge beyond that which is typically received in a MLS program. Library managers must be knowledgeable about basic management strategies and know how to implement them. Being a good reference librarian is *not* the same as being a good manager of a reference department or an evaluator of a program/service.

Knowledge of basic contingency management techniques and strategies (i.e., situational strategies that match unique skills of the individual to the needs and resources of the organization) is essential for the establishment of supportive climates (Kast and Rosenzweig, 1979). Samuels (1982) has detailed specific suggestions for developing a supportive management climate and readying the library organization for change. In fact, the introduction of formal evaluation processes might serve as a catalyst in the development of supportive organizational climates.

The single most important consideration in forming supportive organizational climates for ongoing programs of library evaluation is developing reward structures that encourage change. Staff should be offered "rewards," both intrinsic and extrinsic, for participating in evaluation processes. There should be "pay-offs" from such involvement — both for the library as well as for the individual staff member. Library managers must make certain that the organization provides such reward structures and if it does not, they should develop such strategies.

Evaluation Planning Team. Staff involvement in the evaluation process should be encouraged for a number of reasons:

- Greater involvement in the evaluation process increases their understanding and knowledge of organizational services and activities
- They can better see the relationship among various library services and activities and recognize that the inter-dependency of these activities has an impact on library effectiveness
- Participation in the evaluation may reduce potential fear of such evaluation and assist in the implementation of strategies to change the activity at a later date
- Evaluations that appear to require too much time and effort for one staff member can be accomplished by a team
- Staff have an opportunity to assume new responsibilities, develop increased or expanded skills, and expand their professional horizons

Top library management involvement on the evaluation team is essential. Library staff must see *evidence* that there is both interest and direct involvement by management on the team.

Development of Staff Evaluation Skills.   Another key aspect of the preparation phase is to develop a program of staff training related to basic research/
evaluation methods as well as the necessary designs for evaluating reference
services — including unobtrusive testing techniques. Implementation of ongoing evaluation without corresponding staff skills and competencies significantly
increases the probability for failure in using basic evaluation techniques. Conducting a simple needs assessment of staff skills in this area can be easily accomplished. Based on that assessment appropriate staff training programs and
education can be implemented (Conroy, 1978).

The basic activities described in this section offer a preliminary list of staff
skills and competencies that will be necessary for the successful completion of
evaluations of library services. It should not be assumed that staff have basic
evaluation/research knowledge, data collection and analysis skills, report writing skills, etc. The quality of the evaluations will only be as good as those doing
the evaluation. Management must have basic evaluation skills as well as the
ability to instill these skills in staff who will conduct the evaluations. Rossi and
Freeman (1985) have written one of the best texts on the evaluation process,
and library managers might review it prior to conducting any reference service
evaluation.

Identifying Areas for Evaluation.   Identifying areas for evaluation is com-
posed of two basic components: (1) reviewing the existing quality or performance of library reference services, and (2) developing problem statements. The
review, which is done in the context of existing organizational goals and objectives, is intended to identify *primary* areas where evaluation is necessary. The
process can be either formal or informal, and rely on either objective or subjective evidence; regardless, the intent is to identify areas where evaluation is necessary and begin the process of narrowing down that area to a manageable
problem statement.

Broad questions to consider as a means of identifying areas for possible evaluation include:

- Is existing performance perceived as decreasing or inadequate compared to
  previous performance in this area?
- If the area has never been formally evaluated, then how "good" are its services
  and activities?
- Has the cost or allocation of other resources to this service or activity increased substantially in recent months and cannot staff explain why such increases have occurred?
- Have institutional, clientele, or other external factors which affect this service recently changed; if so, should there be a reassessment of the "appropriateness" or "quality" of the service or activity?

• Is the library considering alternative approaches to improve performance in a given area, and which method or measure will be used to compare these alternatives?

At a more specific level, that of relating possible areas to library goals and departmental objectives, the following questions might be asked:

• How are these services contributing to the accomplishment of organizational goals and departmental objectives?
• How well do these services and activities contribute to meeting the information needs of library clientele?
• Are the resources necessary for the support of these services being spent appropriately or could the resources be better spent elsewhere?
• To what degree is this service or activity "actionable," i.e., does it have the potential for being changed?

Asking these, and related, questions assists library staff in identifying potential service areas for evaluation.

Based on this preliminary assessment, a problem statement should be developed to (1) establish the scope of the service to be evaluated, (2) define key terms related to the service or activity, and (3) begin the process of determining the feasibility of conducting an evaluation of this particular service. An example of a possible problem statement is: *Why has the number of reference questions asked by university faculty, at the main reference desk, dropped off significantly in the last two months, and overall use of the reference materials apparently decreased?*

Generally speaking, problem statements establish parameters for what is to be evaluated; they neither detail specific or expected results to be obtained from the study nor suggest study procedures (the design and methodology).

Literature Review.   The last component of the preparation phase for evaluation is a review of related literature. Although this component is introduced here, in the preparation phase, it will be necessary to return to the literature throughout the evaluation process. The objectives of the literature review are to:

• obtain basic definitions and background information, and determine the current status of research and writing on a topic
• provide the evaluation team members with a common understanding of the topic
• identify evaluation/research designs and methods that might be useful for this particular topic
• revise and refine the problem statement as necessary and assist in the establishment of research questions

The search for literature should include *internal* reports and statistical data from the library as well as *external* literature from the various professional journals, monographs, and other sources.

Phase II: Evaluation Research

The second phase of the evaluation process focuses on data collection. Careful consideration must be given to *what* data will be collected, and *why* and *how* they will be collected. This phase of the evaluation process requires a number of staff skills and competencies in the area of evaluation/research for the assessment to be successful and have an impact on organizational effectiveness.

The specific nature of the evaluation/research to be done, depends, in part, on what types of data need to be examined and why the problem has been selected. Evaluators must recognize that numerous reasons may be put forth for initiating an evaluation — including political justifications, budgetary cutbacks, personnel matters, etc. The evaluation team should gain a sense of why the evaluation has been initiated and take this into account when it develops the research questions and evaluation research design.

Research Questions.   Research questions provide specific guidance to the evaluators about what, exactly, is to be investigated. They narrow the general area to be investigated to specific topics that are manageable; from these topics, possible measures and research designs for the collection of data are formulated. Two example research questions from the problem statement given above are:

- Do faculty perceive the quality of reference service (accuracy of staff answers) provided at the main reference desk as decreasing?
- Is the decline in faculty requests for reference assistance limited to certain academic departments or areas?

Once the research questions are stated, they should be reviewed in terms of their feasibility and utility. For example, the evaluation team should ask: (1) can we realistically answer this question? (2) how will the answer assist us in improving the quality of services, and (3) do we have the physical resources, time, and staff competencies to design a study by which these questions can be answered?

Measurement.   Once the research questions have been established, the next concern is to develop a basis for measuring the service to be evaluated. A number of measures are described elsewhere (Lancaster, 1977; Powell, 1984). Emphasis is given here to *performance* measures that stress the effectiveness, quality, and/or outputs resulting from the various services. While efficiency criteria such as cost and time are certainly important, quality-based measures are crucial during the evaluation process.

Some examples of unobtrusive performance measures that may be useful in assessing various aspects of reference services include:

- *correct answer fill rate* (number of correct answers provided by library staff over all questions asked)
- *correct answers per reference staff hour* (number of correct answers provided by staff over total number of reference hours)
- *cost per correct reference answer* (total cost of reference services for a given time period over the number of correct answers provided by staff during the same time period)
- *duration of correct (incorrect) answers*: (average time spent providing a correct [or an incorrect] answer)
- *referral fill rate*: (number of correct referrals provided by library staff over all referrals given)

These measures are offered as examples. The actual measures selected would depend on the research questions and the nature of the problem under evaluation.

Generally, the evaluation team will establish its own measures for the particular service it wishes to evaluate. A number of sources provide some assistance in developing measures (e.g., Zweizig and Rodger, 1982; Kantor, 1984; McClure and Reifsnyder, 1984). The measures may be simple, e.g., time, cost, and square footage; however, typically, measures for reference services should stress *outputs*, that which is received by the patron rather than *inputs*, the resources contributing to the provision of that service. Once such measures are selected they should be used regularly over time so that the library can produce trend data showing the quality of that service from month to month or year to year.

The choice of measures is *not* limited to those appearing in the literature; the potential is limited only by the evaluation team's imagination (Kaplan, 1964, p. 176):

> . . . whether we can measure something depends, not on that thing, but on how we have conceptualized it, on our knowledge of it, above all on the skill and ingenuity which we can bring to bear on the process of measurement. . . .

Performance measures stress the relative quality or effectiveness of a service and assist library management to make value judgements about the *worth* of a service relative to other services and to the degree that these services facilitate the accomplishment of formal goals and objectives. Every effort should be made to include performance measures in the evaluation process and select appropriate research designs and methodologies to take advantage of these measures.

Evaluation/Research Designs and Methodologies. The primary objectives of the evaluation/research design and method component in the evaluation process is to:

- ensure the collection of reliable and valid data that address the research questions
- describe factors or characteristics of the study's subject in terms of criteria such as quality, utility, effectiveness, and efficiency
- produce data from which recommendations can be developed to improve the quality or performance of that particular service

The selection of an evaluation design depends on the nature of the problem under investigation, the availability of time and resources to conduct the evaluation, the degree of confidence required from the data collection, and the knowledge/competency of those doing the evaluation.

The evaluation design is simply a plan that outlines the procedures by which research questions are answered, the subjects to be studied are identified and selected, and a specific approach such as an experimental design, a case study, or a survey design, is selected for systematically organizing the subjects to be studied. Chapter 4 offered an example of an experimental design combined with unobtrusive testing. The methodology is the manner in which the data are collected—perhaps by interviews, questionnaires, analysis of citation counts, observation, administration of tests, etc. Rutman (1984) provides detailed information about the construction of evaluation designs and methodologies; Rossi and Freeman (1985), Spector (1981), and Patton (1982) offer additional useful information.

Careful attention must be given to the selection of an evaluation/research design and method of data collection to ensure the data are consistent (reliable) and measure what they are supposed to measure (valid). Techniques, such as those identified in Figure 4-2, should be built into the evaluation to ensure the collection of reliable and valid data (Carmines and Zeller, 1979). Regardless of the excellence of the problem statement, the research questions, or other aspects of the evaluation, unreliable and invalid data are not useful for making meaningful assessments about the value of a particular service/program or for developing interventions leading to its improvement.

Self-reported data by any group of individuals should be immediately suspect, the limitations of these data recognized, and proper safeguards employed. Unobtrusive data collection methods are especially useful to obtain valid assessments of library services. These methods offer a "real world" description of activities as opposed to "perceptions" of those activities (a detailed description of unobtrusive methods in both an experimental and non-experimental design appear in Chapters 5 and 3, respectively).

Implementation of the Evaluation Design. The final activity during the second phase of the evaluation process is the actual implementation of the research design and data collection methodology. This phase requires careful scheduling and planning of the evaluation and coordination among the evaluators, the things to be evaluated, and the resources necessary to support the evaluation.

A preliminary activity to implementation may be a pretest or pilot investigation of the evaluation/research design and data collection methodology. If the method calls for the use of a survey, interview, or unobtrusive test, a pretest can:

- determine the amount of time necessary to administer the data collection instrument and/or process and assess its appropriateness
- identify any weaknesses, problems, or inaccuracies with the data collection process or instrument
- attempt to identify any "unanticipated consequences" resulting from the data collection process
- provide insights into the extent to which resulting data are reliable, valid, and useful for library decision making
- ensure that the data actually collected will (1) answer the research questions, and (2) allow computation of the desired performance measures

Investment in a pretest provides excellent returns by saving the evaluation team extra time later, pointing out areas of the evaluation/research design that can be improved *before* it is too late, and allowing the evaluators to tighten controls on the design for improved reliability and validity of the data collected.

The implementation of the evaluation/research design and data collection methodologies can be made more effective with the use of planning and scheduling charts such as GANTT charts, PERT charts, or project managers. A number of these are available in a microcomputer software format and comprise excellent management tools. All of these techniques provide a basis for the evaluators to understand:

- the tasks to be accomplished
- who is responsible for accomplishing the tasks
- when the tasks are to be completed
- how the various parts of the evaluation are related to each other

Scheduling charts, such as that shown in Figure 5-3, assist management in monitoring day-to-day activities related to evaluation and provide benchmark

Figure 5-3 GANTT Planning Chart

Task	Person	Month: 1 2 3	4 5 6	7 8 9	10 11 12
1.					
2.					
3.					
4.					
5.					
6.					
7.					
8.					
9.					
10.					
11.					
12.					
13.					
14.					
15.					

NOTES AND EXPLANATIONS:

dates when the status of the entire evaluation will be reviewed. But perhaps most importantly, it is essential that the evaluation team clearly understand *who* is responsible for each aspect of the evaluation.

Phase III: Organizational Development

The final phase of the evaluation process identifies specific strategies to improve the quality of library services and to increase overall organizational performance. In this phase of the evaluation, value judgements are made about *how well* existing services operate and *what should* the library offer in terms of services and activities. Many librarians ask the "how well" question, but fail to consider the "what should" issue. Yet the "what should" requires careful consid-

consideration and re-evaluation as the library finds itself competing more directly with other non-library information services and products.

Analysis of Data. Data resulting from evaluation are unintelligible until they are analyzed, summarized, and interpreted in terms of *descriptive* statistics, e.g., frequencies, percentages, and averages, and *inferential* statistics, e.g., predictive relationships such as correlations. Producing descriptive statistics is a beginning and essential step; in some instances there will also be a need for producing inferential statistics. Additional guidance on the use of such statistics and on specific techniques for analyzing data are found in a number of texts (e.g., Jaeger 1983; Ary, Jacobs, and Razavieh, 1985; Swisher and McClure, 1984).

Evaluators should also consider using one of the many microcomputer software programs available to analyze data. Although hand analysis is possible, it is not recommended because:

- mistakes are too easy to make
- data cannot be easily re-formatted or reconfigured
- correlations and inferential statistics are not easily computed by hand, and thus, will not be done

There is no reason for library staff to spend endless hours analyzing data by hand when software is easily available and many libraries have access to microcomputers or other institutional computing facilities. Hernon and McClure (1986) provide an overview of the use of microcomputers in the evaluation/research process, for data collection and analysis. They also review selected statistical software programs and project managers.

Another reason for using microcomputers, in analyzing the data is the likelihood of producing descriptive graphics that summarize the findings from the evaluation. Graphics in the form of tables, matrices, pie/bar charts, or X-Y plots can more easily summarize the findings and convey the meaning of the data than descriptive text. Once again, many of the microcomputer-based statistical analysis programs and spreadsheet packages produce such graphics as a matter of course. Hernon and McClure (1986) offer many examples of the use of graphics packages.

Results and Alternative Recommendations. The results of the data analysis, simply stated, are summaries that (1) answer the evaluation/research questions and compute the appropriate measures, and (2) offer alternative recommendations for what the data mean and what should be done about the findings. The results should be brief, concise, and to-the-point. Some library staff and managers may want detailed information about the data and *the process* by which they were collected and analyzed. More likely, they want the "bottom line," or the actual findings.

Alternative recommendations, or actions that management might take as a result of the evaluation, should be developed because:

- a list of alternatives forces comparison among those alternatives regarding which might be "best" in terms of criteria such as cost, time, equipment needs, staff ability to perform the activity, and feasibility
- forcing oneself to list three or more recommendations from the results encourages creativity, innovation, and a fresh perspective on how to improve the service under consideration.

Further, the stating of alternatives may be a catalyst for others reading the recommendations to develop their own approaches to improving the service or activity under consideration.

The recommendations should be as specific as possible and, minimally, offer a basic tasking of each recommendation and comparisons among the recommendations about the:

- costs of implementing the recommendation
- time required to implement the recommendation
- potential impacts and benefits from implementing the recommendation

Adequate descriptive information about each recommendation must be provided so that library staff and management can discuss and analyze the recommendations intelligently.

Reporting. Analyzing the data, stating results, and developing recommendations is *not* the same as reporting those findings and alternative recommendations. Specific techniques to communicate and disseminate the findings of an evaluation study are essential if the evaluator wants to have the recommendations implemented (Anderson and Ball, 1978, pp. 91–109). This reporting process is ongoing, in that library management and staff should be kept informed throughout the evaluation process of its progress. Nonetheless, a written report on the evaluation is essential.

When the evaluation team writes the summary report for the evaluation it should remember the intended audience of the report, that group's level of understanding of both the evaluation process and the service under consideration, the amount of time the group is likely to spend on preparation of the report, and the overall significance of the service in terms of library resources or commitment.

In short, the report should be concise and well-written. It should also include summary graphics and data results, and be written with an easy-to-read style. Figure 5-4 offers a basic outline for the main parts to be included in such a report. Clearly, every effort should be made to write and present the report in a manner that encourages action—the making of decisions and development of

Figure 5-4   Outline for an Evaluation Report

A. Executive Summary of Major Findings and Recommendations

B. Introduction
   • importance of the evaluation
   • relationship of this service to other library activities

C. Evaluation Methodology
   • problem statement, research questions
   • evaluation design and data collection methodology

D. Results
   • analysis of the data (use summary graphics)
   • brief explanatory text

E. Recommendations
   • listing of alternative recommendations
   • discussion of the strengths and weaknesses of each recommendation

F. Appendices (if needed)
   • copies of data collection instruments
   • tabulations/summaries of data
   • supporting documents/information

---

strategies to implement one or more of the recommendations. Such can be done by (Weiss, 1972, pp. 110–128):

• demonstrating the objectivity of the evaluation team throughout the evaluation process
• stressing the feasibility, benefits, and practicality of the recommendations
• being explicit with methods for implementation of recommendations
• making certain that key individuals, opinion leaders, and managers are aware of the findings and recommendations
• avoiding the preparation of reports which make no clear recommendations; if such should occur, the evaluation should be redesigned and re-done.

Factors such as the timing of the release of the report and the political consequences associated with who will do the reporting and to whom the report is presented are also important considerations.

Managerial Review.   After the submission of the written report and perhaps an oral presentation as well, library management must act on the recommendations. At this point, it is essential to restate that library management should have been involved throughout the evaluation process. Factors that management must consider when it reviews the recommendations are:

• *Goals and objectives*: How will the recommendations assist the library to better accomplish stated goals and objectives?

- *Other library data*: How do the results from the evaluation compare to other existing library management data? Are they supportive or contradictory?
- *Politics*: How will the recommendations affect the use and distribution of power within the library as well as how do they impact on external factors such as the governing board or clientele?
- *Budget*: Will the recommended action require additional resources, save resources, or call for reallocation of resources?
- *Increased effectiveness, efficiency, or quality*: To what degree will the recommendations affect these criteria?
- *Feasibility*: Can the recommendations be implemented successfully without significant "stress" on the library? Are the recommendations "do-able"?

The result of the administrative review is either a (1) go or no-go decision concerning which recommendation to implement, and (2) a clear decision about who is responsible for implementing the recommendations.

Implementation of the Intervention. Intervention is any planned effort designed to produce intended change in a target population or study subjects (Rossi and Freeman, 1985, p. 14). As the capstone of evaluation, it represents a significant difference between basic and applied evaluation/research. For example, Chapter 4 describes two types of interventions, a workshop and a slide/script presentation. Simply studying a service by collecting data about it to better understand it often *is not sufficient*. An intervention strategy may be needed to *change* or *improve* the service and increase its overall effectiveness or quality. For this reason, unobtrusive techniques should be used as part of a larger program of self-diagnosis and self-improvement.

Some of the important activities to consider when implementing the intervention include tasking, setting target performance levels, monitoring, evaluating, and reporting.

Tasking. Although the basic tasks necessary for implementing the recommendations are probably included in the evaluation report, a more detailed description of those tasks might be necessary. Once tasks are specified, they should be reviewed in terms of cost and feasibility. Again a GANTT planning-scheduling chart, such as that shown in Figure 5-3, is an excellent tool to detail tasks, responsibilities for accomplishing the tasks, and the time line by which the tasks will be accomplished. All participants involved in an intervention should receive copies of a written tasking for that intervention. Managers should make certain that they understand their responsibilities.

Setting Target Performance Levels. Library management should set target levels for acceptable performance on the service or activity under consideration. If, for instance, the evaluation study determined that the *correct answer fill rate* for the professional reference staff was 45%, the target performance level might be set at 60%. As part of an intervention for a library service, it is essential for staff to have a target level of performance both to aim toward and to assess, later, the effectiveness of the intervention. Discussion regarding an "appropriate" level of performance for a particular service will depend on the values of the library staff and management, the available resources, and the priority of the service relative to goals and objectives for reference.

Monitoring. Library management and/or the specific individual(s) responsible for implementing the recommendations must constantly monitor the success with which tasking is completed. This could involve an informal process whereby library management simply observes the implementation activities on a regular basis, or via a more formal process whereby individuals responsible for particular portions of the intervention provide a written status report on activities at regular intervals. The monitoring process provides an "early warning system" to correct minor problems *before* they become potential disasters.

Evaluating. Based on the target levels of performance that have been set for this particular service, and perhaps other pre-determined criteria as well, the effect of the intervention on the service should be assessed. This assessment should be based on clearly defined performance measures and compared to the measures that described the performance of the service *prior* to actual intervention. The purpose of this particular evaluation process is to determine if the recommended intervention did or did not make a difference in the quality of the services provided.

Reporting. The results of the evaluation as well as an overview of the success of the intervention should be summarized in a short report that:

- assesses the success of the intervention based on specific performance measures
- compares the level of performance for the service before and after the intervention
- offers recommendations for how the service might be improved as a result of what has been learned in the process of implementing the intervention
- discusses the costs and benefits of this intervention compared to other possible strategies that might have been used to improve this service

The report documents the attempt to improve the particular service and provides a written record for library management to refer to when assessing goals and objectives for reference services, developing budgets, and making other types of decisions.

Recycling. The evaluation process has now come full circle. The results of a specific evaluation process and the intervention provide input in developing evaluations for other service areas. Provision of such information as feedback into an ongoing program of evaluation can be enhanced by maintaining a decision support system (an information system that systematically identifies, collects, and analyzes data to assist in library decision making) and reports a broad range of reference service data. Indeed, decision support systems for reference services can be microcomputer-based and assist library management in identifying areas requiring evaluation (Samuels, 1986).

Overview

The components of the evaluation process that have been described in this section are *basic*; library staff engaging in evaluation may wish to modify, expand, re-arrange, or otherwise adapt these components. Such adaption is essential because no treatment of the evaluation process can cover all the possible contingencies and situations that might arise in one particular setting. Thus, there is no substitute for the careful consideration of how to best employ the approach suggested here — individual skills and competencies about the understanding and application of the evaluation process will always be preferred over cookbook adherence to procedures which clearly are inappropriate for a specific setting.

When conducting evaluation studies, issues related to the *quality of the service* must be separated from the *value of that service*. Numerous reference services can be accomplished successfully, and, indeed, an evaluation of such a service can document the degree to which it is effective or of high quality. However, just because a service has high quality and displays certain attributes of effectiveness, it is *not* the same as saying, or judging, that service "valuable." The value of a service, ultimately, is based on the degree to which the service resolves the information needs of library clientele and facilitates the accomplishment of stated service objectives.

SUGGESTIONS FOR IMPLEMENTING
UNOBTRUSIVE EVALUATION

While unobtrusive testing comprises but one type of evaluation to assess the *quality* of library services, it is one of the most robust for producing information that directly assesses the quality of library services. But, unobtrusive techniques are little understood and only infrequently used when assessing library services today. Better understanding of how unobtrusive testing can be utilized, on a practical basis, can assist library managers to implement these techniques on a regular basis.

Basic Types of Unobtrusive Studies

For purposes of the evaluation of library services, Figure 5-5 illustrates four types of unobtrusive studies that realistically might be conducted in a library

Figure 5-5   **Basic Types of Library Unobtrusive Studies***

	UNOBTRUSIVE	TECHNIQUE
Subjects	TESTING	OBSERVATION
Library STAFF	I	III
Library CLIENTELE	II	IV

* Unobtrusive studies of subjects other than library staff or library clientele are possible, but are not the focus of this chapter.

setting. The figure is not intended to be comprehensive. Generally, unobtrusive studies test or observe either library staff or library clientele as subjects. There are numerous possible subgroups within these two types of subjects. For example, library staff may be described as professional or paraprofessional; full-time or part-time; public services, technical services, or management; main or branch library staff; and so forth. Similarly, subgroups for library clientele encompass a wide range of demographic, library use, geographic, or other criteria.

Approach I: Testing Library Staff. This approach is perhaps the best known and has been used in a number of unobtrusive tests of reference services (see Figure 1-1). One version of this approach is described in detail in Chapters 2 through 4 of this book. However, many variations to this approach can be designed depending on the specific skills of the staff that the evaluators wish to assess. For example, they might examine knowledge of specific reference tools, accuracy with which answers are given, or the use of various interpersonal and question negotiation techniques.

Approach II: Testing Clientele. Although some reference librarians may not realize it, clientele are regularly being "tested" as they attempt to resolve their information needs in the library. This approach simply formalizes the procedures by which library staff assesss their knowledge of clientele. For example, awareness, use, and assessment of particular library services can be determined by "testing" library users with two or three predetermined questions which are interwoven into a reference negotiation process or other setting. Or, library staff may work with groups outside the library where students, for example, might be asked questions about the library and its services, or assessed on the extent to which they resolve predetermined problems.

Approach III: Observing Library Staff. Structured observation of library staff activities is a relatively easy and straightforward approach to study unobtrusively the quality of staff performance. Sophisticated methods that employ video cameras which operate on a random basis or that simply require a proxie to sit in the reference or other service area and carefully observe and record the activities of library staff can provide valuable evaluation information about the quality of services provided.

Approach IV: Observing Library Clientele. Structured unobtrusive observations of clientele use of the card catalog, specific equipment — such as microform readers, and other activities in the library are the most common applications of this approach. Similar applications can be used in examining interlibrary loan, patrons' approaching the reference desk, etc. Indeed, in one instance reference librarians were wired with a small microphone and the interview between reference staff and the patrons was recorded for later analysis (Lynch, 1978).

Unobtrusive observation, approaches III and IV, offer a useful means of acquiring qualitative evaluation information. Epstein and Tripodi (1977, pp. 43–58) provide an excellent introductory overview for conducting such observationally based evaluations. They stress the importance of structured, systematic observation in which the purpose of the observation and the activities to be observed are articulated. Moreover, the data recording forms that define those activities, and techniques to enhance the reliability and validity of the observation must be developed. Goodell (1975) summarizes specific examples of how such observational forms can be constructed in a library context, how to determine the number of observations that are necessary to achieve particular reliability levels, and which methods are effective for reporting the results.

Research Opportunities for Unobtrusive Evaluation

A broad expanse of opportunities for unobtrusive evaluation/research is available for assessing the quality of services provided by library staff. Specific aspects that lend themselves to unobtrusive evaluation include the:

- *Accuracy* of answering in-person reference questions: Although existing unobtrusive evaluation has concentrated on general factual and bibliographic questions, evaluators can design the questions to stress:
  a. specific subject areas, e.g., history, science, or literature
  b. levels of difficulty, e.g., questions which are pretested by other librarians to be either "easier" or "more difficult" than typical questions
  c. subgroups of library staff, e.g., professional versus paraprofessional, full-time versus part-time
  d. types of materials, e.g., knowledge of specific information formats, e.g., microforms, maps, periodicals, government publications, or electronic files

- *Accuracy of answering telephone reference questions*: The accuracy or quality of answering telephone queries may be significantly different than answering in-person questions; McClure and Hernon (1983) identify specific areas that can be stressed for answering telephone and in-person reference questions.
- *Accuracy and appropriateness of referrals*: For which types of reference questions are referrals made? Should the referral have been made or could the answer have been obtained from sources available in the library or the department? If a referral was made, was it to the "best" source? How effective are referral sources in answering the questions?
- *Ability to negotiate a question successfully*: Childers (1978) has shown that unobtrusive testing comprises a powerful means to assess library staff's ability in using specific interview techniques related to open-ended questions, the "why" question, listening skills, and other factors (Katz, 1982, pp. 41–52).
- *Use of non-verbal communication or other interpersonal skills*: The best means to assess the library staff's knowledge and application of interpersonal skills in the provision of services is to observe unobtrusively those skills; such factors have been shown to be important considerations in the overall effectiveness of information services (Gothberg, 1974).
- *Use of information resources in the provision of services*: Do library staff have specific "favorites" that they rely on to answer reference questions at the expense of sources which might "better" answer the question but of which they are unaware? Library staff members use of particular types of information sources for specific types of questions has been inadequately considered as a factor in the provision of reference services.
- *Duration of the provision of information services*: Findings reported in this book and elsewhere (McClure and Hernon, 1983) suggest that staff members may have an "internal clock" that determines the amount of time they will spend with a particular client; better understanding of how such "internal clocks" impact on the answering of correct versus incorrect answers, referrals, and interpersonal skills is needed.

These topics are not intended to be comprehensive. Rather, they are suggestive of areas where unobtrusive testing is not only appropriate, but one of the few methods available to obtain data that are reliable, valid, and objectively based rather than perceptual.

Further, the listing of these areas accents the importance of having clearly defined service goals, objectives, and policy statements. The effective evaluation of services in each of these areas depends on having a set of criteria that describe "adequate" or "excellent" performance. Gers and Seward (1985, p. 34) have developed a useful example of an evaluation form that can be used for establishing such criteria and as a means for assessing library staff. Library management is responsible for describing such criteria in terms of "acceptable" or "model" reference services. *Managers* must clarify expectations for what constitutes excellence, be able to operationalize those expectations into observable and definable behaviors, and then base unobtrusive evaluations on those criteria.

Although unobtrusive evaluations for library and information services assess *staff* skills, competencies, and attitudes, the method can also examine library clientele as well. For example, the traffic patterns of clientele can be unobtrusively observed throughout the library, and questions which indirectly assess clientele knowledge of the library or library services can be asked within the context of "typical" exchanges between reference staff and the patron. Further, observation of the sources that clientele use and patron search patterns also lend themselves to unobtrusive evaluation. Knowledge from such unobtrusive evaluation provides important management information for structuring information services intended primarily to *resolve the information needs of library clientele.*

These unobtrusive methods can be combined with a relatively new technique, transaction log analysis, which has potential application in each of the four approaches suggested in Figure 5-5. Transaction log analysis is based on an assessment of the transactions, or procedures that one follows when searching for a record in an online catalog, a bibliographic database, or similar interactive computer system. The computer system is programmed to maintain a record of the subject's transactions while he/she uses the computer system. A log of those activities can then be reviewed, based on a set of specific criteria.

Borgman (1983) has shown that use of this unobtrusive technique has been most successful in assessing patron's knowledge of online catalogs. Tolle (1983) offers a detailed description of the methodology as a means of studying patron's use of OCLC. The approach has great potential for assessing a broad range of library services and the skills of library staff and users regarding specific services.

For example, a number of public libraries now provide public access microcomputers for their clientele. Librarians could ask patrons to leave with the reference staff copies of the search results generated at the microcomputer (transaction logs). Based on an analysis of these transaction logs, the reference librarians could design a series of training sessions that covered specific problems and issues identified by reviewing the copies of the search strategies and results.

Reference department managers could review the search skills of staff on online bibliographic databases, bibliographic utilities such as OCLC and RLIN, or other interactive computer systems with which they come into contact. An analysis of transaction logs constitutes an excellent means for obtaining evaluation information on what *actually* occurs rather than a *perception* of what occurs. Further, the assessment of such logs provides a direct link to developing intervention strategies to remedy identifiable problems. Clearly, however, more evaluation needs to employ multiple data collection techniques.

Unobtrusive testing, when combined with other techniques, provides management with a more complete assessment of the quality of library services and programs.

Administering the Unobtrusive Test/Observation

A key decision that has to be made is who will administer the unobtrusive test/ observation and the data collection instrument to the subjects? In reaching a decision, every effort should be made to (1) ensure that the individuals responsible collect reliable, valid, and objective data, and (2) minimize any ethical concerns about unobtrusive techniques that might arise *after* the availability of the data. The ethical considerations and suggestions to minimize objections to the use of unobtrusive techniques have been discussed elsewhere (Webb et al., 1966; Crowley, 1985).

In some instances, the library staff may serve as data collectors for unobtrusive testing/observation of library clientele. But in instances where library staff are to be unobtrusively tested or observed, administering data collection instruments can be accomplished through a number of different approaches. One approach is for a librarian to administer the unobtrusive test/observation; another is to obtain the services of "proxies."

A proxie is a person who is unknown to the library staff and whose services have been obtained specifically for the purpose of testing or observing the staff. Proxies may be a broad range of individuals: university faculty, students, members from the library community, other librarians, etc. The effectiveness of proxies, however, will be dependent on the extent to which they recognize the importance of the research effort and are trained to perform the unobtrusive test/observation. The evaluator will want to take special care in working with the proxies, observing their work, and refining their activities *before* the actual unobtrusive test/observation. Previous chapters discuss proxie training.

The evaluators, themselves, may wish to administer the unobtrusive test or observation. However, in such instances, it may be extremely difficult to maintain the "unobtrusive" nature of the evaluation if the staff suspect that such an evaluation is being done. Nonetheless, librarians have unobtrusively assessed the quality of reference and referral services by asking factual and bibliographic questions to the library staff via the telephone. Staff can unobtrusively observe the types of referrals given by their colleagues while they are working together at the reference desk. They might maintain a record of those referrals on a data collection form.

Reporting Unobtrusive Results to Staff

The reporting of unobtrusive tests/observations to the same staff members tested may create difficulties and may be a primary reason why unobtrusive testing of library services is performed infrequently. Where staff believe that they perform at a high level of quality, and if they are confronted with evaluation results suggesting less than high quality performance, they may respond defensively. Library managers may lack both the interpersonal and managerial skills to utilize unobtrusive test results in a positive manner — as a catalyst to *improve* the quality of various library services.

Some suggestions that should be considered by evaluators when reporting unobtrusive evaluation results to library staff are:

- *Be able to demonstrate that the data are reliable and valid and that they were collected by individuals who were objective and trained in the data collection process.* Use of consultants or proxies, to assist in the evaluation, who have no personal or political agendas can enhance objectivity.
- *Present findings at a summary or group level of analysis.* The concern is for the department or area as a whole to assess its services; do not focus, or allow the discussion of the results to focus, on performance of individuals. If such discussions are needed, they should be private — between the evaluator and the staff member and not be held in a group setting.
- *Do not link results from unobtrusive testing/observation to salary increases or other personnel evaluation rewards.* Unobtrusive techniques are best used as "self-diagnostics" for a staff as a whole. Linking such techniques to annual personnel evaluations is likely to be counter-productive to encouraging change and improving services.
- *Focus discussions in terms of factors or conditions that might be related to the results and what might be done to change these factors.* This approach directs the discussion to a future perspective, i.e., what interventions can be developed to address the findings, rather than a retrospective perspective, i.e., defending why the results occurred.

Argyris (1985) offers additional suggestions for minimizing defensive responses when promoting organizational change. He describes a range of individual-organizational defensive routines and offers specific strategies for breaking those routines and developing strategies that increase overall acceptance of change and promote organizational effectiveness. In addition to these strategies, library managers will also need patience and perseverance.

But, equally important, the evaluators who present the findings must be conscious of interpersonal and professional issues related to unobtrusive evaluation of library services. Special skills in group processes and team building are also useful. The focus of the discussions should be on (1) what levels of performance can be reasonably provided for particular services, (2) what steps must be taken to reach acceptable performance levels, and (3) how will library staff know when those levels of performance have been reached.

At issue here is that many library staff have never considered what constitutes an acceptable level of performance for particular services. Nor have library managers been committed to developing and using *measures* by which the performance of a service can, in fact, be described. Given different missions, goals, and priorities of libraries, a *correct answer fill rate* of 40% may be acceptable *to that library* if the staff are consciously concentrating their resources on other service areas. It is this larger context of using unobtrusive evaluation for planning and setting service priorities which must be better understood.

THE CONTEXT OF UNOBTRUSIVE EVALUATION

Increased attention to formal programs of reference service evaluation is essential in libraries today. As part of that evaluation, greater attention must be given to the use of non-traditional evaluation designs and data collection methodologies. Simply stated, little use of formal evaluation techniques is common, and reliance on survey methods, perceptual data, and data that do not directly address *qualitative* assessment of library services is excessive. Knowing that "X" number of patrons completed a reference transaction is *not* knowing the *quality* of the service that they received. Unobtrusive evaluation techniques that address qualitative performance criteria, such as accuracy of answering reference questions, are powerful means to assess library services (Crowley, 1985).

But such assessments must consider the broader context of organizational factors. For example, in considering reference services, Lancaster has identified and discussed a broad range of factors that influence the effectiveness of question-answering services in libraries (1984, pp. 95–108). A broader context may assist the evaluator in understanding the inter-connectedness of various factors when conducting qualitative evaluation research.

Figure 5-6 is a typology of organization variables that might be considered when evaluation research is conducted (Walton, 1985, p. 196):

- *contextual variables*: environmental factors over which the organizational members have no or very limited control, e.g., laws and regulations, and state/local/national economic conditions
- *design variables*: factors over which the organizational members have some or a great deal of control; these can be manipulated by the organization, e.g., through organizational structure, management style, and rewards
- *psycho-social organizational variables*: attitudes, group relationships, perceptions, and organizational cultures and climates
- *outcome variables*: factors that describe the results or products from the organization; for libraries, such factors might include benefits for the library community, quality of services, or contribution toward the goals of the parent institution or agency

This chapter has emphasized the importance of the psycho-social variables and stressed the library manager's responsibility in setting organizationl climates

Figure 5-6   Typology of Variables in Evaluation Studies*

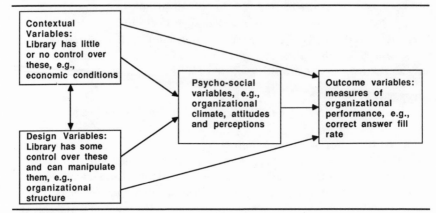

* Adapted from Richard E. Walton, "Strategies with Dual Relevance," in Edward E. Lawler, III, et al., *Doing Research That Is Useful for Theory and Practice* (San Francisco: Jossey-Bass, 1985), pp. 195–197.

and management styles to enhance staff performance. The evaluation process has stressed outcome variables, which in the opinion of the writers of this book, are critical indicators of the *quality* of the library.

Library managers must clearly differentiate among these categories of variables and consider their affect on the provision of library services. For example, it is important to recognize which variables within the library are *contextual*, that is, over which there is little or no control, versus those that are *design* variables, that is, those which can be manipulated. While it is essential to understand which variables are which, it is equally as important to concentrate on design variables, or those which are *actionable* during the evaluation process. Actionable variables form the basis for intervention strategies.

But notice in Figure 5-6 that interventions which rely only on the manipulation of design variables may not affect the desired organizational outcomes *unless* they also consider psycho-social aspects of the organization. Thus, the outcome from a library service, such as *correct answer fill rate,* is based on a composite of contextual, design, and psycho-social variables. Successful evaluations of library services will be the ones that:

- identify the existence of contextual variables and explain their impact on performance levels
- study specific design and psycho-social variables that are likely to be related to the provision of information services
- implement interventions which are based on variables that are actionable and have been shown to be related to the quality with which information services are provided

Library management must assess the organization in terms of these four categories of variables and identify those that appear to have the greatest potential for change. At the same time it must decide which intervention strategies might be most successful.

Research findings that have been presented in both this book and *Improving the Quality of Reference Services for Government Publications* (McClure and Hernon, 1983) suggest that the most important design variables are *individually based*. That is, volume size, staff size, and other institutional characteristics are less important than (1) the psycho-social variables (organizational climate and management style) and (2) individually based design variables such as specific interview skills, knowledge of sources, and interpersonal skills. Thus, it is in these two areas that library managers should concentrate their intervention strategies for improving the quality of the library's information services.

Accuracy, or other qualitative-based criteria, can be best assessed in evaluation research conducted within the organization, and, if possible, by organizational members. Generally, case study designs which are combined with a range of data collection techniques — such as unobtrusive methods — are excellent beginning points for libraries embarking on this process. Case studies are especially powerful because the process suggests intervention strategies — thus, evaluation is directly linked to making recommendations and developing intervention strategies. Yin (1984) offers an excellent practical overview of case study designs and how to implement them in an evaluation study. McClure, Hernon, and Purcell (1986) provide an example of combining a case study design with a number of data collection techniques, including unobtrusive testing.

Evaluators who use case study designs which include unobtrusive methods and who assess the quality of information services within a particular library should not be that concerned with the external validity of their findings beyond that particular library. External validity, or the degree to which the evaluation results can be broadly generalized, is not an objective for practitioner-based library evaluation research. The issue, rather, is to maintain a high degree of reliability and internal validity, that is, the study measures what it is supposed to measure within the organization and findings are correct for *that* particular library at that particular time (Krathwohl, 1985).

While knowledge of strategies that appear to have worked in one library setting may assist in the development of interventions in another library, managers must conduct evaluation research, in *their* particular library setting, that identifies which *particular variables* fall into the categories described in Figure 5-6. One cannot assume that they will be similar for all types of libraries. Indeed, the safer assumption is that the unique settings, range of contextual and design variables, and the uses of different management styles in various organizational climate conditions, combine to describe organizational contexts in which interventions will have to be tailored for each setting. Such is the responsibility of library management.

To first improve the quality of any library service, there must be an awareness that evaluation is essential, a willingness to engage in an evaluation process, and adequate competencies and skills on the part of the evaluators. The existing state of complacency regarding ongoing programs of library evaluation is exemplified by library staff who are "shocked" when they discover that their library has a 35 % *correct answer fill rate.* Perceptions and assumptions about what is thought to be occurring in the provision of library services should be validated by programs of ongoing evaluation research. Librarians must accept this challenge of testing their perceptions and assumptions and determine if, in fact, their intuitive assessments match those resulting from formal evaluations.

Apparently, the techniques of evaluation research and unobtrusive methods have been perceived by library practitioners as inappropriate, unnecessary, or perhaps too difficult to conduct. And, of course, there are literally thousands of reasons to justify and rationalize such hesitancy to engage in ongoing evaluation of library services. But the evidence is clear that the *quality* of library services, especially in the area of reference services, requires immediate attention. A formal program of ongoing evaluation research, based on the suggestions offered in this chapter, is essential if library information services are to be improved. It is the responsibility of library managers to develop and implement such an evaluation program.

CHAPTER 6

THE EDUCATIONAL IMPERATIVE

Both the profession at large and individual library staff members must reassess and reconsider the role of library information services, in general, and reference service, in particular. Findings based on "half-right" answers from unobtrusive studies may be only the beginning of issues broadly related to the quality of services provided by libraries. Quality-based evaluation research has only begun to address such issues. Generally, library managers and staff do not know the quality of their library reference services, do not engage in a regular program of services evaluation, and do not carefully develop interventions that improve the quality of these services. While there may be much talk about a concern for the provision of quality services, there appears to be little direct attention given to it, at the local library level, by schools of library/information science and professional associations, and, at the government level, by the Government Printing Office (GPO) and the Joint Committee on Printing (JCP).

The profession must address, directly, the findings, from a large number of studies (see Figure 1-1), that *correct answer fill rates* average around 55% in academic and public libraries. Based on our experiences administering a number of unobtrusive tests over a period of four years, the authors of this book would suggest that the findings related to *correct answer rate* are only the tip of a larger iceberg in which measures of the *quality* of other library information services may also "shock" members in the professional community.

The areas that have yet to be formally studied and brought to the full attention of the profession include the quality of interpersonal skills of reference staff members, accuracy and appropriateness of referrals, costs for the provision of various information services, use and non-use of information technologies in the provision of services, and the quality of information services beyond "basic" activities such as the answering of factual or bibliographic questions. The profession chooses to believe, intuitively, that everything is fine and that "business as normal" is the rule for the day. The profession also chooses to believe that libraries can accept *new* responsibilities and duties without an assessment of how well *current* responsibilities are being met.

The crux of improving the quality of reference services is evaluation and intervention. There is little justification for conducting a library evaluation simply for its own sake; evaluations must be linked to predetermined statements of library goals and objectives, acceptable levels of performance for specific library services and activities, and methods for maximizing those levels of performance in services which are identified as priorities. Indeed, the operative word here is *priority;* libraries cannot provide all types of information to all types of clientele.

The result of "being all things to all people" is probably best characterized, generally, as mediocre service (Miller, 1984). Mediocre services will continue in many libraries until formal programs of evaluation and interventions are initiated. Interventions, that is, a formal program or programs of activities intended to change existing activities and increase library effectiveness, are primarily the responsibility of library managers.

There are three primary sets of factors that must be considered regarding interventions for improving the quality of library reference services. These factors relate to the: (1) individual library staff member, (2) managerial-organizational setting in the library, and (3) education/training that is provided to professional staff by schools of library/information science. Clearly, there may be other factors affecting the quality of reference services, but the variables within these three categories tend to be "actionable," i.e., they have the potential to effect change and serve as a basis for developing possible interventions.

Libraries wishing to develop *programs* that assist staff to improve the quality of reference services must assess variables within all three of these areas, together, and develop intervention strategies that consider the three sets of factors. Chapter 5 identifies procedures for the evaluation-intervention process and managerial-organizational factors for consideration in implementing programs of evaluation and intervention. Suggestions for such individually-based interventions have been offered in *Improving the Quality of Reference Services for Government Publications* (McClure and Hernon, 1983, pp. 111-160) as well as Katz (1982), Lancaster (1984), Childers (1984), and Schwartz and Eakin (1986).

The purpose of this chapter is to first examine the relationships between schools of library/information science and academic/public libraries in improving the quality of reference services and to offer specific suggestions for strengthening these relationships. The chapter also will suggest the importance of developing recertification programs for academic and public librarians — especially in a reference services context. Specific strategies will be offered by which such recertification programs might be initiated and professional associations and agencies such as the GPO can participate in such programs. Throughout the chapter, the key theme is that conscious strategies to promote ongoing programs of formal and informal education (within the context of evaluation and intervention) must be developed if libraries are to enhance their role as effective providers of information — regardless of its format.

PRELIMINARY CONSIDERATIONS

Findings from the second unobtrusive study reported in this book (see Chapter 4) may offer some insights regarding implications for developing educational programs to improve the quality of academic and public library reference services. These factors should be considered prior to examining the role of schools of library/information science in post-master's education and suggesting specific strategies that may assist the profession in addressing the problem of "half-right" answers to factual and bibliographic reference questions.

Changing Reference Service Behavior

The study reported in Chapter 4 suggests that attempts to change reference service behaviors may be difficult because, despite the interventions,

- the quality of reference service (as measured by *correct answer fill rate* and exit questionnaires) may not improve
- 66% of the questions could have been answered at the main reference desk, but 58% of all questions were referred to the documents department

Administrators, for example, may wish to improve the *correct answer fill rate* or the ratio of referrals to the government documents department. But results from this study and previous research in the area of organizational development (Argyris, 1985; Kast and Rosenzweig, 1979, pp. 563-587) suggest that identifying such problems is much easier than developing effective remedies.

While unobtrusive testing assesses the *correct answer fill rate* for reference services and the overall effectiveness of staff skill-building as a result of an intervention, it does *not* assist administrators in developing strategies for improving the quality of the reference services that their library staff provide. The organizational context, including a broad range of climate conditions (McClure and Samuels, 1985), the personality and interpersonal skills of administrators and staff, the availability of resources, and other factors all have to be considered when developing intervention strategies.

The intervention strategies used in Chapter 4 were not based on an individualized needs assessment of this particular library, staff did not participate in the development of the interventions, and no clear reward structures were established between participation in the intervention and increasing skills/competencies. Decision makers must keep these factors in mind when attempting to develop educational interventions and using unobtrusive testing to assess the effectiveness of those interventions.

Awareness versus Increasing Competencies

Increasing reference staff competencies and changing behavior may be difficult, regardless of the interventions used. It is important to differentiate between increasing awareness and increasing staff skills and competencies. The authors expected an increase in the participants' awareness of government statistical sources in general (see Chapter 4). Although only 30% of the participants *perceived* that the interventions increased their awareness of these sources, the researchers suspect that the simple act of participation in either intervention may have increased staff awareness (or reacquaintance with) certain sources.

Increased awareness is not necessarily the same as increasing staff competencies. Yet the vast majority of educational interventions in which library staff participate are best categorized as one day (or less) "workshops." Without a *program* of ongoing staff development and continuing education and the use of CE delivery formats and mechanisms specially designed for a particular target audience (Conroy, 1978), the vast majority of educational interventions used in libraries will impact on awareness but are not likely to have significant impact on developing competencies. The appropriateness of various educational interventions need to be reconsidered for *both* the criterion of increasing awareness and of increasing competencies.

The Best That Can Be Expected?

The overall *correct answer fill rate* of the library portrayed in Chapter 4 fell within the typical bounds found in other studies. But, strangely, the average *correct answer fill rate decreased,* rather than increased, after the interventions. Regardless of the nature of the interventions, one might have thought that *any* intervention specifically targeted to the area in which unobtrusive testing occurred would improve the *correct answer fill rate* of the participants. Such was not the case in this instance.

This finding does not permit generalization, since the experiment was conducted in only one library setting. However, the researchers' assessment of the two departments examined is that the public service operations here are very similar to those found in many other libraries — in terms of responsibilities, resource allocations, and staffing. Thus, speculation about the failure of the interventions to affect the *correct answer fill rate* is appropriate.

Possible propositions that might explain the failure of the workshop or slide/ script interventions to affect *correct answer fill rate* include:

- *Inadequate research methodology:* The research design inaccurately measured *correct answer fill rate* either in the pretest or the posttest; intervening variables confounded the results.
- *Inappropriate interventions:* Regardless of the reason, the interventions had little educational value and failed to offer substantial learning to participants.
- *Limited motivation of staff to take continuing education seriously:* Except for "professional commitment," there is little reason for library staff to be committed and motivated to participate effectively in *any* type of continuing education.

- *Verification of 50-60% correct answer fill rate:* A 50 to 60% *correct answer fill rate* is the typical range of performance to expect from reference staff and is not likely to be modified significantly.

While other propositions surely can be identified, these four deserve special attention in the context of this particular study and the ongoing research in the area of unobtrusive testing.

Given the range of precautions built into the research design and methodology used for this experiment (see Figure 4-2), and the previous experience of the researchers with unobtrusive testing, it is unlikely that either the design or methodology was so badly flawed that changes resulting from the interventions were not measured. Random error might account for *some* of the variance in the scores but, still, a plus or minus of 3 to 4 percentage points on either score would not change the overall meaning of the scores.[1]

Educational interventions for increasing performance and changing behavior comprise well-known and often-used strategies (Zaltman and Duncan, 1977). However, the assumption is that there are organizational rewards for the increased performance or changed behavior. The two educational strategies used in this study are probably typical of many that library staff "endure," i.e., a half-day workshop on a particular topic or a self-paced instructional script, with or without slides, on a particular topic.

For the study reported in Chapter 4, the staff had no choice but to participate in either one or the other intervention. For the vast majority of continuing education opportunities, staff select those they wish to attend — if they choose to attend any at all. Thus, workshop leaders typically have a highly motivated, self-selected, professionally committed group. Such may not have been the case in this instance. Indeed, a common complaint among continuing education coordinators is that the staff that need the education the most are the ones least likely to attend.

The study reported in Chapter 4 assessed the appropriateness of unobtrusive testing as a method for self-diagnosis and improving the quality of reference service on the criterion of *correct answer fill rate*. The educational interventions, i.e., slide/workbook presentation and workshop, were selected as types of interventions that a library might reasonably employ to analyze and improve, if necessary, the quality of its reference services. Such interventions, however, do not comprise a *program* of continuing education.

While not intended to provide an overview of the difficulties with continuing education for library staff, this discussion suggests that perhaps the quality of the interventions used in this study is as good as the majority of those used in the

---

[1] Additional research needs to estimate the random error and confidence intervals associated with *correct answer fill rates*. It should also use repeated measures and collect longitudinal data. Chapter 4 represents a modest beginning in re-directing unobtrusive methodologies in library settings.

profession. Second, the broad range of skills and competencies that one might encounter from staff providing reference services has a "leveling effect," i.e., under "normal" conditions, the typical library staff will provide correct answers to 50 to 60% of the factual and bibliographic questions.

Thus, the research related to unobtrusive testing is beginning to suggest that, on average, regardless of library type or department, reference staff provide a 50-60% accuracy rate for factual and bibliographic questions. As the Trueswell 80-20 rule proposes that 20% of the collection accounts for 80% of the circulation (Trueswell, 1969), so too can a rule be proposed that "reference staff, regardless of library type or department, correctly answer 55% of the factual and bibliographic questions they receive." The consistency of unobtrusive study findings appears to warrant relabelling the proposition as the 55% reference rule.

Implications of the 55% Reference Rule

If approximately a 55% *correct answer fill rate* is the norm, then perhaps some underlying assumptions on which libraries typically base reference services merit reconsideration. Perhaps libraries need to reconsider the relative importance of "reference services" vis-a-vis other library activities and resource allocation priorities. Since the 1960s, the library community has been aware of the 55% accuracy rate, yet few tangible ongoing strategies have been developed to address the implications from this finding (Crowley, 1985).

The 55% *correct answer fill rate* is typically computed on an "easier than average" or an "average" difficulty level for the questions. What level of performance can be expected from "difficult" questions or questions that require unique or specialized training? How easily and at what cost can the 55% *correct answer fill rate* be improved? Should such an accuracy rate be accepted as "the best that can be reasonably expected" or should the library community carefully consider how to increase the level of performance?

It is ironic that the primary activity of most libraries, i.e., the provision of timely and accurate information that meets the needs of its clientele, is an activity in which "half-right" services appear to be provided. If the 55% reference rule is a fact of life, critical issues about the quality of reference services in a particular library and the role of information services, in general, in the larger professional context must be re-examined.

Perhaps one of the most serious implications from the 55% reference rule is related to the educational background of reference librarians and the degree to which basic educational skills are upgraded and expanded throughout one's professional career. Findings from our 1983 study provided clear evidence that library staff who engaged in an effective reference interview process had answered almost three times the number of questions correctly (after three minutes) than had librarians who were ineffective during the reference interview process (McClure and Hernon, 1983, p. 49).

Reference interview skills, along with a broad range of other reference services-related skills can be learned, improved upon, and upgraded with the development and implementation of educational programs. If there is a concern within the profession about the quality of the reference services academic and public libraries provide, educational strategies will be important components in an overall strategy to improve the quality of reference services. Schools of library and information science will have an important role to play in both designing and implementing such strategies.

ROLE OF SCHOOLS OF LIBRARY/INFORMATION SCIENCE

A discussion of the broad context of library/information education is beyond the scope of this chapter and useful reviews have appeared elsewhere (Stueart, 1984; Hannigan, 1984). But issues regarding the role of library education are related as much to the profession of librarianship as they are to only library education. The success with which librarians address and resolve these issues will depend on how the profession, *as a whole,* determines the types of library education that are necessary and appropriate, the degree to which adequate resources can be made available for those programs, their ability to monitor and evaluate those programs effectively, and their commitment to improving the *quality* of both library education and graduates from library education programs.

Identifying Myths

A first myth to dispell is that, overall, library education is of poor quality and unable to provide leadership or address the profession's future needs. Put in perspective, library education is no better or worse than other areas of librarianship. Further, only recently have practitioners shown significant interest in designing/revising programs in library education (Battin, 1983). Clearly, the practice of librarianship and the teaching of library/information science are sides of a same coin.

A second myth to dispell is that programs of library/information science education have ignored quality, are not concerned with quality, and do little to ensure increased quality of their programs. Despite controversies and problems surrounding ALA's Committee on Accreditation (COA), the process (along with internal university review processes) does provide an important mechanism of self-diagnostics to improve programs both for internal reviews as well as for external accreditation purposes. As an aside, it should be noted that most academic and public libraries have no formal accreditation process, or if they do, it is but a small portion of an institutional accreditation.

Third, the library community assumes that what it does in society is important, that, overall, society recognizes the value of library services, and that libraries are "important" mechanisms for accomplishing larger societal goals. Such simply is not the case. A recent study of the economics of the master's degree in library/information science shows that "library education is a poor investment. Current library school graduates can expect to earn *less* with their MLS degree than the average college graduate" (DeWath, 1985, p. 47). Changes in library education, alone, will not improve societal norms regarding services provided through local libraries.

Fourth is the myth of a "quick fix" that library schools can easily do something by which new graduates will be better reference librarians. The following are typically proposed as "quick fixes":

- *Recruit better students from a broader range of disciplines:* This is unrealistic for the reason DeWath has noted earlier; by and large librarians are self-selected professionals from the humanities and the social sciences.
- *Add more courses specifically related to reference services:* Schools already attempt to cover too broad a range of material and have, typically, only an average of 7 to 9 full-time faculty to cover existing coursework.
- *Send library school faculty out to libraries to find out about "the real world":* While this idea sounds good, sending library school faculty to learn and enhance their skills from the majority of the libraries that the authors have been testing during the last four years would be *counter-productive;* this approach would not contribute to developing graduates with better reference skills; further there are few rewards to encourage library educators to return to the field.
- *Require students to have internships and practicums:* The on-the-job learning process can be important; however, student interns frequently have inadequate training to assume "professional" duties and thus are used in "lower level" skill areas; libraries have inadequate staff time to work regularly with the students; since students are in the library only for a semester, there is no long term pay-off for library staff to instruct them; and library staff rarely are rewarded for assisting in the internship.
- *Include more practitioners in library education:* Being able to *do* something is not the same as being able to analyze and teach about it; "high" quality practitioners would first have to be identified; and, generally, there is little reward for practitioners to participate in library school education.

Proposed quick fixes will not improve the quality of library information services, in general, and reference services, in particular.

Recognizing Realities

One reality in library education is that the typical faculty of 7 to 9 full-time professionals cannot be all things for all people. The perspective from the field is that library schools can specialize at the MLS level to emphasize skills for a particular type of library, e.g., academic librarianship, and within that type of library, for a specific area, e.g., reference services. The reality is that most students take the job that they can get (regardless of setting and coursework), that adding courses for graduation makes the library school less competitive vis-à-vis its neighboring library schools, and there is little agreement on what additional courses can and should be offered.

Second, specialization is likely to be more appropriate and more effective *after* the MLS. A primary purpose of the MLS is to provide *entry* level professional librarians and information specialists for a broad range of information-related work environments. Given the fact that there is no required undergraduate degree, that students frequently come into programs with little practical experience, and that most programs require only 36 credit hours for completion, specialization at the MLS level is difficult indeed.

Library schools, historically (and at present), have been underfunded within their university setting. Realistically, adding additional coursework, investing in examples of new information technologies for teaching purposes, and developing "outreach" programs requires *additional resources*. While some public libraries can request bond votes or obtain other direct revenues from their community, academic libraries and schools of library and information science are essentially barred from going directly to "the people." Thus, changes in library schools, typically, will be financed by *re-allocation* of existing revenues rather than new resources.

A fourth reality is that, by and large, practitioners are both unable and unwilling to be more directly involved in the education process. There are numerous reasons for this — first and foremost being that librarians already have extensive responsibilities and tasks. But, in addition, salaries to pay for teaching adjuncts from the field are minimal, given the amount of work necessary to do a credible teaching job; many libraries are unable to provide "release time" for library staff to participate in library education; and few rewards exist for practitioners' involvement either in the teaching or in the learning processes of library education *after* receiving the MLS.

Let it be admitted that the profession as a whole has little commitment to *ongoing involvement and participation* in library/information science education after obtaining the MLS or equivalent. Participation in advanced degrees and continuing education (CE) is self-determined. Those who need advanced training and education or participation in a regular program of CE are the least likely to be involved in such activities. Library schools cannot force their participation and libraries generally do not reward such involvement. Unlike medical librarians or most school librarians, academic and public librarians have no requirement to return for additional formal education; and most do not.

Sixth, most schools of library and information science must address *both* professional and research-based standards for excellence throughout their programs. However, institutional credibility for the *graduate* programs often comes from productivity in research-related activities. Generally, there is little institutional reward or credibility provided for working with practitioners directly, offering workshops, developing programs of continuing education, and being active in professional associations. Thus, if the library schools must slight either the professional responsibilities or the research-based responsibilities, it is likely to be the former.

Finally, let it be noted that a number of library organizations today systematically stifle individual creativity, innovation, the taking on of additional responsibilities, and taking risks. In addition, some are managed by people who are out of touch with the day to day realities of their library, and, who have never obtained additional formal education since *their* MLS. Thus, fresh, dynamic, enthusiastic, creative, and hard-working new graduates from library schools have an encounter "of the third kind" when accepting their first professional position. Curriculum changes or other changes in library schools, in isolation, will not resolve the problem of library organizations that systematically waste and ignore human resources and reinforce an attitude that the *quality* of library services is not important.

Educational Interventions and Continuing Education

For the effective provision of information services, and reference services in particular, active regular participation in *programs* of formal continuing education *after* the MLS is essential. The experience of the authors during four years of unobtrusive testing suggests that the quality of reference services may be significantly improved by formal instruction to post-MLS library staff that emphasizes:

- *evaluation research techniques:* methods to conduct valid evaluation research in the library, e.g., developing evaluation research questions, collecting and analyzing data, and developing intervention strategies (such as those described in Chapter 5)
- *reference and information services skills:* specific strategies to stay up-to-date and learn new skills, e.g., learning techniques for performing online bibliographic database searching, identifying public service applications of online catalogs, learning to use appropriate microcomputer software or gaining better interpersonal, referral, question negotiation skills

It is likely that many practicing reference librarians *never* obtained such skills or received inadequate instruction in these areas in their MLS program—for a host of reasons *not* having to do with either the competence or quality of the program or the students (Hernon and McClure, 1984, p. 393).

Although many schools of library and information science offer courses, and, in some instances, programs for continuing education, most do not receive heavy enrollment or significant resources from the library school. Except for school librarianship, there is little motivation to participate in, and few tangible rewards to be received from, Sixth Year Certificate Programs. Ironically, the profession generally accepts the notion that the curriculum requirements at the MLS level are inadequate but there is little support to move toward (1) an undergraduate-based professional degree, (2) a two-year master's degree, or (3) certification of academic and public librarians *after* receipt of the master's degree.

THE ATTITUDE OF CONTINUING EDUCATION

The belief in and the perceived importance of continuing education is based, in large part, on attitudes. An operational definition of continuing education incorporates the following concepts (Stone et al., 1974):

- the implication that lifelong learning is necessary to keep the individual employee up-to-date and productive
- the necessity for the individual to assume the basic responsibilities for his/her own development
- the opportunity for the individual to diversify to new areas of interest
- the encouragement of employees to become involved in educational activities beyond those considered necessary for entrance into the profession
- the inclusion of all library personnel in the continuing education process

An individual library has a number of responsibilities, or roles, to fulfill if it is to participate in programs of continuing education:

- *identifying:* determining the specific continuing education needs of the staff
- *coordinating:* linking staff to CE programs on the local, state, and national levels
- *providing:* sponsoring institutes, workshops, etc.
- *supporting:* assigning staff within the library to assume continuing education planning and development for their peers
- *facilitating:* encouraging staff to participate in continuing eduction programs through a wide range of reward structures

These library roles comprise an attitude toward continuing education pro-grams, i.e., an ongoing program of developing objectives and implementing activities intended to improve the skills and competencies of library staff.

Such in-house interventions are possible strategies, but only in a larger con-text of continuing education. Perhaps it is unrealistic to expect significant change to occur on a measure of performance such as *correct answer fill rate* from one brief intervention. More likely, increased performance and the develop-ment of specific competencies result from an ongoing program of continuing education, with carefully selected interventions implemented to address the specific needs of library staff over an extended period of time.

Library administrators may wish to keep this in mind when assessing the im-pact of one particular intervention by means of unobtrusive testing (or any other technique). At the same time, the assumption that a carefully planned and implemented "one-shot activity" of continuing education will sufficiently increase a library's *correct answer fill rate* (or other appropriate performance mea-sures) over time is suspect and deserves additional investigation.

The profession of librarianship has a spotty record, at best, of cooperation between schools of library and information science wtih practitioners in the area of *programs* of continuing education. There is much talk about the impor-tance of continuing education and the need for more and better *programs* in li-brary continuing education, and for greater numbers of librarians to be engaged in ongoing continuing education. Realistically, academic and public librarianship is not committed to continuing education after the master's degree.

THE ROLE OF EVALUATION

Given this lack of commitment to post-master's continuing education by either the library schools or practitioners, there has been little assessment of what continuing education needs exist in particular library settings. Without unobtrusive testing in a particular academic library, the staff may not be aware that their *correct answer fill rate* is 35%, for example. Once this is known, a strat-egy should be developed to improve the score. But this level of performance would be unknown if the evaluation of the service had not occurred *first*.

Although there are some efforts, most notably by state library agencies, to assess continuing education needs of public librarians (DuMont, 1986), gener-ally, schools of library and information science design continuing education courses in terms of:

- topics that can be taught by available instructors
- *perceived* importance of a particular topic, or if the subject is currently a "hot" one
- available resources to teach the course.

Thus, there may be a large chasm between the clearly identified educational needs of the library and the courses/programs offered by the library school.

Better coordination between the library schools' continuing education programs and the identified educational needs of the libraries is necessary. Indeed, continuing education strategies typically are not targeted at individual library settings because they are unlikely to be self-supporting. Yet continuing education programs implemented over time for a particular library, with particular educational needs, and in a particular setting, are most likely to have a direct pay-off in terms of increased performance and productivity for that library.

NEED FOR CONTINUING EDUCATION PROGRAMS

Participation in one day or half-day workshops is not likely to increase skills or change behavior significantly. *Programs* of education which link formal courses with directed practicums are needed to do this. At best, most one-day (or less) workshops typically offered at library schools and state and national conferences are "battery-chargers"; they get participants excited about a specific topic and increase their awareness of the importance of that particular topic. If better on-the-job skills are the desired outcome, listening to an instructor discuss the topic for a half-day is unlikely to have the intended effect.

Continuing education programs must address *both* education and training. Training suggests the teaching of specific operations and procedures, and may tend to be more practice oriented. Education, however, stresses the ability to identify and critically analyze issues—to think, and to engage in successful problem solving. Both perspectives are important in programs of continuing education.

For library schools and library managers to make a commitment supporting *programs* of *post-master's degree* continuing education library managers must:

• provide resources to support those librarians who attend programs of continuing education, e.g., release time and reimbursement for continuing education expenses such as tuition
• develop reward structures by which increased salaries and other benefits are provided to those who participate in continuing education
• establish programs to recertify librarians on a regular basis after completing the professional degree

Faculty at schools of library and information science should support the "Policy Statement on Continuing Library and Information Science Education," (1981) adopted by the then Association of American Library Schools (now Association for Library and Information Science Education). Appendix I reprints this statement. It outlines the role of the Association as well as that of member schools in the following areas:

• programs and policies
• communication outside the library school
• evaluation
• faculty development

However, commitments by library managers to continuing education are essential if schools of library and information science are to justify programs of continuing education and dedicate significant resources to their operation.

Even with such commitments, a program of recertification is necessary to formalize methods by which librarians could demonstrate completion of minimum levels of ongoing continuing education. Close cooperation among library managers, library schools, professional associations, and practicing librarians would be necessary for such to occur. But, realistically, a commitment to ongoing education after the master's degree is likely to occur *only* through programs of recertification whereby librarians are recertified on a regular basis to maintain "membership in good standing" within the profession.

RECERTIFICATION OF LIBRARIANS

Issues related to certification and recertification of librarians are numerous and controversial. Willet has provided an overview of these issues as they pertain specifically to library/information science education. He notes that "lifetime certification earns no one's respect; recertification is a means of ensuring that professional librarians are keeping up with their ever-changing profession" (1984, p. 19). Recertification also will force libraries and schools of library/information science to enter into a meaningful discussion regarding continuing education beyond the post-graduate degree.

Generally, library schools are not involved effectively in the post-MLS education of library practitioners. This state of affairs has numerous negative impacts on *both* libraries and library schools:

• There are few incentives or rewards for librarians to continue their education and further develop specific skills or for educators to address post-MLS learning needs.
• Library schools are unable to mount "sixth year certificate programs" or other formal programs of continuing education successfully without minimum levels of enrollment in such programs.
• There is decreased communication and exchange of ideas between practicing librarians and library school educators.

- Research and teaching may not be closely related to practitioners' perceptions of issues and topics that are most important.
- Advanced skills, especially in the areas of evaluation research, information technologies, and management are not delivered to those practicing librarians who need them the most, i.e., those who have been out in the field 5 to 10 years.

Until there is a formalized incentive program such as an ongoing recertification program of librarians, it is unlikely that academic and public librarians will obtain additional formal education after their MLS degree.

In United States academic and public librarianship, once an individual receives the professional degree, there is no formal requirement to participate in ongoing education. Thus, it is not only possible, but extremely likely, that once a person receives the master's degree, he/she will never participate in another formal course related to his/her job again. Improving the quality of basic library services, such as reference, will require a professional commitment to develop continuing education programs where academic and public librarians are recertified on a regular basis. Such recertification can be developed in a number of contexts.

State and National Recertification of Academic and Public Librarians

As suggested earlier, models exist for recertification of librarians at both the state and national levels. The Medical Library Association (MLA) requires recertification of health sciences librarians every five years by one of two options: completion of 35 contact hours of approved continuing education, or a passing score on the current Certification Examination of the Medical Library Association.

"Requirements for Recertification for Health Sciences Librarians" (n.d.) describes a carefully developed program for recertification. This booklet details criteria for "approved continuing education" and procedures to be followed to obtain the recertification. As stated in the introduction to the booklet, the purpose "for the recertification of librarians is to assure [their] continuing competence" (p. 1). Interestingly, similar programs for recertification of academic and public librarians have not been developed by either the American Library Association (including the Association of College and Research Libraries and the Public Library Association) or any of the state library associations.

At the state level, many states have recertification requirements for school/media librarians (Burks, 1985). Although it is difficult to generalize about the recertification criteria, they generally require librarians to enroll in a certain number of formal courses and/or approved continuing education activities. A number of the recertification booklets available from the individual state agencies make clear statements about the concern of the state to assure the competency of school librarians by requiring such recertification. There are also clear and straightforward descriptions of the procedures and activities necessary for recertification.

Recertification of Reference Librarians

Another possible approach is to develop a recertification process in specific functional areas of the library, e.g., reference services. If members of the American Library Association (ALA), Reference and Adult Services Division (RASD), are concerned about assuring the competency of reference librarians, they could develop criteria for such recertification. Requirements for such recertification could be based on enrolling in a predetermined number of courses and/or approved hours of continuing education broadly related to reference services.

Numerous organizations and agencies might be involved in recertification of reference librarians. For example, the Government Documents Round Table (GODORT) of ALA might take responsibility for developing and implementing a recertification plan. Similarly, the Government Printing Office through the depository library program could require recertification of depository librarians as part of the regular inspection process for each depository library. Clearly, such recertification programs must be carefully developed and implemented. However, the GPO's current stance of non-involvement appears to be untenable.

The GPO, under the direction of the Joint Committee on Printing, must assume some responsibility for education, continuing education, or certification/recertification of government documents librarians—especially in light of evidence that the quality of reference services for government publications in academic and public libraries is less than should be acceptable. In 1986, GPO's Depository Library Council to the Public Printer explored possible educational/training alternatives for government documents librarianship. However, the results of this deliberation have not been released. Nonetheless, in sum, the stance of the GPO has been that it is not responsible and will not provide resources for education and/or certification of government documents librarians. This stance must be changed.

Closely related to the idea of recertifying reference librarians is that of accrediting a library's reference services. Vavrek (1984) has proposed that such a process be developed specifically for reference services. Building from his ideas, an accreditation process could be developed whereby academic and public libraries could request from a national agency (similar to that of the Committee on Accreditation for Schools of Library and Information Science) the accreditation of the quality of their reference services.

Such an accreditation could be based on both qualitative and quantitative criteria. A number of qualitative statements exist such as "A Commitment to

Information Services: Developmental Guidelines" (1979). But, in addition, unobtrusive testing such as that suggested earlier in this book could be used as one technique in the accreditation process. Based on such processes, the accreditation agency could then produce a listing of academic and public libraries that have requested and obtained accreditation of their reference services.

Recertification within the Library

Individual libraries need not wait for professional associations or state agencies to develop recertification procedures. Criteria for recertification can be developed within a library and used for staff in that particular library. An excellent model for such a program, although it is not currently being used for "recertification," is being developed at a Midwestern public library.[2]

The purpose of the project is to prepare the public library staff to "provide quality service through a structured course of study in library and information skills, philosophy of service, and personal development." The program describes five course clusters of topics and a final independent study activity. Staff may select courses which are especially appropriate for their needs and educational delivery systems for the course selected. Completion of courses within the various clusters provides the staff with "incentive points." As currently configured, one time monetary awards will be given at the completion of each course cluster and permanent salary increases will be awarded with every 100 incentive points.

In effect, this program combines elements of a formalized and structured continuing education program and a recertification system. Interestingly, the program can be used by both professional and para-professional staff. Further, very clear reward structures have been incorporated into the program. Although participation in the program is not required to maintain employment, the benefits of participation — both tangible and intangible — are clear. This program is an excellent example of an in-house managerial strategy that encourages ongoing continuing education and rewards participants for such involvement.

Starting Points for Recertification Programs

The sections discussed above offer a number of starting points to develop recertification programs, e.g., Medical Library Association and state school library/media recertification programs. But one of the single most useful sources of information is the Continuing Library Education Network and Exchange, Inc. (CLENE). Its programs and activities were *not* developed in the

---

[2] The following information is based on a program being developed, in 1986, at the Topeka Public Library, Kansas.

context of recertification. However, much of its material can provide important insights and suggestions for those developing such programs.

One area that might be especially useful is the provider approval system (Continuing Library Education Network and Exchange, Inc. [CLENE], 1980). A report describing it provides an excellent discussion of criteria for continuing education programs and activities to assure the quality and appropriateness of such programs. The report details the component parts that comprise a "quality" continuing education opportunity. It also suggests criteria for continuing education providers, i.e., the process and resources appropriate for providing high-quality continuing education programs.

CLENE's Voluntary Recognition Service provides "a mechanism for recognizing educational attainment [of librarians] and builds a system for encouraging better quality continuing education activities" (CLENE, 1981, p. 1). The system was designed to maintain a record-keeping mechanism for an individual's participation in approved continuing education activities, in terms of contact hours. Participants could receive a "transcript" of their CE activities. These and other related documents from CLENE provide an excellent groundwork in developing post-master's educational programs.

The limitation to much of these CLENE initiatives is the lack of motivation and reward structures by individual librarians to participate. National, state, or professional recertification requirements would force involvement in such activities. Library managers and faculty at schools of library/information science would also be encouraged to coordinate educational opportunities. Indeed, without such structures to "encourage" participation, one is not surprised that the CLENE initiatives have garnered little support from the profession.

Moving toward a Recertification Program

The lack of recertification programs, and programs of required continuing education to maintain one's professional status in academic and public librarianship, is evidence of the limited existing commitment to assuring the competency of members in the profession. A number of models from a national, state, and individual library level exist by which recertification can be implemented.

Although this section has stressed the importance of recertification of librarians, there may also be a need to certify the quality of faculty members in schools of library and information as continuing education instructors. The CLENE approved provider program offers one possible method to assure that programs of continuing education meet basic criteria. But more generally, programs by which the faculty are educated on a regular basis are as important as ongoing continuing education of practitioners.

Library managers, leaders in professional associations, state agencies, and faculty in schools of library/information science must work together toward developing programs of recertification of academic and public librarians. Until the profession as a whole endorses and participates in such programs that *require* ongoing and regular upgrading of skills and knowledge, there will be little involvement by academic and public librarians in *programs* of continuing education. And, as a result, the quality of overall library services — and most importantly, reference services — is not likely to improve.

COOPERATIVE LIBRARY-LIBRARY SCHOOL STRATEGIES: ONE SCENARIO

Opportunities are present for partnerships between schools of library and information science and libraries to improve the quality of library services. But this partnership relies on library managers taking responsibility for *wanting* to assess and improve their staff's level of performance. Thus, before the strategy listed below can be used as a means of improving the quality of library reference services, a cooperative attitude of commitment and partnership between libraries and library schools must be fostered.

Program Outline

One approach to provide direct education to library staff is contracting with an outside individual to provide a program of on-site education. The benefits of such an approach include:

- The individual with whom the library contracts can be selected for a particular area of expertise that has to do with a key educational area needed in the library; the specific content of the educational package is negotiated between the library and the instructor.
- The library management signals to staff that it is willing to make an investment in developing improved service.
- The education specifically addresses the needs of the library staff.
- Library staff can relate the education to *specific* topics or problems in the library with which they must currently address.
- The cost/benefit ratio of such an approach is excellent since a large number of library staff can participate in the education at the same time without having to leave the library and the education can be targeted at specific library-related topics.
- The strategy encourages library staff to work together in a team approach and help each other in the educational process.

This approach of on-site educational programming should *not* be confused with consulting although there are some similarities. In consulting, the primary objective is to solve a particular problem, whereas in an on-site education program, the primary objective is to increase the skills and competencies of library staff regarding a particular subject or topic. A secondary benefit, however, might be the resolution of particular library problems/concerns.

Generally, the process by which on-site educational programming occurs is as follows. First, library management, with input from library staff, assess their educational needs. This can be accomplished simply by group discussions, management assessment of educational needs, or evaluating particular library services/activities (as described in Chapter 5). A clearly written statement of the desired education, in terms of specific skills or topics, can then be developed.

Based on this statement, library management can negotiate a level of involvement with a particular outside educator.[3] This person then develops a written proposal for library management that minimally describes:

- specific learning objectives to be accomplished
- assignments and learning activities of participants
- amount of time and description of resources required to implement the program
- format and delivery of the education
- a time line for what specific activities are to occur and at what point in time during the program
- a method to evaluate the effectiveness of the educational program
- the fee for providing the educational program

Based on such a document, the educator and library management negotiate a written agreement.

The in-house educational program should be based on identified educational needs of staff. However, part of the educational program may include a process by which the educator assesses existing competencies and skills as a basis for developing the educational program. Indeed, it may be useful for the educator to reach his/her assessment of the educational skills necessary for a particular area or problem and compare that assessment with that of library management.

Based on this clear statement of educational needs, the educator then develops a *program* of training sessions, learning activities, independent studies, projects, or other learning opportunities (e.g., visiting another library), to accomplish the objectives of the program. It must be stressed that successful on-site educational programs are *more* than simply having someone come to the library and give lectures on a particular topic. The on-site education is likely to be more successful if:

---

[3] The term "educator" is used here to mean any person who conducts the program and not just educators from schools of library/information science.

- a combination of educational formats and delivery techniques are used, e.g., hands-on training, simulations, lectures, demonstrations, guest speakers, independent projects, practicums, and field trips
- the learning opportunities are tailored to the unique educational needs of library staff
- mechanisms are incorporated that provide regular feedback and informal evaluation of the participants' progress
- the educator can be flexible and modify the learning opportunities as the program develops

In short, the educator conducting the program must have both knowledge of a particular topic *and* an ability to design and implement an educational program.

Another important component of on-site educational programming is to allow adequate time for the program. In the experience of the authors of this book, "one-shot," one or two-day workshops with large groups of participants are the least likely method to increase educational skills *and* enable staff to apply those skills in a work context. Time is required for the information presented to be digested, reviewed, questioned, and considered. The interaction between the educator and the participant, on a regular basis and over a sustained period of time, is essential if the on-site educational programming is to make a difference in the individual's ability to apply the education to a particular problem or concern in the library.

At the completion of the on-site educational program, the educator should prepare a written report that:

- summarizes the learning activities employed to accomplish the various educational objectives
- presents summary evaluation data on the degree of success with which the participants accomplished the learning objectives, and which of the learning activities appeared to be most successful
- offers recommendations for sustaining the education that has been gained as a result of the program, or additional areas where educational programming might be appropriate

Such on-site educational programming can be an extremely valuable means for increasing staff competencies and skills.

For example, in the area of education and training for improving skills related to the reference interview, an educator could develop an entire program of learning activities over a 3 to 6 month period of time, specifically for a particular reference staff in a particular library setting. Both instruction *and* practice can be molded together in such a program to assure increased staff competencies on this particular topic. The direct involvement of the staff with such an educational program would increase their knowledge of various aspects of the reference interview process and their skills in conducting successful reference interviews.

The type of program suggested above cannot occur without a direct commitment from library management to identify areas for the educational development of staff and to commit resources for that development to take place. As suggested in Chapter 5, in-house evaluation of library services can identify educational needs. Library managers must take the initiative in organizing a process such as that described above if on-site educational programming is to be seriously considered.

Generally, the view of the authors of this book is that the MLS degree, at best, is an entry level certification that a particular graduate has certain basic competencies and knowledge, and under the tutelage of a good library organization, has the potential to be a "good" librarian. Primary roles where library schools can work in a partnership with libraries to improve, specifically, the quality or library services must be developed in the context of a post-MLS setting. Librarians must accept the notion that 36 to 40 hours of library/information science coursework is inadequate as lifetime preparation to be a librarian or information professional and prepare that individual for the wide range of challenges he/she is likely to encounter.

Psychological Factors in Program Development

Regardless of the approach taken, one of the major behavioral understandings about problem solving is that (1) people appear to solve problems and learn new behaviors more effectively when the perceived complexity of a problem is narrowed and defined, and (2) a number of psychologically based responses to a "crisis" have to be addressed when resolving the crisis. People may respond to a "crisis" in the quality of reference services in a number of ways: they may be simultaneously concerned about the problem but be immobilized by the problem's complexity.

When problems are defined in crisis proportions in an effort to motivate action, the gravity of the problem may "disable the very resources of thought and action necessary to change them" (Weick, 1984, p. 40). Reasons for this immobilization can be drawn from recent research on "denial," "arousal," and organizational problem solving.

Denial is a commonly employed mechanism and generally takes two forms: (1) refusal to pay attention to the threatening situation, and (2) re-interpreting the situation in a less threatening way (Holmes, 1984, p. 348). Arousal is a concept which psychologists use to describe the physiological response to threatening or stressful circumstances — the state of alertness and readiness for action. Studies show that moderate arousal improves individual problem solving, but as arousal increases, attention to the problem decreases and performance declines (Weick, 1984, p. 41).

Organizational psychologists studying organizational and individual responses to crises find that as arousal increases, organizations and individuals can become *inflexible* so that old solutions and behaviors are reinforced rather than developing new or innovative behaviors to resolve the problem (Staw et al., 1981, pp. 502-507). Studies find that people's arousal levels are influenced by the manner in which they *approach* problems. People most effectively solve problems and learn new behaviors when tasks are broken down into increments for solution. As the perceived complexity of the problem is reduced, arousal decreases and so performance becomes more effective (Bower et al., 1978, pp. 578-580).

Considering these factors in light of responses by reference librarians to unobtrusive testing results helps to explain negative reactions such as:

- giving insufficient attention to the problem (e.g., ignoring or disputing unobtrusive test findings; or doing nothing to address reference accuracy problems, giving up)
- resisting new solutions (e.g., ignoring possible applications of new technologies, continuing a "caretaker" role at the reference desk, or disputing responsibility for the problem)
- acknowledging that such reference service problems may exist in other libraries, but not in *their* library
- perceiving only the large scope of the problem (e.g., poor library management, the complexity of the issues, and feeling overwhelmed by administrative and service demands)

Thus, strategies responding to problems in the quality of reference services must consider these, and other, psychologically based research findings. This brief discussion is not intended to review the vast literatures on organizational and individual responses to crises and problem solving. It does suggest, however, that for meaningful responses to occur to the crisis in the quality of reference services, the following factors should be considered during strategy development (Argyris, 1985):

- define carefully the scope of the crisis and the specific problems that must be resolved
- address psychologically based factors related to crises and problem solving such as denial and arousal
- minimize the perceived complexity of the problem by developing incremental steps for how the problem can be resolved and clarify expectations for each step

- determine, in advance, expectations for solving the problem and possible criteria to know when, in fact, the problem is resolved (at least for the particular setting)

The cooperative library/library school program suggested in this section attempts, in part, to address these factors. But, by and large, there have been few serious efforts to develop specific strategies for addressing the "crisis" in the *quality* of reference services as measured by unobtrusive testing.

IMPROVING THE QUALITY OF REFERENCE SERVICES

While a myriad of factors likely affect the quality with which reference staff answer reference questions correctly and numerous strategies might control these factors (Batt, 1985), three broad areas deserve careful attention. The first has to do with developing the individual skills and attitudes of reference librarians (discussed in McClure and Hernon, 1983, Chapter 5). A second set comprises the managerial and organizational factors that affect reference services and the ability of library staff to engage in ongoing evaluation of reference services (discussed in Chapter 5 of this book). And a third set that is important both for its own right and because it can affect the previous two mentioned are educational concerns (discussed in this chapter).

Comprehensive strategies to improve the quality of reference services must address, minimally, factors in each of these three areas. But the view of the authors of this book is that post-graduate continuing education has been ignored in academic and public libraries. Specific strategies for reorganizing reference administrative units, setting improved organizational climates, conducting ongoing formal assessments of existing levels of reference services, and numerous other topics *require* skills, knowledge, and competencies that are best learned through a program of continuing education.

Many academic and public library staff simply will not meet professional responsibilities in the area of continuing education unless they are required to do so. Recertification programs appear to be one approach to encourage continued education after the professional degree. But it should be stressed that ongoing programs of continuing education, alone, cannot change attitudes of library managers who believe that ongoing evaluation of the quality of services is not necessary, developing positive organizational climates are unimportant, or that continued educational development is either unnecessary or cannot be rewarded.

Many library staff simply lack the necessary knowledge and skills to provide high quality services. For example, in the area of evaluation, a recent study of the use of and perceptions toward performance measures by public service, middle management, academic librarians, reported the following conclusions (McClure, 1986):

- They are not, at this time, likely to use costing and performance measure techniques in decision making processes.
- There are few rewards and benefits for middle management, public service, academic librarians who provide empirical evidence justifying the quality of public services.
- They distrust the use of performance measure data and are unlikely to utilize the data, if available, and generally believe that even when such data are available, their decisions are not affected.
- Intuitive assessment of performance is perceived to be as accurate as empirical assessments.

The last conclusion is especially disconcerting in the context of unobtrusive testing. In each of the four unobtrusive studies conducted by these authors, many readers of study results simply could not believe that libraries could possibly be providing *correct answer fill rates* in the range of 20 to 60%.

Developing additional skills related to unobtrusive testing and applying the technique in academic and public libraries will force librarians to address issues regarding:

- the 55% reference rule
- the appropriateness of incorporating formal mechanisms of evaluation into library services
- the perceptions of the quality of reference services *from the user's perspective*
- the research competencies of library staff to conduct evaluation studies and design strategies to implement findings

Such issues must be addressed in the larger context of library staff's attitudes toward evaluation and the degree to which they really want to know how well they provide information services, are willing to change behaviors and improve services, and are willing to increase their skills and knowledge related to reference services.

Unobtrusive testing has great potential to assist library staff in assessing the quality of a broad range of services — including those in areas other than public services, e.g., use of online catalog systems. This potential can be realized by demonstrating the importance of regular ongoing programs of evaluation, and developing the necessary research competencies in library staff to conduct such evaluation. With successful strategies in these areas, libraries can better identify and meet the current and long-range information needs of their clientele and ensure the provision of high quality information services.

While unobtrusive testing is an excellent means to increase awareness of the quality of reference services, its use, alone, is not likely to increase the quality of reference services. Necessary ingredients for improving the quality of reference services should be based on a comprehensive program of activities that addresses, minimally:

- the commitment of library management to develop positive organizational climates and engage in ongoing evaluation of reference services
- cooperation between schools of library/information science and librarians regarding programs of continuing education
- recertification of academic and public librarians that requires ongoing participation in formal programs of continuing education

Although significant methodological strides have been made in recent years regarding library unobtrusive testing, evaluation, and uses of performance measures, by and large, they are methods in search of a practice.

The quality of reference services can be improved if there is a commitment to do so from the profession. It is unclear, as yet, if such a commitment is present or if the profession will continue to accept 55% accuracy on factual and bibliographic questions as normal. However, the challenges of (1) directly confronting the issue of the *quality* of academic and public library reference services, and (2) developing strategies to improve existing levels of quality, are critical for the overall health and future growth of the profession in the information age. These challenges are likely to shape the overall degree of credibility that society places in academic and public libraries and the profession cannot afford to ignore these challenges.

Basing managerial decisions regarding reference services on perceptions rather than a realistic appraisal is a disservice to library clientele and a myopic stance that continues to impede the development of *quality* reference services. Maintenance of a status quo mentality on the issue of reference quality in light of a 55% reference rule is also myopic. Academic and public libraries, schools of library and information science, professional associations, individual librarians, and agencies such as the GPO must work together to develop effective strategies, including recertification, to improve the quality of reference services. Such strategies are both feasible and essential for the long-term health of the profession.

APPENDIX A

CATEGORIZATION OF CRITICAL RESPONSES TO McCLURE AND HERNON (1983), WITH A BRIEF ASSESSMENT OF EACH ASSERTION[1]

A. DOCUMENTS LIBRARIANSHIP AND UNOBTRUSIVE TESTING

1. A different paradigmatic structure exists between government publications and "most other types of reference endeavor."

This assertion is debatable and requires substantiation from a body of research. Nonetheless, the assertion underscores that government publications have long been regarded as a special or unique resource.

2. Objection could be made to the practice of unobtrusive testing.

Such testing has been used since the 1960s. It is important that neither researchers nor library managers misuse the findings. The names of the test sites should not be disclosed. Annual salary and staff promotion should not be linked to test performance. Beyond these concerns, objecting to the use of unobtrusive testing simply becomes a "cop-out" for not implementing ongoing and effective evaluation procedures.

B. RESEARCH DESIGN

1. "Correctness" might not translate into an overall gauge of the quality of service provided.

The authors concur. However, *correct answer fill rates* should be recognized as an extremely important component of the overall reference process.

2. The authors failed to address local, unique situations within a library that might affect the ability of the staff to answer questions correctly.

---

[1] The points discussed in this appendix were derived from a content analysis of the reviews to the 1985 monograph.

Such a charge provides a rationale for the status quo and for maintaining that "we are doing the best that we can." Users judge service on the basis of personal experiences and should not have to take unique factors into consideration.

3. The sampling frame is too small; it only included 17 libraries. Are conclusions drawn from the small sample size valid?

The study did not benefit from outside funding. Rather, the authors absorbed all costs themselves. Moreover, external validity is important, but only to a point. Greater attention should be given to internal validity and reliability. Validity of a sample is also based on the sampling technique used; the carefully developed stratified random sample enhanced the validity of the study.

Questioning whether valid conclusions can be drawn from a small sample size confuses external validity with internal validity. Whatever the number of libraries represented, every effort should be made to draw valid conclusions for those libraries (internal validity). Whether the conclusions can be extended to a larger group raises the external validity issue. Further, there is the need to protect the anonymity of the libraries tested. Internal validity was deemed more important than a clear delineation of external validity.

C. METHODOLOGY

1. The representativeness and the degree of difficulty of the questions were called into question. Are the questions fair?

It should be stressed that: (1) a group of practicing librarians in both regions reviewed the questions and approved them, (2) the questions were pretested prior to their use, (3) the questions were developed according to specific criteria and only required the use of basic reference sources — ones mostly listed in the *Guidelines for the Depository Library System* (1977), and (4) no questions called for the use of microfiche sources except for the *Publications Reference File* (PRF). Without a clarification of the concept of fairness, it is difficult to respond, except to once again request that readers review the criteria for the development of the test questions, the steps taken for conducting a pretest, and the procedures used in administration of the test questions.

2. There is no guarantee that either professional librarians or trained paraprofessionals answered all the questions.

This is true. However, it is beside the point. "Real-life" patrons request answers to their questions, from whomever is staffing the reference desk. If a staff member cannot handle a particular question, he/she should make referral to another member of the staff. The reviewer also assumes that library patrons are all familiar with the duties, functions, and roles of librarians, and that they can distinguish among types of library employees.

If paraprofessionals answer questions, they contribute to the "average" quality of reference service provided by that library.

3. There are serious questions concerning the applicability and administration of the test.

The reviewer never explained the questions or concerns. What specifically did he/she have in mind? Levelling such charges without specifying these "serious questions," in light of the detailed account of the procedures used, is irresponsible and does not allow for a meaningful response.

Another reviewer stated: "Was the degree of difficulty fair to judge the quality of reference service, or to make a fair comparison with other studies? I think not." Subjective opinion comprises an insufficient basis for an effective challenge to a study. Factual and bibliographic questions are generally recognized as two of the easier types of reference questions. More importantly, the questions were developed to meet specific criteria and tested staff's ability to negotiate factual and bibliographic questions related to GPO publications.

4. A flaw in the nature of unobtrusive testing is that the supposed users seem to have been instructed to act in a very passive way. "The questioners were virtually instructed not to demonstrate any real need to know the answers to their questions, nor to lift a finger to help themselves. This is hardly real life. In real life, I would expect a supplementary to a response of 'Dunno' [to be along] the lines of 'Well, . . . ring up the airport then.' "

Unobtrusive testing is not flawed because proxies refuse to suggest types of sources or places where the answer can be obtained, argue with staff, or press the staff for an answer. Research has shown that many users of academic and public libraries are not aggressive. The researchers could have had the proxies vary their behavior and their dress. However, then confronting variables might explain study findings. If researchers can isolate such variables, it might be productive to explore their possible impact.

5. "There is no thought that the users might begin (or try) to find their own way around, use the bibliographic aids themselves, or bang on the counter or ask for the boss."

These suggestions are beside the point. The research tested staff responses. Banging on the counter might result in confrontation — a topic for a different study. How many library users ask for the boss — is this a department head or the library director? What would be the outcome of seeking out such a person?

6. "The authors paid little attention to the practical juggling act of providing reference service to a variety of patrons (on the phone and in-person) simultaneously. While this should not be reflected in the accuracy of information eventually provided, it does have something to do with the methods employed to provide answers. In academic libraries, the reference librarian may provide the answer, or may consider the reference encounter a teaching opportunity and have the patron find his/her own answer."

The proxies were instructed to approach library staff who did not appear preoccupied with another information request, be it from a telephone or in-person query. Instead, they waited until there was no other patron at the reference desk before asking their question. Even academic staff who prefer to educate patrons to find their own answers do not apply this philosophy in every instance.

D. DATA ANALYSIS AND FINDINGS

1. The frequency of correct responses was not correlated to the size of the collection or the library budget.

Correct responses were compared to the percentage of GPO item categories selected. Determination of the number of documents holdings is a very imprecise process and devoid of real significance. Correct responses were indeed compared to library budget.

2. A comparison of findings to organizational variables indicated some differences to previous studies.

This is not surprising since there are differences in the management, collection, processing, and servicing of government documents and general reference collections.

3. The data were suspect because they were so different from one region to another — 49% to 20%.

The validity of the data are not "suspect" because one group outperforms another. There are numerous possible propositions that could be tested to explain why the results indicated such differences. However, such was not the purpose of the exploratory study.

4. None of the variables studied indicated why staff performance was not higher, herein the study "falters."

The study comprised descriptive research and could not directly examine causality. However, the authors offered a number of possible explanations for poor performance. They also stressed personal/individual competencies/skills.

E. THE REPORTING OF STUDY FINDINGS AND THEIR IMPLICATIONS

1. Focus more on specific learning strategies used in government documents and reference courses in library schools and on "the basic intellectual equipment of students who choose to enter a graduate library school program and eventually find themselves in responsible positions in documents reference work."

This reviewer had his/her own research agenda — one that did not match the test and its stated purposes. Perhaps this reviewer will appreciate the study reported in Chapter 4 of this book and will explore the use of experimental designs for the teaching of government documents and reference courses in library schools.

2. Since study findings indicated that the individual library staff member is the single most significant factor affecting the quality of reference service, conventional continuing education may correct any deficiencies.

Apparently some of the reviewers believed that the final two chapters of the 1983 book suggested routine remedies to improve staff competencies/skills, but offered "more significant and creative suggestions" for dealing with the entire depository program. Chapter 4 of this book suggests that we as well as others still have a lot to learn about effective remedies to complex issues.

3. The book outlines "an ambitious research agenda for documents reference." "Time may run out before so much research can be completed and its results applied. If development in artificial intelligence progresses more rapidly than such research, librarians may no longer be needed for reference work, and the quality of automated service will be both high and uniform."

This belief contains assumptions that might be productive to examine.

4. "The recommendation to shift from Guidelines to performance measures is fundamentally sound. However, it is naive to expect the GPO to lead in this direction. The inspection program has been ineffectual not just because the guidelines are vague but also because, as credible rumors tell it, members of Congress intervene in the process to guarantee passing grades for libraries in their districts. The lead must come instead from individual libraries whose administrators and documents librarians care passionately about the quality (including the accuracy) of their reference services."

Perhaps our recommendation that either the GPO or the Joint Committee on Printing assume a leadership stance was wishful thinking. Although they are currently preparing to redesign the *Biennial Survey,* they have not developed program goals and objectives. Chapters 5 and 6 of this book address the concern that library managers and staff must "care passionately" about the quality of the services provided.

5. "Reagonomics also favours cutting public expenditures, and this gloomy study could be prayed in aid of a drastic pruning programme. 1,365 is a lot of libraries . . . , and I have no idea what the 'right' number may be, but the authors seem to ignore the value of the mere existence of these depository collections and the possibility that some people may make them work if only in spite of their reference staff. . . . It would be a pity if a study based on rather unreal questioning procedures were used to deprive users of the possibility of any access at all."

The procedures conformed to previous uses of unobtrusive testing. At the same time, the authors took steps to ensure the collection of reliable and valid data. What the reviewer seems to be saying is "Keep Quiet" or there might be cutbacks in the depository program? Such a response is simplistic and ignores the historical commitment of the government to the depository program and the legal basis of the program in Chapters 1-19, Title 44, of the *United States Code.*

The central issue is that we must first ascertain the *correct answer fill rate* that depository libraries provide before attempting to improve that percentage or level of service. The reviewer encourages an attitude of anti-evaluation in cases where the findings might not be pleasant or have negative implications. Unfortunately, we cannot identify outcomes prior to conducting research/evaluation.

APPENDIX B

THE FIFTEEN TEST QUESTIONS

A. THOSE ADMINISTERED TO DOCUMENTS PERSONNEL

1. For a term paper in history, I am studying the laws on the imprisonment of free Black seamen in the South prior to the Civil War. It is my understanding that the government published a report on the topic in the 1840s. Please help me find it.

[Answer is correct if staff locate the 1843 document or, for outside referral, provide serial set and document numbers.]

Answer: Serial Set Number 426, House document number 80. "Colored seamen, free, laws in Southern states on"

Sources: Benjamin Perley Poore's *A Descriptive Catalogue of the Government Publications of the United States* (1885), p. 468; *Tables of and Annotated Index to the Congressional Series of the United States Public Documents* (1902); *Checklist of United States Public Documents, 1789-1909* (1911); or *CIS U.S. Serial Set Index,* pt. 1, p. 1726.

2. I am interested in ordering a copy of the publication *Microcomputers: Introduction to Features and Uses.* What is the current cost to order it?

[*Hint:* It is a recent publication from the National Bureau of Standards.]

[Answer is correct if staff member identifies the cost as $4.25.]

Answer: Microcomputers: Introduction to Features and Uses (National Bureau of the Standards, 1984) is available from the sales program of the Superintendent of Documents, under the stock number 003-003-02560-7. The Sudocs number is C13.10:500-110.

Sources: Monthly Catalog, October 1984 (84-20376) and *Publications Reference File.*

3. I would like the number of high school dropouts for Black youths between the ages of 16 and 17 for the years 1968, 1975, and 1982.

[Answer is correct if the staff member provides the correct data or the title and page number of the source answering the question.]

Answer: 1968: 110,000; 1975: 116,000; 1982: 66,000.
Source: Statistical Abstract of the United States, 1984, p. 160; 1985, p. 148.

4. What was the total production of bituminous coal in the U.S. for the year 1868?

[Answer is correct if the staff member mentions the actual number. Proxies must get staff member to answer the question and not merely refer to the table in the source. The table states 16,244 × 1,000 so the answer is not 16,244.]
Answer: 16,244,000 tons
Source: Historical Statistics of the United States, Part I, p. 590.

5. Who is the Administrator, Agricultural Marketing Service, U.S. Department of Agriculture, and what is his/her mailing address.?

[Answer is correct if the staff member gives Highley's name and office address.]
Answer: Vern F. Highley
Agricultural Marketing Service
Department of Agriculture
South Building, between 12th and 14th Streets, SW
Washington, D.C. 20250
Sources: Congressional Directory, 1983-84, p. 603; *U.S. Government Manual,* 1983-84, p. 94; 1984-85, p. 92 and 105; *Federal Executive Directory,* Sept./Oct. 1984, p. 87; *Federal Staff Directory,* 1984, p. 69; *Congressional Staff Directory,* 1984, p. 660; or *Washington Information Directory,* 1984-85, p. 492.

6. The Federal Aviation Administration issued *Air Traffic Control Staffing Standard System* in the mid 1970s. Can you help me locate a copy?

[Answer is correct if a copy is found or if the Sudocs number is discovered.]
Answer: The Sudocs number of this 1975 document is TD4.8/2:1380.33A.
Source: Monthly Catalog, May 1982, p. 291 (82-11490); or OCLC.

7. Where can I find the USDA regulations for the handling of lemons grown in Arizona and California?

[Answer is correct if actual *CFR* citation is given.]
Source: 7 *Code of Federal Regulations,* Part 910.

8. In 1983, President Reagan established a Task Force on Food Assistance. I would like to know its specific charge or function.

[*Hint:* The Task Force was established by Executive Order in September 1983.]
[Answer is correct if charge or function is located.]
Answer: Executive Order 12439 (September 8, 1983): ". . . analyze Federal and other programs intended to render food assistance to the needy and shall make recommendations . . . with respect to how such programs may be improved."
Source: Weekly Compilation of Presidential Documents (September 8), p. 1212; and 3 *Code of Federal Regulations* 205 (1984).

B. THOSE ADMINISTERED TO GENERAL REFERENCE PERSONNEL

9. Where can I find the text of the act which created the U.S. Office of Science and Technology Policy?

[*Hint:* The Office was created in the mid-1970s.]

[Answer is correct if the staff member locates the text or provides the reference to the *Statutes at Large.*]

Answer: 90 *Stat.* 463 (1976)

Source: U.S. Government Manual, 1983-84, p. 91.

10. I would like to know the percentage of vehicles exceeding 55 m.p.h. for every year, from 1945 to 1970. Also what was the average speed of passenger cars for those years? Where can I find *summary statistics?*

[Answer is correct if the title and page number of the appropriate source is given.]

Source: Historical Statistics of the United States, Part II, p. 718.

11. Within the State Department, there is the Office of the Historian. Who is the Historian and what is the mailing address of the Office?

[Answer is correct if his name and mailing address are given.]

Answer: William Z. Slany
Office of the Historian
Rm. 3100
Columbia Plaza Office Building
2401 E. St., N.W.
Washington, D.C. 20520
or
State Annex 1, Room 3100
Washington, D.C. 20520

Source: Federal Staff Directory, 1983-84, p. 562; *Congressional Directory,* 1983-84, p. 513; or State Department Telephone Directory.

12. In 1980, a public law was enacted and it provided universities and small businesses with the right to obtain patents for inventions which their faculties and staffs created with the use of Federal funds. Please help me locate a copy of the law.

[Answer is correct if the public law number or law itself is located.]

Answer: December 12, 1980; Public Law 96-517, *Statutes at Large.* Also see *U.S. Code and Administrative News* (USCCAN) and 94 *Stat.* 3019. *Congressional Quarterly Almanac* (1980), p. 405, identifies the public law number.

13. Please help me locate *Policy Implications of Information Technology.*

[*Hint:* It is by R. K. Salaman and E. C. Hettinger, and was recently issued.]

Answer is correct if title is located, the Sudocs number is found, or referral is made to a source which answers the question correctly.]

Answer: A publication of the National Telecommunications and Information Administration (1984). The Sudocs number is C60.10:84-144.

Source: Monthly Catalog, Aug. 1984, p. 56 (84-16713); or OCLC.

14. Please help me locate the book *Computer-Based National Information Systems?*

[*Hint:* The subtitle is "Technology and Public Policy Issues" and it was published in the early 1980s.]

[Answer is correct if the staff member identifies the title as a government publication.]

Answer: A publication of the Office of Technology Assessment, Congress (1981), Y3.T22/2:2C73/6.

Source: Monthly Catalog, February 1982, (82-002583); *Publications Reference File*; or OCLC.

15. In March 1984, Glenn English gave a speech in which he identified public policy issues related to electronic information. Can you please help me find a copy of the issues which he identified?

[*Hint:* He is a Member of the House of Representatives and his topic was "Electronic Filing of Documents with the Government: New Technology Presents New Problems."]

[Answer is correct if a copy is located or if the staff member identifies the actual date and page number of the *Congressional Record.*]

Source: Congressional Record, March 14, 1984, H1614-15.

APPENDIX C

QUESTIONS PRETESTED BUT NOT USED

A. THOSE FOR DOCUMENTS STAFF

1. Who is the Historian, House of Representatives, and what is his mailing address?

[Answer is correct if his name and mailing address are given.]

Answer: Raymond W. Smock
House Historian's Office
Cannon House Office Building
Washington, D.C. 20515
 or
Historian
Office for the Bicentennial
U.S. House of Representatives
Washington, D.C. 20515

Source: U.S. House of Representatives Telephone Directory, Spring 1984, p. 285; or *Congressional Staff Directory,* 1984, p. 290.

2. I understand that the Office of Management and Budget has developed a set of "Guidelines for the Use of Consulting Services." I need to know where I can get a copy and what the latest revision of the guidelines is.

[Answer is correct if staff member mentions OMB's address and telephone number. The person need not give the date of April 14, 1980.

Source: Office of Management and Budget, A-120 was last issued April 14, 1980. See OMB's Index of circulars and Federal management directives or *Federal Register Abstracts* (DIALOG). The 1982 *Index to CFR* mentions *41 CFR* 1-4.8 (1980) which is on microfiche. It mentions OMB circular A-120 but not by name.

3. Where can I find the text of the act which created the U.S. Office of Science and Technology Policy?

[*Hint:* The Office was created in the mid-1970s.]

[Answer is correct if the staff member locates the text or provides the reference to the *Statutes at Large.*]

Answer: 90 *Stat.* 463 (1976)

Source: U.S. Government Manual, 1983-84, p. 91.

4. I would like to know the percentage of vehicles exceeding 55 m.p.h. for every year, from 1945 to 1970. Also what was the average speed of passenger cars for those years? Where can I find *summary statistics?*

[Answer is correct if the title and page number of the appropriate source is given.]

Source: Historical Statistics of the United States, Part II, p. 718.

5. Where can I obtain a copy of President Reagan's proclamation of May 25, 1983 making that day Missing Children Day, whereby he encouraged government officials and law enforcement agencies to be alert to the implications of lost children?

[Answer is correct if title and page number of a source answering the question is given.]

Source: Weekly Compilation of Presidential Documents, May 25, 1983, p. 774; or *Code of Federal Regulations,* 3 (1984): 58.

6. Can you help me locate a copy of Seastrum's report, *Summary of Trade and Tariff Information?*

[*Hint:* Carl F. Seastrum's report provides statistical data on the luggage industry. It is in two volumes.]

[Answer is correct if title is itself located or if the staff member finds the Sudocs number for the 1977 edition.]

Answer: Prepared by the U.S. International Trade Commission. The subtitle of this 1977 work is "prepared in terms of the tariff schedules of the U.S.: luggage, TSUS items 706.06-706.30 and 706.60." The Sudocs number is TC1.26/2:7-1-1.

Source: Monthly Catalog, November 1982, p. 204 (82-026682). There is also a 1980 edition on handbags (82-016865), TC1.26/2:7-1-8, and a 1983 edition on luggage (84-013153), ITC1.11:7-1-1/second supp. The 1977 edition is not in OCLC. OCLC gives second supplement to this. However, we want the 1977 edition only. The 1977 edition is available on microfiche.

7. Boyatzis has written a report on drunk driving and the rehabilitation of alcoholics in the U.S. Can you help me locate a copy of this report?

[*Hint:* The author is Richard E. Boyatzis and the report, *A System for Diagnosis, Referral, and Rehabilitation of Persons Convicted of Driving While Intoxicated,* was published in late 1970s.]

[Answer is correct if staff member finds the report or identifies the Sudocs number.]

Answer: Issued in 1978, the Sudocs number is TD8.2:D54/6/v.1-2.

Source: Monthly Catalog, Nov. 1982, p. 230; also in OCLC. The document is available on microfiche.

8. In August 1948, the Ambassador to China sent a telegram to the State Department noting the deterioration of the political scene in China and offering recommendations for the future U.S. course of action. Can you help me locate a copy?

[*Hint:* Ambassador was J. Leighton Stuart.]

Source: Foreign Relations of the United States, 1948, volume 7, p. 405.

9. In July 1984, the Small Business Administration exempted its SBA Investigation Files — SBA 360 from compliance with provisions of the Privacy Act. Can you help me find the proposed rule which the agency submitted for general comment?

[*Hint:* The files are maintained by the Investigations Division, Office of Inspection General, Small Business Administration. It can be mentioned that the SBA made its exemption during the last two weeks of July.]

[Answer is correct if the proposed rule is located or if the title page number of the appropriate source is given.]

Answer: The proposed rule was issued April 24, 1984.

Source: Federal Register, July 25, 1984, p. 29944; see also the same source for April 24, 1984, p. 17516. See also *Federal Register Index.*

10. Within the State Department, there is the Office of the Historian. Who is the Historian and what is the mailing address of the Office?

[Answer is correct if his name and mailing address are given.]

Answer: William Z. Slany
   Office of the Historian
   Rm. 3100
   Columbia Plaza Office Building
   2401 E St., N.W.
   Washington, D.C. 20520
    or
   State Annex 1, Room 3100
   Washington, D.C. 20520

Source: Federal Staff Directory, 1983-84, p. 562; *Congressional Directory,* 1983-84, p. 513; or State Department Telephone Directory.

11. My wife (husband) is writing a paper on Federal support of Research and Development activities and copied down from some source that: "Real Federal support for research and development rose by 4.2 percent in 1977 and by 2.6 percent in 1978, while total spending for this purpose increased to 4.4 and 2.8 respectively in these two years. This amounts to a two-year gain almost three times as great as the rise in the previous ten years." Please help me verify the accuracy of these statistics.

[Answer is correct if quote is verified or source giving answer is identified.]
Answer: The quote is accurate.
Source: Economic Report of the President, 1979, p. 132.

12. Can you help me find a source which highlights legislation pertaining to Federal information policy during the 96th Congress?
[Answer is correct if the staff member finds the title "Federal Information Policy."]
Source: Information Policy, 1981, Y4.H81/3: In 3/2/981; *Monthly Catalog* 81-012491; also *CIS Index* (1981, H422-3).

13. In March 1984, Glenn English gave a speech in which he identified public policy issues related to electronic information. Can you please help me find a copy of the issues which he identified?
[*Hint:* He is a Member of the House of Representatives and his topic was "Electronic Filing of Documents with the Government: New Technology Presents New Problems."]
[Answer is correct if a copy is located or if the staff member identifies the actual date and page number of the *Congressional Record.*]
Source: Congressional Record, March 14, 1984, H1614-15.

14. What was the total production of plastic bottles in the U.S. in 1983 and how much of an increase or decrease is this from 1982?
[Answer is correct if the actual statistics given or if the title of a work giving the statistics is suggested.]
Answer: An estimated 16.2 billion units in 1983 and this represented an increase of 4.5% from the previous year.
Source: U.S. Industrial Outlook, 1984, p. 6-7; *Current Industrial Reports,* C3.158.M30E:(83)-13 — the summary for 1983; or *American Statistics Index.*

15. Please help me locate *Issues in Information Policy,* which was recently published?
[*Hint:* It is edited by Helen A. Shaw and Jane Yurow. I have no idea of the exact year of publication; however, it was in the 1980s.
[Answer is correct if the title is located or if the Sudocs number is found.]
Answer: A publication of the National Telecommunications and Information Administration, Department of Commerce (1981).
Source: Monthly Catalog, 81-011679 (October 1981, p. 27); *Publications Reference File;* or OCLC.

16. Please help me locate *Policy Implications of Information Technology.*
[*Hint:* It is by R. K. Salaman and E. C. Hettinger, and was recently issued.]
[Answer is correct if title is located or if the Sudocs number is found.]

Answer: A publication of the National Telecommunications and Information Administration (1984). The Sudocs number is C60.10:84-144.

Source: Monthly Catalog, Aug. 1984, p. 56 (84-16713); or OCLC.

17. Under the Paperwork Reduction Act (1980), the Office of Management and Budget must grant approval for the information which agencies collect. Approval is based on the "practical utility" of the information. Please help me locate a definition of this term and a list of the criteria used in applying the term.

[Answer is correct if both the definition and criteria are located.]

Answer: "Practical utility" means the actual, not merely the theoretical or potential, usefulness of information to an agency, taking into account its accuracy, adequacy, and reliability, and the agency's ability to process the information in a useful and timely fashion. OMB will take into account whether the agency demonstrates actual timely use for the information either to carry out its functions or to make it available to the public, either directly or by means of a public disclosure or labeling requirement, for the use of persons who have an interest in entities or transactions over which the agency has jurisdiction. In the case of general purpose statistics or recordkeeping requirements, practical utility means that actual uses can be demonstrated" (a direct quote from *CFR*).

Source: 5 *Code of Federal Regulations* 1320.7q.

Same answer but different wording: *Federal Register,* 48 (March 31, 1983): 13677; *Statutes at Large,* vol. 94, pp. 2812-2826 *United States Code,* title 44, chapter 35 *U.S. Code and Administrative News,* 2nd sess, 1980, pp. 6279-80 (96th Cong., 2nd sess.)

18. I am looking for a publication "The Shootdown of KAL007: Moscow's Charges and the Record." Please help me locate a copy.

[Answer is correct if a copy is located or if the Sudocs number is found.]

Answer: Sudocs number is IA1.2:K84/3.

Source: U.S. Information Agency (1983?); a nine page pamphlet. *Monthly Catalog* (84-010949) or OCLC.

19. I am working on a paper dealing with the Soviet downing of Korean Air Lines Boeing 747 on August 31, 1983. Is there some "official" source reprinting the major publicly available comments of the State Department from September 1-16, 1983?

[Answer is correct if the source is actually found.]

Answer: Yes, there is an official source.

Source: Department of State Bulletin, October 1983, p. 1-21. Also *Weekly Compilation of Presidential Documents* (September 3, pp. 1197-1198; September 5, pp. 1199-1202; September 7, pp. 1208-1209; September 8, p. 1211; September 15, p. 1257; and September 16, p. 1266).

20. In September 1983, President Reagan established the Task Force on Food Assistance. Whom did he intend on designating as its chairperson?

[Answer is correct if staff member supplies his name.]

Answer: James La Force Jr.

Graduate School of Management

University of California, Los Angeles

Source: 3 *Code of Federal Regulations* 204 (1984) mentions that the President selected the membership and refers to *Weekly Compilation of President Documents* (September 8, 1983), p. 1212.

B. THOSE PRETESTED FOR GENERAL REFERENCE STAFF

1. I understand that Coco has written a workbook on legal research for laypersons. I would like to order a personal copy. Is it still in print and what is the cost?

[*Hint:* Can indicate that it was published in the early 1980s and that the author is Al Coco.]

[Answer is correct if staff member identifies that the title is no longer in print from the GPO; therefore no cost].

Answer: Finding the Law (Washington, D.C.: GPO, 1982) was issued for the Bureau of Land Management. It is now out of print; it used to be available from the Superintendent of Documents for $8.50, as stock number 024-011-00148-4.

Sources: Monthly Catalog (83-017749), *Publications Reference File,* or OCLC.

2. Who is the Administrator, Agricultural Marketing Service, U.S. Department of Agriculture, and what is his/her mailing address?

[Answer is correct if the staff member gives Highley's name and office address.]

Answer: Vern F. Highley

Agricultural Marketing Service

Department of Agriculture

South Building, between 12th and 14th Streets, SW

Washington, D.C. 20250

Sources: Congressional Directory, 1983-84, p. 603; *U.S. Government Manual,* 1983-84, p. 94; 1984-1985, p. 92 and 105; *Federal Executive Directory,* Sept./Oct. 1984, p. 87; *Federal Staff Directory,* 1984, p. 69; *Congressional Staff Directory,* 1984, p. 660; or *Washington Information Directory,* 1984-85, p. 492.

3. I would like the number of high school dropouts for Black youths between the ages of 16 and 17 for the years 1968, 1975, and 1982.

[Answer is correct if the staff member provides the correct data or the title and page number of the source answering the question.]

Answer: 1968: 110,000; 1975: 116,000; 1982: 66,000.

Source: Statistical Abstract of the United States, 1984, p. 160; 1985, p. 148.

4. Where can I obtain a copy of President Reagan's proclamation of May 25, 1983 making that day Missing Children Day, whereby he encouraged government officials and law enforcement agencies to be alert to the implications of lost children?

[Answer is correct if title and page number of a source answering the question is given.]

Source: Weekly Compilation of Presidential Documents or *Code of Federal Regulations*, 3 (1984): 58.

5. What was the total production of bituminous coal in the U.S. for the year 1868?

[Answer is correct if the staff member mentions the actual number. Proxies must get staff member to answer the question and not merely refer to the table in the source. The table states 16,244 × 1,000 so the answer is not 16,244.]

Answer: 16,244,000 tons.

Source: Historical Statistics of the United States, Part I, p. 590.

6. Can you help me locate a copy of Seastrum's report, *Summary of Trade and Tariff Information?*

[*Hint:* Carl F. Seastrum's report provides statistical data on the luggage industry. It is in 2 volumes.]

[Answer is correct if title is itself located or if the staff member finds the Sudocs number for the 1977 edition.]

Answer: Prepared by the U.S. International Trade Commission. The subtitle of this 1977 work is "prepared in terms of the tariff schedules of the U.S.: luggage, TSUS items 706.06-706.30 and 706.60." The Sudocs number is TC1.26/2:7-1-1.

Source: Monthly Catalog, November 1982, p. 204. The 1977 edition is not in OCLC. OCLC gives Sudocs: ITC 1.11:7-1-11, which is a later supplement to this. However, we want the 1977 edition only. The 1977 edition is available on microfiche.

7. Boyatzis has written a report on drunk driving and the rehabilitation of alcoholics in the U.S. Can you help me locate a copy of this report?

[*Hint:* The author is Richard E. Boyatzis and the report. *A System for Diagnosis, Referral, and Rehabilitation of Persons Convicted of Driving While Intoxicated,* was published in late 1970s.]

[Answer is correct if staff member finds the report or identifies the Sudocs number.]

Answer: Issued in 1978, the Sudocs number is TD8.2:D54/6/v.1-2.

Source: Monthly Catalog, Nov. 1982, p. 230; also in *Government Reports Announcement and Index* and OCLC. The document is available on microfiche.

8. Who is the Historian, House of Representatives, and what is his mailing address?

[Answer is correct if his name and mailing address are given.]

Answer: Raymond W. Smock
            House Historian's Office
            Cannon House Office Building
            Washington, D.C. 20515
                or
            Historian
            Office for the Bicentennial
            U.S. House of Representatives
            Washington, D.C. 20515

Source: U.S. House of Representatives Telephone Directory, Spring 1984, p. 285; or *Congressional Staff Directory,* 1984, p. 290.

9, Please help me locate *Postal Service Electronic Mail.*

[*Hint:* The subtitle is "The Price Isn't Right," and the work was published in the 1980s.]

[Answer is correct if the staff member locates the title, provides the Sudocs number, or makes a referral whereby the question is answered completely.]

Source: U.S. Congress. House. Committee on Government Operations. 97th Cong., 2nd sess., 1982, H.Rept. 97-919. Y1.1/8:97-919. *Monthly Catalog* 83-612304, May 1983, p. 204; also see OCLC.

10. What was the total production of plastic bottles in the U.S. in 1983 and how much of an increase or decrease is this from 1982?

[Answer is correct if the actual statistics given or if the title of a work giving the statistics is suggested.]

Answer: An estimated 16.2 billion units in 1983 and this represented an increase of 4.5% from the previous year.

Source: U.S. Industrial Outlook, 1984, p. 6-7; *Current Industrial Reports;* C3.158.M30E:(83)-13 — the summary for 1983; or *American Statistics Index.*

11. Where can I find the USDA regulations for the handling of lemons grown in Arizona and California?

[Answer is correct if actual *CFR* citation is given.]

Source: 7 Code of Federal Regulations, Part 910.

12. I am looking for a publication "The Shootdown of KAL007: Moscow's Charges and the Record." Please help me locate a copy.

[Answer is correct if the staff member recognizes this as a government document.]

Source: U.S. Information Agency (1983?); a nine page pamphlet. *Monthly Catalog* (84-010949) or OCLC.

13. I am working on a paper dealing with the Soviet downing of Korean Air Lines Boeing 747 on August 31, 1983. Is their some "official" source reprinting the major publicly available comments of the State Department from September 1-16, 1983?

[Answer is correct if the source is actually found.]

Answer: Yes, there is an official source.

Source: Department of State Bulletin, October 1983, p. 1-21; or *Weekly Compilation of Presidential Documents.*

14. Please help me locate *Issues in Information Policy,* which was recently published?

[*Hint:* It is edited by Helen A. Shaw and Jane Yurow. I have no idea of the year of publication.]

[Answer is correct if the staff member recognizes this title as a government document.]

Answer: A publication of the National Telecommunications and Information Administration, Department of Commerce (1981).

Source: Monthly Catalog, 81-011679 (October 1981, p. 27), *Publications Reference File,* or OCLC.

APPENDIX D

REFERENCE QUESTION TABULATION SHEET

Sheet Number _____

Library Name _____

Total Library Volumes _____

Government Does FTE Support Staff Answering Ref. Questions _____

General Reference FTE Support Staff Answering Ref. Questions _____

Percentage of Items Selected _____

Person Administering Questions _____

Dates Administered _____

Total Budget _____

Government Does FTE Professionals _____

General Reference FTE Professionals _____

Total Library Professional Staff _____

Reference Question	Academic or Public Library	Does or Reference Dept.	Time Question Asked	Total Time of Reference Interview	Library Owned Source	Staff Checked OCLC	Correct Answer

	Other Than Totally Correct Answer				Referral							
Wrong Answer	Don't Know	Claimed Source Not Owned	Claimed Source Not on Shelf	Other (Describe)	To Does Dept.	To Another Dept.	To Govt. Agency	To GPO Bkstore	To Another Dept.	Please Return Later	Other (Describe)	Referral Source Gave Corr. Ans.

COMMENTS OR ADDITIONAL EXPLANATION:

APPENDIX E

PARTICIPANT QUESTIONNAIRE

We want to thank you for participation in our instructional program and to invite your feedback on the instructional unit which you received. Our purpose is to improve upon the methods of instruction; for this we need your comments and suggestions.

Please check whether you received:

(a) _____ the slide presentation (and script)

(b) _____ the workshop

I.   On the following scale, please indicate the extent to which you believe the instructional unit (the slide presentation or workshop) accomplished the following: (circle the correct response)

1.   increased your awareness of *basic* U.S. government document statistical publications

                    Not at All   Very Much
                         1 2 3 4 5

2.   showed you ways to use *basic* U.S. government document statistical sources more effectively

                    Not at All   Very Much
                         1 2 3 4 5

3.   increased your awareness of the strengths and weaknesses among a selection of *basic* U.S. government document statistical publications

                    Not at All   Very Much
                         1 2 3 4 5

II. FOR GENERAL REFERENCE STAFF **ONLY**: Do you think that the instructional unit that you received improved your ability to answer *basic* U.S. government document statistical questions directly rather than to refer such questions to the documents department?

                    Not at All   Very Much
                         1 2 3 4 5

FOR GOVERNMENT DOCUMENTS STAFF **ONLY**: Do you think that the instructional unit in which you participated will improve the ability of general reference staff to answer *basic* U.S. government document statistical questions directly rather than to refer such questions to you?

Not at All   Very Much

1 2 3 4 5

III.   In your opinion, has the instructional program increased your ability to answer questions related to U.S. government statistical sources?

Not at All   Very Much

1 2 3 4 5

IV.   What suggestions have you for improving the instructional unit you received prior to its use again?

V.   Would you like to see an instructional unit similar to the one that you received developed for other topics related to government publications?

(a)   Yes _____

(b)   No _____

If you checked "yes," would you like to see it for: (check as many as you believe applicable)

a.   more complex statistical sources   Yes _____ No _____

b.   conducting legislative histories   Yes _____ No _____

c.   gaining access to report literature   Yes _____ No _____

d.   searching for patents   Yes _____ No _____

e.   using basic indexes to government documents   Yes _____ No _____

f.   conducting online searching of government documents databases   Yes _____ No _____

g.   Other (Please Specify)   Yes _____ No _____

_____ Yes _____

_____ Yes _____

_____ Yes _____

VI.   Do you think that library staff at other institutions would benefit from access to an instructional unit such as the one that you received? Yes _____ No _____ . Please explain your answer and take into account the fact that such a service probably would not be free.

VII. Other Comments?

THANK YOU FOR YOUR ASSISTANCE

APPENDIX F

INTRODUCTION TO UNITED STATES GOVERNMENT STATISTICAL REFERENCE SOURCES: A SELECTED LIST*

INTRODUCTION

This annotated bibliographic guide to U.S. government publications provides an *introduction* to *selected* works and indexes typically used in answering reference questions of a statistical nature. Each publication listed here is described both by a brief annotation and a number of slides. Since the slides are coordinated with specific sections of the text, users of the guide should follow the instructions for relating the appropriate slide to the annotation. After reading through the guide and viewing the slides, you may wish to examine the actual reference sources discussed.

The sources discussed in this guide are listed below. In addition, Joe Morehead, *Introduction to United States Public Documents,* third edition (Littleton, CO: Libraries Unlimited, 1983), describes many of these reference sources in greater detail.

INDEXES

American Statistics Index
Index to U.S. Government Periodicals
Statistical Reference Index
Index to International Statistics

SOURCES

Agricultural Statistics
Annual Energy Outlook 1984 with Projections to 1995

---

*Slides and Annotated Bibliography developed by Charles R. McClure and Peter Hernon, with the assistance of Michele McKnelly, Government Documents Department, Oklahoma State University.

Annual Survey of Manufacturers
Business Statistics
The Condition of Education: A Statistical Report
County and City Data Book
County Business Patterns
Crime in the United States: Uniform Crime Report
Digest of Educational Statistics
Economic Indicators
The Handbook of Economic Statistics
Handbook of Labor Statistics
Historical Statistics of the United States: Colonial Times to 1970
Labor Force Statistics Derived from the Current Population Survey: A
   Datebook
Census Catalog
1980 Census of Population—Vol 1. Characteristics of the Population.
   Chapter A. Number of Inhabitants
1980 Census of Population—Vol 1. Characteristics of the Population.
   Chapter B. General Population Characteristics
1980 Census of Population—Vol 1. Characteristics of the Population
   Chapter C. General Social and Economic Characteristics
1980 Census of Population—Vol 1. Characteristics of the Population.
   Chapter D. Detailed Population Characteristics
1982 Census of Agriculture—Vol 1. Geographic Area Series
1980 Census of Housing—Vol 1. Characteristics of Housing Units Chapter
   A. General Housing Characteristics
1980 Census of Housing—Vol 1. Characteristics of Housing Units Chapter
   B. Detailed Characteristics
1980 Census of Population and Housing: Census Tracts
1980 Census of Population and Housing: Congressional Districts of the 98th
   Congress
Sourcebook of Criminal Justice Statistics
Statistical Abstract of the United States
Survey of Current Business
Vital Statistics of the United States
The World Factbook
World Military Expenditures and Arms Transfers

Instead of presenting these titles in alphabetical order, the guide clusters
them by broad subject:

• indexes
• general works
• agriculture
• business and economics

- crime
- education
- energy
- information about other countries
- the labor force
- population, housing (census data), and demographics

Nevertheless, some titles may contain information pertinent to other topical categories.

INDEXES

[SLIDE 1: ASI Cover]
   1. Congressional Information Service. *American Statistics Index* Bethesda, MD: Vol. 1- , 1973- . Annual.

The *American Statistics Index* (ASI) is the most comprehensive guide to statistical information published by the U.S. government. ASI appears both in a print and an on-line version (available through DIALOG at $90 per on-line connect hour). With the 1974 Annual and Retrospective Edition, the index's coverage dates back to the 1960s.

The ASI Abstract volume contains a user's guide [SLIDE 2: User Guide], which includes explanations, search suggestions, and sample searches [SLIDES 3-4; Sample of ASI Search, Suggestions]. The Congressional Information Service sells microfiche copies of all documents listed in ASI, unless otherwise noted in the abstract [SLIDE 5: Microfiche]. If one does not have access to an ASI microfiche collection, and the document is not available in the local depository library, titles may be obtained from the ASI Documents on Demand Service (see Annual Supplement of ASI for complete details).

From 1974 through the present, ASI has issued an Annual Index, with Monthly Supplements, to provide current information throughout the year [SLIDE 6: Monthly Supplements]. The 1983 Annual Index abstracted approximately 6,500 titles. The Congressional Information Service expects to issue a quinquennial cummulation of ASI (1980-1984) soon.

ASI indexes individual monographs, periodical articles, annual reports, and publications in series. In contrast, the *Monthly Catalog* does not index these works; it may only list works by title in the annual Serial or Periodical Supplement. ASI indexes publications of Federal agencies and their regional offices [SLIDE 7: Issuing Agencies]. Publications are defined as ". . . all printed or duplicated materials that may be distributed by an agency to members of the public, whether on a broad or limited basis" (1983 ASI Annual Supplement, p. xviii). ASI indexes some materials which are not sent through the GPO depository library program.

ASI does not index:

- scientific and technical data disseminated by NTIS, NASA, ERIC or NLM
- most contract studies published by the GPO or NTIS
- classified and confidential data

ASI only includes congressional publications that contain significant statistical information; the *CIS Index* offers a more complete record of the publications of Congress. Addresses for individual agencies that publish statistical materials are also given in the prefatory matter of the index volume under "Where to Write for Statistical Publications."

One may search the ASI index using four different methods:

- *Subject and Name Index,* which includes subject terms, place names, corporate bodies, and personal names (as authors and subjects)
- *Category Index* [SLIDE 8: Index by Categories], which includes geographic, economic, and demographic breakdowns
- *Title Index*
- *Agency Report Number Index* [SLIDE 9: Index by Agency Report Numbers]

The linking of portions of the ASI index to terms listed in the Standard Industrial Classification (SIC) [SLIDE 10: Guide to Standard Classifications] allows greater specificity in searches. ASI's index includes appropriate SEE and SEE ALSO references. Index entries do not generally include the exact title of the document; instead, the user must refer to the abstract for this information.

The abstract portion [SLIDE 11: Sample Abstract] includes: the ASI accession number and analytics describing individual tables (See Organization of ASI Abstracts and Indexing in the Annual Supplement for a full explanation of the structure and meaning of the accession numbers [SLIDE 12: Sample ASI Accession Number]); issuing agency and publication type (Header information); pagination; paper copy availability information and price; availability for depository distribution (the appearance of a black dot before an item number); depository item number; ASI microfiche availability and unit count; stock number; Sudoc number; LC card number, *Monthly Catalog* entry number (when available); descriptions of publications as a whole; title and page locations for individual tables; and description of individual articles. Abstracts in the index also include specific statistical data and tables contained in the publication [SLIDE 13: Example Entry].

To recap, use of ASI involves a two-step process. First, check the index volumes and select a publication entry. Each entry is followed by an accession number. Second, locate the accession number in the abstract volume and ascertain if the publication probably contains the desired information.

The abstracts are arranged in accession number sequence and grouped by agency. Each publication or series receives a unique number and recurring titles generally have the same number each year. The description of the contents of a publication is very detailed.

Many of the publications included in ASI are available through the GPO depository library program. The publication are also available from the Congressional Information Service and its microfiche service.

2. Infordata International Inc. *Index to U.S. Government Periodicals* Chicago, IL. vol. 1- . 1970- . Annual.
[SLIDE 14: IUSGP Cover]

The *Index to U.S. Government Periodicals* (IUSGP), known as the Reader's Guide to government documents, provides author and subject access to articles in a variety of periodicals published by the U.S. government. The periodicals included "offer substantive articles of lasting research and reference value." Many of these periodicals are available through the GPO depository library program; the others can be obtained from the issuing agency. The publisher offers all the periodicals on microfiche.

Explanatory information about the index's format is given at the beginning of each volume [SLIDE 15: IUSGP Preface]. Users should note that the *Monthly Catalog* does not index periodicals; it merely lists them by title in the yearly *Periodical* (or *Serial*) *Supplement to the Monthly Catalog*. The *Index to U.S. Government Periodicals* does not index materials that are specifically about statistics, although much statistical data are included [SLIDE 16: Sample Entries]. Rather, IUSGP is a general index covering nearly 200 Federally published periodicals. These titles are listed on the front and back cover of the index. This list signifies whether a title is available from the GPO or the issuing agency and provides the Sudocs classification number, where relevant.

3. Congressional Information Service. *Statistical Reference Index*. Bethesda, MD: vol. 1- , 1979- . Annual. Coverage dates from 1980.
[SLIDE 17: SRI Cover]

The *Statistical Reference Index* (SRI) follows the format and organization of ASI. It indexes and abstracts statistical publications that are *not* issued by the U.S. government. The 1984 SRI covered 1,800 titles. The SRI is intended to review current statistical publications issued by major U.S. professional, industry and trade associations, institutions, businesses, commercial publishers, independent research centers, *state* government agencies, and universities. SRI includes publications which present business and social statistics of general research value and having national, regional, or statewide breadth of coverage; materials which contain statistics regarding topics that are not covered by Federal data (e.g., religion); and material which may be limited in scope, but authoritative in nature [SLIDE 18: SRI Contents].

The data contained in SRI complement coverage of ASI. In some cases,

Federal data are reported through commercial publishers, independent research organizations, state government agencies, university and affiliated research centers, and associations. SRI may pick up and report these data.

The User's Guide explains how to use this index [SLIDE 19: User Guide]. SRI is used in a manner similar to ASI. In terms of subject coverage SRI and ASI are similar; the main difference is the *source* of the material (Federal government versus non-Federal government). SRI includes a subject and name index, an index by categories,, an index by issuing sources, and an index by titles. About 90% of the SRI publications covered are available in the SRI Microfiche Library on a subscription basis.

An entry in the bibliographic data section of each abstract describes the microfiche status of a publication as:

- *complete* — the entire publication is available in the SRI Microfiche Library
- *excerpts* — only statistical portions have been filmed and included in the library
- *not filmed* — the publication is copyrighted and not included
- *complete, delayed, excerpts delayed* — the issuing agency has stipulated that SRI must not distribute the microfiche copy for a specified period of time, as a condition of granting reproduction rights

4. Congressional Information Service. *Index to International Statistics.* Bethesda, MD: vol. 1- , 1983- . Annual.

[SLIDE 20: IIS Cover]

The *Index to International Statistics* (IIS) covers English language publications of international, intergovernmental organizations (IGO's). IGO's publish data on population, business, finance, trade, education, industrial production, demographic and political characteristics of nations and the world, etc. IIS indexes comprehensively between 1,300 to 1,500 titles, including 100 periodicals [SLIDE 21: IIS Size]. IIS covers a variety of publication types, including official sales and non-sales publications, current mimeographed documents, and working papers.

The coverage complements ASI and in some cases the data gathered and reported were from U.S. publications. The U.S. government is a major producer of the information that other countries and international organizations use.

IIS is used in the same manner as ASI, but patrons should consult the user's guide [SLIDE 22: Users Guide] for additional information[SLIDE 23: IIS Contents]. IIS includes five indexes:

- subjects, names, and geographic areas
- categories
- issuing sources
- titles
- publication numbers

Issued monthly, there are quarterly and annual cumulations. The major difference between IIS and other CIS indexes is that the monthly and quarterly index and abstract parts are placed together in a single volume. The index by publication number is particularly crucial, since often patrons do not have the correct title for the documents they need. Documents indexed in IIS are available to libraries on a subscription basis; the publisher offers all the periodicals on microfiche. An especially helpful feature of IIS is its inclusion of a list of the countries which are members of selected IGOs.

GENERAL WORKS

5. U.S. Department of Commerce. Bureau of the Census. *Statistical Abstract of the United States* Washington, D.C.: GPO. Annual. C3.134:year.

[SLIDE 24: Cover]

Statistical Abstract is the most comprehensive and useful of all the general statistical sources that the GPO publishes. Issued since 1897, it includes summary statistics "on the social, political, and economic organization of the United States"; many of the tables are derived from non-Federal sources. Since this source almost always identifies the publications from which its information is gathered [SLIDE 25: Table with Source Information], users have an indirect method for accessing additional relevant statistical information. The data presented in the *Statistical Abstract* are generally the most recent; for example, the 1985 edition is largely based on 1984 figures.

Statistical Abstract contains a table of contents with information arranged by broad categories such as population or education. The body of the work consists of tables of data on each subject. At the beginning of each section a short text summarizes the subject matter. For example, in the section of population, the constitutional mandate for the census is explained and a brief description of census materials is presented. There is a lengthy index at the back of the *Statistical Abstract,* but it has major shortcomings: (1) there are few cross references from unused or related terms, and (2) subentries under major headings are not detailed. Consequently the user must consult numerous tables that may be relevant.

Statistical Abstract contains a section entitled "Recent Trends," which reports trends in:

- population
- vital statistics and health
- education and law enforcement
- labor force and income
- federal income
- federal income security programs

- government
- defense
- elections
- commerce
- science
- communications and transportation
- energy and agriculture

This section provides brief data on each subject and graphically displays the information [SLIDE 26: Example Graphs].

Appendix 1, "Historical Series-Index to Tables in Which Historical Statistics Series Appear" [SLIDE 27: Index] contains the equivalent table number from *Statistical Abstract* to *Historical Statistics*. Appendix 2, "Metropolitan Area Concepts and Components," explains MSA's and other Office of Management and Budget designations used for gathering statistical data. A list of MSA's, and their components, is appended. Appendix 3 explains the methods used in data collection and the reliability of data reported in the work. Appendix 4, a "Guide to Sources," lists additional statistical publications arranged by the subjects covered [SLIDE 28: Guide to Sources].

Although *Statistical Abstract* is indexed in ASI, the primary utility of this ready reference source is that it often serves as a finding guide to more detailed statistical information. Source footnotes for each table and Appendix 4 are enormously useful in this respect.

6. U.S. *Department of Commerce. Bureau of the Census. Historical Statistics of the United States: Colonial Times to 1970.* Washington, D.C.: GPO, 1970. C3.134/2: H62/789-970/pt. 1 & 2.

[SLIDE 29: Cover]

This work contains summary statistics, for the U.S., on a broad range of topics, including:

- population
- vital statistics, health and medical care
- migration
- labor
- prices and price indexes
- national income and wealth
- consumer income and expenditures
- social statistics
- land, water, and climate
- agriculture
- forestry and fisheries

- minerals
- construction and housing
- manufactures
- transportation
- communications
- energy
- distribution and services
- international transactions and foreign commerce
- business enterprise
- productivity and technological development
- financial markets and institutions
- government
- colonial and pre-Federal statistics

A special section covers colonial and pre-Federal statistics.

Historical Statistics has both a table of contents [SLIDE 30: Contents] and an index [SLIDE 31: Subject Index]. Each general topic is introduced by prefactory information, which includes references to additional sources, and [SLIDE 32: Health and Medical Care] data are presented in tabular form. Each table includes special notes on the scope or accuracy of the data [SLIDE 33: Example Table]. Additionally, a time period index [SLIDE 34: Time Period Index] is useful for locating topical data for specific time periods.

7. U.S. Department of Commerce. Bureau of the Census. *County and City Data Book*. Washington, D.C.: GPO, 1983. C 3.134/2: C 83/2-983.

[SLIDE 35: Cover]

The *County and City Data Book* presents a vast range of information for regions, divisions, states, counties, and cities for 25,000 or more people, and for Minor Civil Divisions (MCD's). Table header information about the specific topics covered is given [SLIDE 36: Column Headings for Cities], and summary data are taken from the decennial and quinquennial censuses as well as from a large number of governmental and private agencies.

Tables are clear and easy to read [SLIDE 37: Sample Table]. The work includes maps for states and area components of Standard Metropolitan Statistical Areas (SMSA's). There is no index to the work, but rather a detailed Table of Contents and a set of column headings for each table. Special features include a list of the highest ranking counties by selected subjects [SLIDE 38: Highest Ranking Counties] and a ranking of the 75 largest cities on selected topics, such as median household income.

The *County and City Data Book* is indexed in ASI and is also available from the Bureau of the Census on floppy diskette.

AGRICULTURE

8. U.S. Department of Agriculture. *Agricultural Statistics* Washington, D.C.: Government Printing Office. Annual. A 1.45: .

[SLIDE 39: Cover]

Agriculture Statistics covers agricultural production supplies, consumption, facilities, costs and returns, farm resources, and finance and price supports. It also includes conversion tables for weights and measures, e.g., the number of pounds in a bushel of corn. The 1984 edition includes 738 tables, many of which refer to further source information at the bottom of the table. [SLIDE 40: Sample Entry]. Since the statistics in each issue are limited to the last ten years, a person needing older data must consult back issues. Footnotes for each table clarify terms and explain data collection problems and statistical techniques. The work has both an index and a general table of contents [SLIDE 41: Contents].

9. U.S. Department of Commerce. Bureau of the Census. *1980 Census of Agriculture— Vol. 1. Geographic Area Series:* State name. Washington, D.C.: GPO, Issued July 1984.

[SLIDE 42: Cover]

The *Census of Agriculture* is conducted every five years; since 1978, it has been conducted concurrently with the Census Bureau's various economic censuses. The first *Census of Agriculture* was done in 1840, and until 1920 this census was part of the decennial census; quinquennial censuses have been conducted beginning in 1925. From 1954 to 1974 the *Census of Agriculture* was conducted in years ending with 4 and 9.

The *Census of Agriculture* is the leading source of statistical information on the nation's agricultural production, and the only source of comparable data on agriculture on a state, county, and national level [SLIDE 43: Example Table]. The *Census of Agriculture 1982* includes a table of contents, an index, [SLIDE 44: Index] and appendices which define technical terms and data collection techniques. The index is divided into state and county data; the left portion of the column applies only to the state data tables and the right portion only covers county data.

BUSINESS AND ECONOMICS

10. U.S. Department of Commerce. Bureau of the Census. *Annual Survey of Manufactures.* Washington, D.C.: GPO, 1984. Annual (except for the year in which the economic census is issued). C 3.24/9-2: 980-81.

[SLIDE 45: ASM Cover]

The *Annual Survey of Manufactures (ASM),* which began publication with the 1949/51 edition, includes a table of contents, but has no index. Since most data in the current *ASM* have been collected in a similar manner since 1977, trend data can be constructed. *ASM* contains data related to key measures of manufacturing activities (e.g., value added by manufacture, employment, and plant hours) by industry and geographic area. The *ASM* contains estimates of general statistics, such as:

• number of employees
• payrolls for industry groups
• individual industries and states
• broad industrial and geographical totals for gross assets
• rental payments
• supplemental labor and fuel costs

Additionally, *ASM* supplies data for important classes of products shipped by manufacturing establishments [SLIDE 46: Industry Classification]. *ASM* contains six tables arranged by Standard Industrial Codes (SIC) [SLIDE 47: Sample Table]. *ASM* defines terms and describes survey samples and the statistical methods used. Five appendices further clarify terms and methods used.

11. U.S. Department of Commerce. Bureau of the Census. *County Business Patterns.* Washington, D.C.: GPO, 1943- Annual. C 3.204:82- .

[SLIDE 48: Cover]

This continuing series of annual reports presents statistical information on industries, employment, and payroll by state, county, and SMSA [SLIDE 49: General Explanation]. The series includes fifty state reports, a summary issue for the U.S., and an issue for Puerto Rico. Data are tabulated by types of business, as characterized in the *Standard Industrial Classification Manual* (1972 edition plus the 1977 supplement) [SLIDE 50: Example Table]. Any issue includes useful information, such as an explanation of the reliability of the data [SLIDE 51: Reliability of Data].

12. U.S. Department of Commerce. Bureau of Economic Analysis. *Survey of Current Business.* vol. 1 (1921)— Monthly. C 59.11: vol. and nos.

[SLIDE 52: Cover]

The *Survey of Current Business* provides monthly information on trends in industry, the business outlook, and a vast range of statistical data relevant to the U.S. economy. Tables on current business statistics include:

• GNP changes
• manufacturing data
• price deflators

- finance
- labor force data
- U.S. and international transactions
- industry statistics [SLIDE 53: Example Table]

Each issue presents updated information for the last six quarters. The July issue features revised estimates of the National Income and Product Accounts. Each monthly publication also includes various essays/articles [SLIDE 54: Essay], and has an index at the back of each issue.

13. U.S. Department of Commerce. Bureau of Economic Analysis. *Business Statistics*. Washington, D.C.: GPO. Biennial. C 59.11/3:year.
[SLIDE 55: Cover]
This supplement to the *Survey of Current Business* presents historical data and methodological notes for numerous series appearing in the *Survey*. The main body of the work presents monthly and annual data, while the appendices offer selected monthly data.
Examples of topical areas covered include general business indicators, commodity prices, construction and real estate, domestic trade, labor force employment and earnings, labor conditions, unemployment insurance programs, finance, foreign trade of the U.S., transportation and communication, chemicals, electric power and gas, food and kindred products, leather and products, lumber, metals petroleum and coal, pulp and paper products, rubber products, clay and glass products, and textile products.

14. Congress. Joint Economic Committee. *Economic Indicators*. Washington, D.C.: GPO. Monthly. Y4.Ec 7:Ec 7/year-month.
[SLIDE 56: Cover]
This publication provides monthly data on leading indicators such as prices, wages, business activity, credit, Federal finance, money, employment and unemployment and production. *Economic Indicators* also covers the Gross National Product (GNP) and international transactions. Both tables and figures may identify the sources for which the information is gathered.

CRIME

15. U.S. Department of Justice. Federal Bureau of Investigation. *Crime in the United States: Uniform Crime Reports*. Washington, D.C.: GPO, 1983. J1.14/7:year.
[SLIDE 57: Cover]
The Uniform Crime Reports (UCR) provides the general public and law enforcement community with data on the nature, extent, and seriousness of

crime. It gives a nationwide view of crime based on statistics contributed by state and local law enforcement agencies. The UCR does not include an index but the Table of Contents analyzes the tables according to the type of crime they cover [SLIDE 58: Contents]. The UCR contains a summary of the Uniform Crime Reporting Program, the Crime Index Offenses Reported, Crime Index Offenses cleared, a section on Persons Arrested, and Law Enforcement Personnel. Each section contains written comments, charts, and tables.

The publication contains six appendices:

- table methodology
- offenses in Uniform Crime Reporting
- Uniform Crime Reporting definitions
- Age-Specific arrest rates by sex
- Index of Crime, Standard Metropolitan Statistical Area
- Directory of State Uniform Crime Reporting Programs

The UCR is particularly useful since the statistical data are correlated with population size and since it includes excellent graphics [SLIDE 59: Example Graphic].

UCR and the *Sourcebook of Criminal Justice Statistics* (see next entry) cover many of the same topics. The *Sourcebook,* however, is easier to use; it contains an index within the volume, while UCR does not.

16.   Timothy J. Flanagan and Maureen McLead, eds., *Sourcebook of Criminal Justice Statistics.* U.S. Department of Justice. Bureau of Justice Statistics. Washington, D.C.: GPO, 1984. J 29.9:SD-SB-12.

[SLIDE 60: Cover]

The eleventh edition comprises a comprehensive reference source for statistical data concerning criminal justice. This work is noteworthy because it contains an excellent subject index [SLIDE 61: Index], a thumb index, a general table of contents and a list of figures, and an explanatory figure describing the availability of Criminal Statistics [SLIDE 62: Overview of Data]. The *Sourcebook* includes source notes that enable the user to locate more detailed information as needed [SLIDE 63: Example Table with Source Notes]. The *Sourcebook* contains primarily tabular data, but does have a few graphs and maps, and covers:

- Characteristics of the Criminal Justice System
- Public Attitudes toward Crime and Criminal Justice-Related Topics
- the Nature and Distribution of Known Offenses
- Characteristics and Distribution of Persons Arrested
- Judicial Procession of Defendants
- Persons under Correctional Supervision

The *Sourcebook* has sixteen appendices, e.g., Crime in the United States-Definition of Terms and Children in Custody.

EDUCATION

17. U.S. Department of Education. National Center for Education Statistics. *Digest of Educational Statistics 1983-1984.* Washington, D.C.: GPO, 1983. ED 1.113: 983-84.
[SLIDE 64: Cover]
The *Digest,* which provides statistical data from the pre-kindergarten to graduate level, contains statistical data on topics such as:

- the number of schools and colleges
- teachers
- enrollments
- graduates
- educational attainment
- finances
- Federal funds for education
- employment and incomes of graduates
- libraries
- international education

The data are derived from both governmental and non-governmental sources. To be included in the *Digest,* reports must be nationwide in scope and of current interest and value. Each table includes a source note to assist users seeking additional information. The *Digest* has a table of contents [SLIDE 65: Contents] and an index. Data are presented in tabular form with a brief explanation at the beginning of each chapter.

18. U.S. Department of Education. National Center for Educational Statistics. *The Condition of Education: A Statistical Report.* Washington, D.C.: GPO. Annual. ED 1.109:year.
[SLIDE 66: Cover]
This report to Congress presents detailed data on enrollment, staff, achievement, curriculum, and finances, for all levels of the educational structure in the United States [SLIDE 67: Contents]. It also includes information on the effects of education on employment. *The Condition of Education* provides key data for decision making on a state, local, and Federal level. Information is presented in a non-technical format for use by a general audience.

Data are presented in both a graphic and tabular form [SLIDE 68: Example Data Presentation]. The *Condition of Education* also includes notes on the information content of tables. Additionally, there is a section on the "Data Sources, Sources and Reliability of Estimates," and definitions of selected terms. Since *The Condition of Education* does not always cover the same data from year to year, the index [SLIDE 69: Cumulative Index] covers not only the current issue but also the three latest issues.

ENERGY

19. U.S. Department of Energy. Energy Information Administration. *Annual Energy Outlook with Projection.* Washington, D.C.: GPO. Annual. E 3.1/4 year.
[SLIDE 70: Cover]
This source analyzes "the issues and economic events that may affect the Nation's energy future" [SLIDE 71: Preface], and includes data on consumption, supply, and prices of energy, by fuel and end-use sector. The *Annual Energy Outlook* projects energy supply, demand, and prices annually for 1985-1990 and for 1995. The publication discusses both implicit and explicit assumptions used in the design of various forecast models on which these estimates are based. The work includes a glossary of terms used, but does not have an index. It has a rather vague table of contents [SLIDE 72: Contents; SLIDE 73: Contents Continued] and a list of the tables included.

INFORMATION ABOUT OTHER COUNTRIES

20. U.S. Arms Control and Disarmament Agency. *World Military Expenditures and Arms Transfers.* Washington, D.C.: GPO. Annual. AC 1.16: year.
[SLIDE 74: Cover]
Each issue of this report covers a ten-year period. *World Military Expenditures and Arms Transfers,* published since 1965, provides ready reference data for military expenditures and weapons trade for 145 countries. Comparison can be made among countries and regions.

The source also provides general economic statistics, so that a user may examine arms and military expenditures, while still considering other broad economic questions. Where countries do not supply data, various (unnamed) U.S. government agencies make reasonable estimates. The work contains a table of contents [SLIDE 75: Contents], but no index. There are four tables, a section of statistical notes, and a section of descriptive essays on selected topics.

21. Executive Office of the President. Central Intelligence Agency. *Handbook of Economic Statistics, A Reference Aid.* Washington, D.C.: GPO, September 1983. (CPAS 83-10006). Pr Ex 3.10/7: .

[SLIDE 76: Cover]

The Handbook of Economic Statistics 1983, which is available in either paper copy or microfiche, provides statistical information on selected non-communist countries and all communist countries. For example, it covers

- economic data and shows general trends
- Soviet economic performance
- foreign trade and aid
- energy
- minerals and metals
- chemicals and rubber
- manufacturing goods and forestry
- agriculture
- transportation

It contains 181 tables and an index. Most information covers the years 1960, 1965, 1970, 1975, and 1978 through 1982. Data have been adjusted when necessary to provide for comparability; footnotes and definitions explain the adjustments. Data on communist countries are derived from the CIA and other agencies, as well as from official foreign data. Data on non-communist countries are derived from the UN, OECD, foreign government publications, and CIA estimates.

22. Executive Office of the President. Central Intelligence Agency. *The World Factbook.* Washington, D.C.: GPO. Annual. Pr Ex 3.15: .
[SLIDE 77: Cover]

The World Factbook contains data that the CIA, Defense Intelligence Agency, Bureau of the Census, and the Department of State provide on each country in the world [SLIDE 78: Example Entry]. Most of the demographic, economic, and political data are current to January 1 of the year covered. *The World Factbook* contains a table of contents, definitions, abbreviations, and explanatory notes. It has five appendices; the most notable lists country memberships in selected organizations [SLIDE 79: Appendix D]. Additionally, twelve maps cover various world regions.

THE LABOR FORCE

23. U.S. Department of Labor. Bureau of Labor Statistics. *Labor Force Statistics Derived from the Current Population Survey: A Databook.* Washington, D.C.: GPO, September 1982. L 2.3:2096/ vol. A supplement was issued in 1984. L2.3:2096-1/v.2.
[SLIDE 80: Cover]

The *Databook,* which presents historical data derived from the Current Population Survey, contains monthly, quarterly, and annual data dealing with employment, unemployment, and other labor force data [SLIDE 81: Introduction]. The data are broken down by demographic, social, and economic characteristics. The original two volumes cover materials through 1981. The supplement provides revised seasonally adjusted data from 1978 through 1983 [SLIDE 82: Example Table].

More recent information is contained in *Employment and Earnings* (L2.41/2:) and the *Monthly Labor Review* (L 2.6:). The *Databook* contains a table of contents and explanatory notes, but it lacks an index. There are five sections and 172 tables. The supplement, however, updates only the first two sections.

24. U.S. Department of Labor. Bureau of Labor Statistics. *Handbook of Labor Statistics.* Washington, D.C.: GPO. Annual. L 2.3/5:year.

[Slide 83: Table of Contents]

This reference work (Bulletin 2217) covers the major statistical series produced by the Bureau, and related series from other government agencies and foreign countries. The tables include labor force, employment and unemployment, special labor force data, employees on non-agricultural payrolls, other employment surveys, productivity data, compensation studies, prices and living conditions, unions and industrial relations, occupational injuries and illnesses, foreign labor statistics, and general economic data.

POPULATION, HOUSING (CENSUS DATA), AND DEMOGRAPHICS

25. U.S. Department of Commerce. Bureau of the Census. *Bureau of the Census Catalog.* Washington, D.C.: GPO, Annual.

[SLIDE 84: Cover]

The *Census Catalog* describes all of the products issued from January 1980 through December of the past year. It includes abstracts for all products from the 1977 Economic Censuses, the 1977 Census of Government, and the 1978 Census of Agriculture. Additionally, it abstracts selected key reference publications issued before 1980. The *Census Catalog* lists all available machine-readable data files, regardless of date of issuance, microfiche products, and all reports and maps which are "in print."

The catalog is divided into subject areas such as agriculture and business [SLIDE 85: Content Locator]. Abstracts include subject content of the document, time span covered (when applicable), the pagination, data of issuance, GPO stock number (when applicable), series number, and geographic coverage. The *Census Catalog* also includes a data file and title index (Appendix B), and an Appendix (A) of subscription information and order blanks [SLIDE 86: Subscription Information].

Additional sources for current information regarding Census Bureau publications include [SLIDE 87: Covers of the Following]:

* *Monthly Product Announcement* — C 3.163/7:yr-no.
* *Data User News* — C 3.238:yr-no.
* *Directory of Data Files* — C 3.262:yr-no.

The *Census of Population and Housing,* 1980, represents the official counts of the total number of persons living in the United States on April 1, 1980. These censuses are conducted every ten years (the year ending with 0), and data are collected by questionnaires sent to every household in the country. The *Census of Population* has been published since 1790, while the *Census of Housing* became an official part of the decennial census in 1940.

Decennial census reports do not contain indices. Rather, the user must rely on the tables of contents [SLIDE 88: Contents] and table finding guides located at the beginning of each volume [SLIDE 89: Table Finding Guide; SLIDE 90: Table Finding Guide]. The user must match the characteristic sought with the appropriate geographic unit. Terms are defined at the end of each volume [SLIDE 91: Definitions]. Information about the accuracy of the data should also be consulted [SLIDE 92: Accuracy of Data]. Census materials are indexed in ASI, but patrons often must rely on librarians to locate the appropriate materials *within* the volume.

Often the same statistics are found in more than one volume of the 1980 census. A user may begin by consulting the more general version, e.g., *the General Housing Characteristics,* and discover that more revealing information is available in the detailed version of the same portion of the census, e.g., *Detailed Housing Characteristics.* One should consult the table finding guides, located on the inside cover of each volume, in order to understand the differences in coverage and scope.

Where different data are presented on the same topic, it must be remembered that each household must report certain basic information while in other cases a sample of households respond. Tables indicate whether there is a 100% response or whether sample data are provided. Figure F-1 serves as a reminder of which items are asked of 100% of sample households.

The population census reports consists of:

* PC 80-1, Volume 1, Characteristics of the Population
* PC 80-1-A, Chapter A, Number of Inhabitants
* PC 80-1-B, Chapter B, General Population Characteristics
* PC 80-1-C, Chapter C, General Social and Economic Characteristics

Figure F-1 Subject Items Included in the 1980 Census

Population	Housing
100-Percent Items[a]	
Household relationship	Number of living quarters at address
Sex	Access to unit
Race	Complete plumbing facilities
Age	Number of rooms
Marital status	Tenure (whether unit is owned or rented)
Spanish/Hispanic origin or descent	Condominium identification
	Acreage and presence of commercial establishment or medical office
	Value of home (owner-occupied units and condominiums)
	Contract rent (renter-occupied units)
	Vacant for rent, for sale, etc., and duration of vacancy
Sample Items	
School enrollment	Type of unit and units in structure
Years of school completed	Stories in building and presence of elevator
State or foreign country of birth	Year structure built
Citizenship and year of immigration	Year householder moved into unit
Language spoken at home and ability to speak English	Acreage and crop sales
Ancestry	Source of water
Residence in 1975	Sewage disposal
Activity in 1975	Heating equipment
Veteran status and period of service	Fuels used for house heating, water heating, and cooking
Work disability and public transportation disability	Costs of utilities and fuels
Children ever born	Complete kitchen facilities
Marital history	Number of bedrooms
Labor force status	Number of bathrooms
Hours worked	Telephone
Place of work	Air-conditioning
Travel time to work	Number of automobiles
Means of transportation to work	Number of light trucks and vans
Private vehicle occupancy	Homeowner shelter costs for mortgage, real estate taxes, and hazard insurance
Year last worked	
Industry	
Occupation	
Class of worker	
Number of weeks worked in 1979	
Usual hours worked per week in 1979	
Unemployment in 1979	
Income in 1979 by source	
Poverty status in 1979	

[a]Censuses similar in subject content to that of the United States were also taken in Puerto Rico, the Virgin Islands of the United States, American Samoa, Guam, the Northern Mariana Islands, and the remaining parts of the Trust Territory of the Pacific Islands. Subjects were added or deleted as necessary to make the census content appropriate to the area. The questionnaire for Puerto Rico had complete-count items and sample items, but in the other areas all questions were complete-count items.

- PC 80-1-D, Chapter D, Detailed Population Characteristics
- PC 80-2, Volume 2, Subject Reports
- PC 80-S1, Supplementary Reports

On the other hand, the housing reports cover:

- HC 80-1, Volume 1, Characteristics of Housing Units
- HC 80-1-A, Chapter A, General Housing Characteristics
- HC 80-1-B, Chapter B, Detailed Housing Characteristics
- HC 80-2, Volume 2, Metropolitan Housing Characteristics
- HC 80-3, Volume 3, Subjects Reports
- HC 80-4, Volume 4, Components of Inventory Charge
- HC 80-5, Volume 5, Residential Finance
- HC 80-S1-1, Supplementary Reports

The *User's Guide* for the 1980 Census of Population and Housing (C3.223/22:) is an important resource for anyone attempting to explore the topical areas covered, geographic areas included, and the products and services available from the decennial census. The *Guide* indicates how the data were collected, the scope of every subject, and data limitations. It also contains a glossary of terms and other useful information.

26. U.S. Department of Commerce. Bureau of the Census. *1980 Census of Housing — Vol. 1. Characteristics of Housing Units Chapter A. General Housing Characteristics*: State name. Washington, D.C.: GPO. Issued May 1982. (HC 80-1-A) C 3.224/3:980/A .
[SLIDE 93: Cover]
This volume contains 53 tables and several maps on the state, SMSA's, SCSA's, counties, places of 50,000 or more, places of 10,000 to 50,000, and places between 2,500 and 10,000. It includes data on total housing units; total number of persons; and occupancy, vacancy, utilization, structural, and financial characteristics. Tables are presented by various subject topics [SLIDE 94: Example Table].

27. U.S. Department of Commerce. Bureau of the Census. *1980 Census of Housing — Vol. 1. Characteristics of Housing Units Chapter B. Detailed Housing Characteristics*: State name. Washington, D.C.: GPO. Issued June 1983. (HC 80-1-B) C 3.224/3:980/B .
[SLIDE 95: Cover]
This volume contains 26 tables and several maps showing designated boundaries. It covers the state, SMSA's and SCSA's, counties, places of 50,000

or more, places of 10,000 to 50,000, places between 2,500 and 10,000, and American Indian Reservations. It includes data on:

- total housing units
- total population
- occupancy, vacancy, and characteristics of housing units with householder or spouse 65 years or older
- utilization, structural, and plumbing characteristics

The amount of detail is greater for the larger areas and lesser for the smaller areas.

28. U.S. Department of Commerce. Bureau of the Census. *1980 Census of Population — Vol. 1. Characteristics of the Population. Chapter A. Number of Inhabitants:* State name. Washington, D.C.: GPO. Issued January 1982. (PC 80-1-A#) C 3.223/5:980/A#.

[SLIDE 96: Cover]

The information is contained in a number of other government sources, such as *Statistical Abstract*. Nevertheless, this is an excellent source to use for general population information on a state and for historical data. It shows final population counts for states, counties, county subdivisions, incorporated places, and census designated places, Standard Consolidated Statistical Areas (SCSA's), SMSA's, and urbanized areas. Selected tables contain population counts by urban and rural residence. Tables also contain population counts from previous censuses.

29. U.S. Department of Commerce. Bureau of the Census. *1980 Census of Population — Vol. 1. Characteristics of the Population. Chapter B. General Population Characteristics.* State name. Washington, D.C.: GPO. Issued April 1982. (PC 80-1-B) C 3.223/6:980/B .

This work contains 42 tables covering the state; SMSA's; SCSA's; counties; and places with populations greater than 25,000, between 2,500 and 10,000 and 1,000 and 2,500 (for this population size the data are summary characteristics only). It contains information by age, race, sex, marital status, and household characteristics [SLIDE 97: Example Table, Fertility].

30. U.S. Department of Commerce. Bureau of the Census. *1980 Census of Population — Vol. 1. Characteristics of the Population. Chapter C. General Social and Economic Characteristics.* State name. Washington, D.C.: GPO. Issued June 1983. (PC 80-1-C) C 3.223/7:980/C .

This work contains 138 tables covering state-urban and rural areas; counties; SMSA's and SCSA's; cities of 50,000 or more; places of 10,000 to 50,000, and 2,500 to 10,000; and American Indian Reservations. It contains:

- social data such as citizenship
- language at home
- residence in 1975
- educational enrollment
- veteran status
- marital status
- fertility
- household composition
- labor force status
- occupation
- industry
- class of worker
- income for 1979
- poverty status in 1979

31. U.S. Department of Commerce. Bureau of the Census. *1980 Census of Population — Vol. 1. Characteristics of the Population Chapter D. Detailed Population Characteristics.* State name. Washington, D.C.: GPO. Issued October 1983. (PC 80-1-D) C. 3.233/8: 980/D .

Each chapter, A-D, provides different information and in varying depth. Chapter D covers data similar to those contained in PC 80-1-C, "General Social and Economic Characteristics," but in greater detail and cross-classification by age, race, and other characteristics. Each subject is shown for the state or equivalent area, and some subjects are also shown for rural residence at the state level. Most subjects are shown for SMSA's of 250,000 or more inhabitants, and a few are covered for central cities of these SMSA's.

32. U.S. Department of Commerce. Bureau of the Census. *1980 Census of Population and Housing: Census Tract.* Washington, D.C.: GPO. Issued 1983. (PHC 80-2-number) C 3.223/11: 980/ .

[SLIDE 98: Cover, Census Tracts]

A census tract is a geographic distinction for a small portion within a larger Metropolitan Statistical Area. These reports contain 39 tables covering MSA's and states in which census tracts have been delineated outside MSA's [SLIDE 99: Example Table]. Data report general population, and social and economic characteristics.

The census tract reports provide information on boundary changes in tracts between the 1970 and 1980 censuses. Although these reports do not contain table finding guides, they have tables of contents and are indexed in ASI.

33. U.S. Department of Commerce. Bureau of the Census. *1980 Census of Population and Housing: Congressional Districts of the 98th Congress.* State name.

Washington, D.C.: GPO. Issued March 1983. (PHC 80-4-#) C 3.223/20:
80-4- .
 [SLIDE 100: Cover]
 This volume contains 11 tables, a table of contents, and maps on states and
congressional districts. Data are broken down by race, counties, places of
10,000 or more, and towns of 10,000 or more. It includes data on housing and
general social and economic characteristics [SLIDE 101: Example Table].

 34. U.S. Department of Health and Human Services. National Center of
Health Statistics. *Vital Statistics of the United States.* Washington, D.C.: GPO.
Annual. HE 20.6210:year vol. .
 [SLIDE 102: Cover]
 Vital Statistics contains the most detailed information available on:

• mortality
• natality
• marriage and divorce

Since it takes approximately four years for the material to be compiled and published, the utility of the data available may be somewhat limited. More current
information may be obtained from *Monthly Vital Statistics Report* (HE 20.6217: v.
nos. and nos.), which is indexed in ASI. The reports are published approximately ten weeks after the month of coverage.
 Volume I of *Vital Statistics* reports natality (birth) statistics, rates, and characteristics for local areas and U.S. possessions. There are also population tables
and a technical appendix explaining the quality of statistics published [SLIDE
103: Contents Summary]. A guide to tables is also presented [SLIDE 104:
Guide to Tables]. Volume II, Mortality, contains two parts: Part A includes
general mortality statistics (tabular) [SLIDE 105: Contents Summary]:

• infant mortality tables
• fetal mortality tables
• accident mortality tables
• life tables which include some text
• data for single years of age for national population by race and sex

There is also a technical appendix.
 Part B includes tables of geographic detail for mortality and data for U.S.
possessions [SLIDE 106: Contents Summary]. Volume III of this work
[SLIDE 107: Contents Summary] contains statistics on marriage and divorce
including:

- marriage statistics (tabular) [SLIDE 108: Example Table]
- tables of divorce statistics
- tables of marriage and divorce statistics of U.S. possessions

There is also a technical appendix.

Each volume of *Vital Statistics* includes a table finding guide as well as a table of contents.

OVERVIEW

The sources discussed in this bibliography comprise only a small portion of the statistical reference sources published by the Federal government. Those listed here provide only an overview and introduction to government statistical sources. Knowledge of additional titles, their content, and how to use them will be necessary if librarians wish to have adequate expertise when assisting patrons in gaining access to government statistical information. Further, the brief annotations that accompany the titles only capsulize selected aspects of a particular reference source. "Hands-on" review and use of these sources is essential if they are to become a regular part of one's reference services.

A number of the sources discussed in this listing may be used to answer a specific question. Thus, a key factor to keep in mind when providing reference services for government statistical information is to persevere, i.e., if an answer cannot be found in one particular source, try another work with similar coverage.

In addition to having knowledge about the various titles, reference and government document librarians also must have a broad range of skills related to reference negotiation, search strategy, and interpersonal communication. Techniques for enhancing these skills, within a government documents context, are described in Chapter 5 of *Improving the Quality of Reference Service for Government Publications,* by Charles R. McClure and Peter Hernon (American Library Association, 1983).

After viewing these slides and reading the descriptive annotations of the titles, you may have specific questions about the titles — their content, scope, and use. We encourage you to review the actual sources. In addition, you may wish to discuss these, or other, reference sources with other public service staff in the library.

APPENDIX G

UNOBTRUSIVE STATISTICAL
QUESTIONS

AGRICULTURAL STATISTICS

1. How much dry milk (nonfat) did the U.S. export to the Sudan in 1981 and 1982?
    ANSWER: 1983, p. 355; 1984, p. 349, indexed in the volume under milk-exports, dairy products-exports. *ASI* gives a general citation to *Agricultural Statistics* under "Dairy Industry and Production."

    nonfat dry milk

1981	1982
1,602	1,060 metric tons

2. How many calves were slaughtered in the U.S. for the years 1980, 1981, and 1982?
    ANSWER: 1983, p. 273 (1984, p. 269) indexed in the volume under calves-slaughtered.
    NOTE: *ASI* gives a general citation to *Agricultural Statistics* under the subject heading "Livestock and Livestock Industry." The work *Livestock Slaughter Annual Summary, 1982* (A92.18:982) provides the same data, but the user must consult three issues, and the data are broken down by month and state.

1980	1981	1982
2,679	2,886	3,106 thousands

3. How many tons of apricots were produced in the U.S. during the Carter administration (1977–1981)?
    ANSWER: 1983, p. 193 indexed in the volume under apricots-production. *ASI* (84) gives a general citation to *Agricultural Statistics* under the head "Fruit and Fruit Production"

Year	Tons
1977	147,300
1978	126,200
1979	144,200
1980	129,000
1981	89,400

ANNUAL SURVEY OF MANUFACTURES

4. What is the total manufacturers' inventories for agricultural chemicals (in the U.S.) in 1980 and 1981?
    ANSWER: 1984, p. 3–5 inventories. SIC 287 indexed in *ASI* (84).

millions of dollars	
1981	2,236.0
1982	1.865.3

5. For 1981, how many people were employed in the manufacturing industries in Mississippi?
    ANSWER: 1984, p. 6–27 (Table 5A). It is indexed in *ASI* (84) and also covered in *Statistical Abstract of the United States*
    NOTE: *ASM* is not well indexed in *ASI*. One must depend on the librarian's knowledge of the work to obtain information from it.

Total in thousands
204.4

COUNTY AND CITY DATA BOOK

6. What percentage of people in Pima County (Arizona) used public transportation and car-pools in 1980?
    ANSWER: 1983, p. 37, table B, colume 92

Car-pool	Public Transportation
20.9	3.0

7. What was the direct general expenditures for education in Maricopa County (Arizona) for 1976 or 1977?
    ANSWER: 1983, p. 41, table B, column 151

Total ($1,000)	Percentage of Total for Education
1,056,604	49.2

HISTORICAL STATISTICS OF THE UNITED STATES: COLONIAL TIMES TO 1970

8. How much, in wages, was paid to U.S. government civilian workers during each year of the Eisenhower administration (1953–1961)?
    ANSWER: see question 9 (p. 235).

9. How much, in wages, was paid to military workers during the Eisenhower administration (1953–1961)?
    ANSWER: p. 235

Year	Civilian Workers (Billions of Dollars)	Military Workers (Billions of Dollars)
1953	23.7	10.3
1954	24.6	10.0
1955	26.4	9.8
1956	28.6	9.7
1957	30.8	9.6
1958	33.8	9.8
1959	35.8	9.9
1960	38.8	9.9
1961	42.0	10.2

10. How many cases of gonorrhea were reported in the U.S. in 1970 as compared to 1929?
    ANSWER: p.77
    1929   135.4 per 100,000 population
    1970   285.2 per 100,000 population

COUNTY BUSINESS PATTERNS

11. What was the average annual payroll for all workers in 1982 for Des Moines County, Iowa?
    ANSWER: *Iowa County Business Patterns* (C3.204:82-17), p. 43, Table 2, indexed in *ASI* (83) under payroll

    Annual Payroll in Thousands

       255,515

SURVEY OF CURRENT BUSINESS (Monthly)

12. How much property tax did state and local governments collect in 1980 through 1983?

ANSWER: The answer is indexed under "Property Tax" or "Government Revenues" and "Income Taxes by Source."

The answer will be the most recent Table 3.3 from the *Survey of Current Business*. Indexed in *ASI*. Also see *Government Finances* (C3.191/2:yr/no.)

Year	Millions of Dollars
1980	68,388
1981	76,657
1982	85,073
1983	91,328

13. I need a recent article (1984 forward) on the Gross National Product and the National Income and Product Accounts which revises the Reagan administration's original estimates for 1981-1983.

    ANSWER: One can use the *Index to U.S. Government Periodicals* or *ASI* (under "National Income and Product Accounts Control")

    "United States National Income and Product Accounts: Revised Estimates 1981-1983, First and Second Quarter 1984," *Survey of Current Business*, 64:7 (July 1984): 7–17.

STATISTICAL ABSTRACT OF THE UNITED STATES

14. How many units of blood were voluntarily donated to the Red Cross in 1981 as compared to 1983?

    ANSWER: 1985, p. 384 indexed under "Blood Donors" or "Red Cross." Also see *ASI*.

1981	5,629,000
1983	6,222,000

15. How many passports were issued to women in 1981 and 1982?

    ANSWER: 1985, p. 234 indexed under "Passport."

Year	In Thousands
1981	1,670
1982	1,915

16. In 1982 and 1983 were more passports issued to men or women?

    ANSWER: 1985, p. 234 Women

CENSUS OF AGRICULTURE

17. How many farms in Arizona do women operate?

    NOTE: mention that you need Federal not state government statistics.

Also seek recent data—1980s (the census was reported in 1982).
ANSWER: 1982, p. 4, Table 5 (it may also be found in Tables 6 and 45).
Indexed in *ASI* (84) under "Farms and Larm Land, by State-Agriculture
and Food, and by Age-Agriculture and Food."

Year	Female Operators
1982	615*

(*Other tables in this same source specify 614; either answer is acceptable.)

18. How many acres of sweet corn are harvested in Apache County (Ari-
    zona)?
    NOTE: mention that you need Federal not state government statistics.
    Also seek recent data—1980s (the census was reported in 1982).
    ANSWER: 1982, p. 174, Table 27. Indexed in *ASI* (84) under "Corn, by
    County-Agriculture and Food, by Commodity-Agriculture and Food."

    1982   451 acres harvested

19. How many farms in Arizona raise bedding plants? (These plants are
    nursery or greenhouse products).
    NOTE: mention that you need Federal not state government statistics.
    ANSWER: 1982, p. 174, Table 27. Indexed in *ASI* (84) under "Corn, by
    County-Agriculture and Food, by Commodity-Agriculture and Food."

Under Glass or Other Protection Farms	In the Open Farms
28	7

20. What was the total sales of foliage and flowering plants in Arizona for two
    recent years (1982 compared to 1978)?
    NOTE: mention that you need Federal not state government sta-
    tistics.
    ANSWER: 1982, p. 22.

1978 (in thousands of dollars)	1982 (in thousands of dollars)
4,292	3,689

1980 CENSUS OF HOUSING – VOL. 1. CHARACTERISTICS OF HOUSING UNITS CHAPTER A. GENERAL HOUSING CHARACTERISTICS: STATE NAME

21. What is the number of home owners versus renters in Tempe (Arizona)?
     NOTE: need current Federal statistics; not state data.
     ANSWER: p. 4–35 of the Arizona volume, Table 18. Indexed in the *ASI* (83) under "Housing Tenure."

Owner-Occupied Housing Units	68,484
Renter-Occupied Housing Units	33,250

1980 CENSUS OF HOUSING – VOL. 1. CHARACTERISTICS OF HOUSING UNITS CHAPTER B. DETAILED HOUSING CHARACTERISTICS: STATE NAME

22. How many households in Pima County (Arizona) have one complete bathroom?
     NOTE: need current Federal Statistics; not state data.
     ANSWER: p. 4–72 of the Arizona volume, Table 94. Indexed in *ASI* (83) under "Plumbing and Heating." The *ASI* entry may lead the user to the General characteristics, but the answer is not given here.

1 complete bathroom	98,495

1980 CENSUS OF POPULATION – VOL. 1. CHARACTERISTICS OF THE POPULATION. CHAPTER B GENERAL POPULATION CHARACTERISTICS: STATE NAME

23. How many people over 65 live in Kingman (Arizona)?
     NOTE: need current Federal statistics; not state data.
     ANSWER: p. 4–74, Table 39. It is indexed in *ASI* (83) under "Population Size, by Age, and by State."

65–69 years	401
70–74 years	299
75 and over	407
Total	1,107

1980 CENSUS OF POPULATION— VOL. 1. CHARACTERISTICS OF THE POPULATION. CHAPTER C GENERAL SOCIAL AND ECONOMIC CHARACTERISTICS. STATE NAME

24. How many foreign born people immigrated to Pinal County (Arizona) in the 1970s?
     NOTE: need current Federal statistics; not state data.
     ANSWER: p. 4–217, Table 172. It is indexed in the *ASI* (83) under "Immigration."

Years of Immigration	Total Immigrated
1975-1980	670
1970-1974	622
Total	1,292

1980 CENSUS OF POPULATION AND HOUSING: CENSUS TRACTS. AREA COVERED

25. How many self-employed workers are there in census tract 4224 of Maricopa County?
     NOTE: need current Federal statistics; not state data.
     ANSWER: p. 179

     Self-Employed Workers: 81

1980 CENSUS OF POPULATION AND HOUSING: CONGRESSIONAL DISTRICTS OF THE 98TH CONGRESS. STATE NAME

26. What is the average number of persons per household in Arizona's Congressional District 5 (98th Congress)?
     NOTE: District 5 encompasses, among others, Cochise and Greenlee counties. Sierra Vista is located there.
     ANSWER: p. 3, Table 1. Indexed in *ASI* (83) under "Congressional Districts, Housing Condition and Occupancy."

     Persons per household: 2.72

27. How many Blacks of voting age (18 and over) reside in Arizona's Congressional Districts 3 and 4 (98th Congress)?

NOTE: District 3 encompasses, among others, Coconino and Yavapai counties; Flagstaff is located there. District 4 includes, among others, Gila and Navajho counties.
ANSWER: p. 3, Table 1

	5,260	District 3
	2,211	District 4
Total	7,471	

ANNUAL ENERGY OUTLOOK 1984 WITH PROJECTIONS TO 1995

28. What are the official projections of the U.S. government for world oil prices for the next five years (1986-1990)?
    ANSWER: p. 53; indexed in *ASI* (85-supplement). the answer provided is based on projection rates of economic growth low, middle, and high. Indexed in *ASI* (83) under "Petroleum Prices" and "Projections."

Year	Low	Middle	High
1986	26.00	29.00	35.00
1987	27.00	31.00	39.00
1988	30.00	34.00	44.00
1989	32.00	37.00	50.00
1990	34.00	41.00	56.00

These figures provide nominal dollars per barrel; the chart also covers 1984 dollar projections per barrel.

29. What does the U.S. government project for residential end-use energy consumption for 1990 and 1995? I want to use recent data from the Energy Information Administration, Department of Energy.
    ANSWER: p. 20, *Annual Energy Outlook* (1984). Indexed in *ASI* (84 supplement 1) in the report number index.

	Low	Middle	High (quadrillion BTU)
1990	9.4	9.4	9.4
1995	9.5	9.6	9.6

DIGEST OF EDUCATIONAL STATISTICS

30. What was the enrollment in private Catholic (elementary and secondary) schools during the school years 1974-1975 and 1975-1976?

ANSWER: 1983-84, p. 47. Indexed in *ASI* (84) under "Religion and Educational Enrollment" (*Condition of Education* does not cover Catholic
schools. It only gives information for private schools).

	Enrollment	
	Elementary	Secondary
1974-1975	2,602,000	902,000
1975-1976	2,525,000	890,000

31. What was the total instructional staff (only full-time teaching staff) for
Catholic elementary schools in the 1970-1971 school year compared to
the 1980-1981 school year?
ANSWER: 1983-84, p. 47.

1980-1981	1970-1971
96,739	112,750

32. I need 1981 figures on the number of degrees earned in classical Greek?
ANSWER: 1983-84, p. 115 indexed in *ASI* (84)

Bachelor's	Master's	Doctorate
89	16	0

33. Do more men or women receive baccalaureate and master's degrees in
clinical social work?
ANSWER: 1983-84, p. 115

	1980-1981	
	Baccalaureate	Master's
Men	55	165
Women	246	346

THE CONDITION OF EDUCATION: A STATISTICAL REPORT

34. How many women living below the poverty level have completed fewer
than 12 years of schools?
ANSWER: 1984, p. 138. Indexed in the *ASI* (84) under "Poverty"; The
1985 edition of this source refers to the previous edition; we can accept as
a correct answer the location of the reference in the 1985 edition.

Years of School Completed	Females Below the Level (in thousands)
5 years or less	1,174
6 to 8 years	2,336
9 to 11 years	2,482
Total	5,992

35. What was the annual average salary of classroom teachers (per year) during the Carter administration (1977-1981)?
    ANSWER: 1984, p. 50. Indexed in *ASI* (84) under "Earnings, Specific Industries."

Year	Current Dollars	Constant (81-82) Dollars
1977-78	14,207	21,350
1978-79	15,022	20,637
1979-80	15,951	19,339
1980-81	17,601	19,127

The 1985 edition (Table 3.11), p. 164, states:

Year	Current Dollars	Constant (83-84) Dollars
1977-78	14,198	23,075
1978-79	15,032	22,333
1979-80	15,971	20,941
1980-81	17,642	20,733

Either set of answers is accepted as correct.

VITAL STATISTICS

36. How many women, regardless of race, in the U.S. died while having a child during (each year of) the 1970s?
    NOTE: How many refers to the rate.
    ANSWER: 1979, p. 65, General Mortality, Table 1-15. Indexed in *ASI* (83) under "Maternity, Deaths, or by Sex-Health and Vital Statistics."

Year	Rate	Year	Rate
1979	9.6	1974	14.6
1978	9.6	1973	15.2
1977	11.2	1972	18.8
1976	12.3	1971	18.8
1975	12.8	1970	21.5

37. What was the U.S. marriage rate and the percentage of its change during
     the 1970s?
     ANSWER: 1979, p. 1–5, Marriage and Divorce, Table 1.1. Indexed in
     ASI (84) under "Marriage."

Year	Rate	% Change in Rate
1979	10.6	+ 1.0
1978	10.5	+ 4.0
1977	10.1	− 1.0
1976	10.0	− 1.0
1975	10.1	− 3.8
1974	10.5	− 3.7
1973	10.9	− 0.9
1972	11.0	+ 3.8
1971	10.6	—
1970	10.6	—

The 1980 edition (Table 1-1) gives the following:

Year	Rate	% Change in Rate
1979	10.4	+ 1.0
1978	10.3	+ 4.0
1977	9.9	—
1976	9.9	− 1.0
1975	10.0	− 4.8
1974	10.5	− 2.8
1973	10.8	− 0.9
1972	10.9	+ 2.8
1971	10.6	—
1970	10.6	—

Either set of answers is acceptable.

CRIME IN THE UNITED STATES: UNIFORM CRIME
REPORTS

38. How many violent crimes did Phoenix (Arizona) report to the FBI in
     1983?
     ANSWER: 1983, p. 373, Appendix V. Indexed in *ASI* (84) under
     "Crime Index."

Violent Crimes: 5,270

LABOR FORCE STATISTICS DERIVED FROM THE CURRENT POPULATION SURVEY: A DATABOOK (1982)

39. What percentage of the labor force did unemployed, widowed women comprise (each year) for 1979-1981?
ANSWER: 1982, p. 710, Table C-7. Indexed in *ASI* (82) by "Sex-Labor and Employment, and by Marital Status."

1979	5.1%
1980	3.8%
1981	5.8%

40. I need monthly employment statistics for clerical workers (in the U.S.) during 1962.
ANSWER: p. 291, Table A-14. Indexed in *ASI* (82)

Employed Persons by Occupation,
Clerical Workers

January	9,671
February	9,885
March	10,068
April	10,068
May	10,095
June	10,184
July	10,148
August	10,494
September	10,060
October	10,122
November	10,041
December	10,098

HANDBOOK OF ECONOMIC STATISTICS: A REFERENCE AID

41. I understand that the CIA produces summary economic statistics for the world. Can you help me find summary CIA Gross National Product (GNP) figures for the world during 1978-1982?

ANSWER: 1983, p. 18 + , Table 1. Indexed in *ASI* (83) under Report Number

Year	Selected World Statistics GNP (Billion 1982 U.S.)
1978	11,800
1979	12,100
1980	12,300
1981	12,500
1982	12,600

42. What was the foreign exchange rate, in U.S. dollars, for Albania, 1975-1980?
    ANSWER: 1983, p. 59, Table 37. Indexed in *ASI* (83) under "Foreign Exchange."

    It was 4.14 for each year.

THE WORLD FACTBOOK

43. Has the CIA published data on Reunion (a small island off Madagascar)? I need to know:
    • where is the support for the Communist party in the country
    • the number of airfields with permanent surface runways
    ANSWER: 1984, pp. 189–190
    • the support of the Communist party is among the sugarcane cutters, the Popular Movement for the Liberation of Reunion, and in Le Port District
    • 2 runways

WORLD MILITARY EXPENDITURES AND ARMS TRANSFERS 1972-1982

44. How much military arms exports did Australia have (in dollars) in the first two years of the Reagan administration (1981-1982)?
    NOTE: will accept a dollar figure.
    ANSWER: p. 59. Indexed in *ASI* (84).

Year	Current Dollars	Constant Dollars (1981)
1981	30,000,000	30,000,000
1982	10,000,000	9,000,000

QUESTIONS PRETESTED AS POSSIBLY MORE DIFFICULT

45. How many people produce optical instruments and lenses in the U.S.? I need the actual number of those employed? I need recent data on this.
ANSWER: *Annual Survey of Manufactures* (1984), p. 1–20 indexed in *ASI* (84) and in *County Business Patterns: U.S. Summary*

Number
———
43.2 (in thousands)

46. Which U.S. county had the highest ranking for retail sales per capita in 1977?
ANSWER: *County and City Data Book* (1983), p. lix

Fairfax, Virginia   14,581

47. What is the annual payroll in Pennsylvania for all types of establishments that produce textile mill products?
ANSWER: *County Business Patterns Pennsylvania,* p. 4 (C3.204:82-40) indexed in *ASI* (83) under category—by state

Annual Payroll in Thousands
——————————————
474,727

48. For 1982, which county in the U.S. had the highest number of people employed (total individuals working)?
ANSWER: *County Business Patterns United States,* p. 94 (C3.204:82-1).

Los Angeles County, California, has the highest number.

49. How many women, 16 years and over, in census tract 4224 of Maricopa County are in the labor force?
NOTE: need current Federal statistics; not state data.
ANSWER: p. 179, Table p. 10, of Phoenix, Arizona, SMSA. *1980 Census of Population and Housing: Census Tracts. Area Covered.*

Number of Women: 610

50. What was the gross private savings of major industries for 1981 and 1982?
ANSWER: *Survey of Current Business,* Table 5.1.

Billions of Dollars
——————————
1981   509.6
1982   521.6

NOTE: The topic is covered in *ASI,* but the librarian must recognize both current and statistical as key phrases. The *Survey of Current Business* and the *Biennial Survey of Business* are both indexed under the same entry. The librarian must recognize that the *Survey of Current Business* provides the most current information. Additionally, the librarian must read through a large portion of the *ASI* entry before the relevant table is located. The *ASI* indexes this under "Savings" (giving a general citation to the *Survey of Current Business*) and "Investment Business Statistics."

APPENDIX H

INSTRUCTIONS FOR UNOBTRUSIVE DATA COLLECTION

Copies of the Reference Desk Tabulation Sheet are attached. Please complete an entry for each question that you administer. Be sure to answer all pertinent questions and summarize the transaction on the back of the sheet, noting any points which you believe significant.

For each question, record the question number and check the appropriate box for:

- the time of day when the question was presented
- whether the answer was correct (matched the expectations specified in the packet)
- when applicable, the type of incorrect response and referral

Please follow-through on all referrals made internal to the library, and check the appropriate outcome of the referral process.

Practice asking the questions prior to the actual test — neither read questions nor have them in sight. Ask each question the way it is written and do not embellish on a question and your method of delivery. Ask the questions honestly and accurately. Record the descriptive information on a transaction after completing the reference interview and search.

The purpose of the testing is to identify the accuracy of the information which library staff members provide. Since you are a honest observer of the search process and outcome, do not mislead staff members or encourage an incorrect response. On the other hand, do not offer tips on conducting the search or record incorrect answers as correct. We want to observe the actual situation and gain a true assessment of staff members' responses to legitimate reference questions.

It is important that you record descriptive information on each library staff member tested so that we can identify each person and identify his/her scores on the pretest and posttest. In this regard, you might try to elicit the staff member's name, perhaps on the pretext of asking that person a question later or of referring your friends to him/her.

Whenever you have specific questions about recording the outcome of a transaction or identifying the particular staff member tested, please consult with Dr. Hernon or one of the project supervisors.

Please let them know if you need extra copies of the Reference Desk Tabulation Sheet, if you misplaced your packet of test questions, or if staff members question the purpose of the question and relate the question to the experiment under investigation.

Once the results of the transactions have been completed, please return the Reference Desk Tabulation Sheets to Dr. Hernon and go over each completed transaction with him. At that time, please share with him your impressions of the way you were treated, the interpersonal communication skills of the librarians tested, the reference interview, librarians' search strategies, and the search outcome. Since we are interested in your subjective assessment of the situation, please record any relevant comments on the Reference Desk Tabulation Sheet.

Thank you for your assistance in data collection.

APPENDIX I

AALS* POLICY STATEMENT ON CONTINUING LIBRARY AND INFORMATION SCIENCE EDUCATION**

BACKGROUND STATEMENT

AALS for some years has shown leadership in its concern for the continuing education of members of the library/media/information science field. In 1972 it adopted one of the first statements on continuing education approved by any library association. The 1973 statement was based on the premise that "present day developments, including changes in our society, the accelerated growth of new knowledge, the implications of new technology, and the increasing demands for additional or changing types of library, information and communication services support the assumption that continuing library education is one of the most important problems facing librarianship today."[1] That first statement addressed the general continuing education concerns of the profession. This revised statement, based on the same assumptions as the 1973 statement, addresses more specifically the role of AALS and its member schools in continuing education.

ROLE OF AALS

The role of AALS is to provide leadership in encouraging library/media/ information programs to provide not only basic education for the profession, but also continuing education programs and activities for the field.

---

* Association of American Library Schools, now Association for Library and Information Science Education.

** Reprinted from *Journal of Education for Librarianship,* 21 (Spring, 1981): 351-352. A position paper developed by AALS 1980-81 Continuing Education Committee. Approved by the AALS Board, June 28, 1981.

[1] AALS Position Paper on Continuing Library and Information Science Education — 1973, p. 1.

Because of this commitment, AALS has responsibilities in the following areas:

Programs and Policies

Encourage library education programs, i.e., library schools, to develop strong continuing education policies including a statement of the school's responsibility and the range of continuing education services.

Encourage examination and adjustment of university reward structures to reflect the importance and academic legitimacy of faculty involvement in the provision of continuing education.

Encourage COA [Committee on Accreditation, ALA] to consider faculty involvement in continuing education important evidence of the 1972 Standards requirement that faculty maintain "close and continuing liaison with the field."[2]

Communication among Organizations

Maintain close alignment, through affiliation and other means, with associations concerned with the continuing education of library and information science personnel to increase communication and solve common problems.

Collaborate with groups from other professions who are concerned with professional continuing education.

Evaluation

Encourage research on methods of improving continuing education needs assessment, delivery, and evaluation.

Encourage the adoption by library education programs of criteria to maintain quality control of continuing education activities.

Faculty Development

Encourage faculty of schools of library and information science to continue their own education.

Provide faculty development opportunities.

Provide opportunities for discussion of continuing education activities and research through mechanisms set up by AALS.

ROLE OF MEMBER SCHOOLS

AALS recommends that member library education programs provide continuing education programs and activities for the field, encourage evaluation of continuing education programming, and foster faculty development.

---

[2] A.L.A. Committee on Accreditation. *Standards for Accreditation,* 1972, p. 7.

Because of this commitment, library schools have the responsibility to encourage students at the master's level to accept responsibility for their continued professional development.

Programs and Policies

Clarify the continuing education role of the school, develop a strong continuing education policy and include it in the goal statement of the school.

Develop a total continuing education program; offer both regular courses and special short term CE offerings at times and places which are convenient to the needs of the continuing education audience.

Assign responsibility for coordination of CE activities.

Provide sufficient human and fiscal resources to assure high quality.

Set priorities appropriate to the needs of the CE audience in the service area.

Communication Outside Library School

Designate appropriate client groups who will be served by the continuing education programs (these may include alumni, library personnel in a specific geographical area, state or national clientele, etc.). Maintain contact with alumni and offer special services that take account of their special talents and needs.

Coordinate planning and priorities with other library continuing education providers and library development planners serving the area.

Collaborate as appropriate with other professional schools and disciplines in the university.

Evaluation

Monitor the quality of continuing education programming offered by the school.

Incorporate practitioner input in the planning and evaluating of continuing education.

Faculty Development

Encourage library/information/media faculty to meet their own learning needs through continued participation in learning opportunities.

BIBLIOGRAPHY

Anderson, Scarvia B. and Samuel Ball. *The Profession and Practice of Program Evaluation.* San Francisco, CA: Jossey-Bass, 1978.

Argyris, Chris. *Strategy, Change and Defensive Routines.* Marshfield, MA: Pitman Publishing Inc., 1985.

Ary, Donald, Lucy C. Jacobs, and Asghar Razavieh. *Introduction to Research in Education.* 3rd ed. New York: Holt, Rinehart and Winston, 1985.

Batt, Fred. "Uneven Reference Service: Approaches for Decreasing This Source of Conflict at the Reference Desk," in *Conflicts in Reference Service,* edited by Bill Katz and Ruth Fraley. New York: Haworth Press, 1985, pp. 49–63.

Battin, Patricia. "Developing University and Research Library Professionals: A Director's Perspective," *American Libraries,* 14 (January 1983): 22–25.

Blalock, Hubert M., Jr. *Conceptualization and Measurement in the Social Sciences.* Beverly Hills, CA: Sage Publications, 1982.

Borgman, Christine L. *End User Behavior on the Ohio State University Libraries' Online Catalog: A Computer Monitoring Study.* Dublin, OH: OCLC Online Computer Library Center, Inc., 1983 [report number OCLC/OPR/RR-83-7].

Bower, Gordon H., Kenneth P. Monteiro, and Stephen G. Gilligan. "Emotional Mood as a Context for Learning and Recall," *Journal of Verbal Learning and Verbal Behavior,* 17 (October 1978): 573–585.

Bundy, Mary Lee and Amy Bridgman. "A Community Based Approach to Evaluation of Public Library Reference Service," *The Reference Librarian,* 11 (Fall/Winter 1984): 159–174.

Burks, Mary Paxton. *Requirements for Certification.* 15th ed. Chicago, IL: University of Chicago Press, 1985.

Carmines, Edward G. and Richard A. Zeller. *Reliability and Validity Assessment.* Beverly Hills, CA: Sage Publications, 1979.

Chase, Clinton I. *Elementary Statistical Procedures.* 2nd ed. New York: McGraw-Hill, 1976.

Chen, Ching-chih and Peter Hernon. *Information Seeking: Assessing and Anticipating User Needs.* New York: Neal-Schuman, 1982.

Childers, Thomas A. *The Effectiveness of Information Service in Public Libraries: Suffolk Co., Final Report.* Philadelphia, PA: School of Library and Information Science, Drexel University, 1978.

_____. *Information and Referral: Public Libraries.* Norwood, NJ: Ablex Pub. Corp., 1984.

_____. "The Test of Reference," *Library Journal,* 105 (April 15, 1980): 924–928.

_____. "Trends in Public Library I&R Services," *Library Journal,* 104 (October 1, 1979:2035–2039.

_____. "A Commitment to Information Services: Developmental Guidelines." Chicago, IL: American Library Association, Reference and Adult Services Division, 1979.

Continuing Library Education Network and Exchange, Inc. *Program for Quality in Continuing Education for Information, Library, and Media Personnel: Policy Statement. Criteria for Quality and Provider Approval System.* Washington, D.C.: National Council on Quality Continuing Education Information, Library, Media Personnel, 1980.

_____. *Voluntary Recognition Service.* Washington, D.C.: Continuing Library Education Network and Exchange, Inc., 1981.

Conroy, Barbara. *Library Staff Development and Continuing Education: Principles and Practices.* Littleton, CO: Libraries Unlimited, 1978.

Crowley, Terence. "Half-Right Reference: Is It True?," *RQ,* 25 (Fall 1985): 59–68.

_____ and Thomas Childers. *Information Service in Public Libraries: Two Studies.* Metuchen, NJ: Scarecrow Press, 1971.

DeWath, Nancy. "The Return on the Investment in Library Education," *Library and Information Science Research,* 7 (January-March 1985): 31–52.

Donald, Archie. "On the Stating of Goals," *Journal of Systems Engineering,* 4 (January 1976): 89–95.

DuMont, Rosemary Ruhig. "Continuing Education and the State Library Agency," in *State Library Services and Issues,* edited by Charles R. McClure. Norwood, NJ: Ablex Pub. Corp., 1986, pp. 114–131.

Edgar, Neal L. and Rosemary D. Herrick. "Thoughts on Policy Manuals for Reference Services," in *Reference Services Administration and Management,* edited by Bill Katz and Ruth A. Fraley. New York: Haworth Press, 1982, pp. 55–60.

Epstein, Irwin and Tony Tripodi. *Research Techniques for Program Planning, Monitoring, and Evaluation.* New York: Columbia University Press, 1977.

Gers, Ralph and Lillie J. Seward. "Improving Reference Performance, Results of a Statewide Study," *Library Journal,* 110 (November 1, 1985): 32–35.

Goodell, John S. *Libraries and Work Sampling.* Littleton, CO: Libraries Unlimited, 1975.

Gothberg, Helen M. *User Satisfaction and Librarian's Immediate and Non-Immediate Verbal-Non Verbal Communications.* Ph.D. dissertation. Denver, CO: University of Denver, 1974.

Government Depository Libraries. Washington, D.C.: GPO, 1983.

Guba, Egon G. and Yvonna S. Lincoln. *Effective Evaluation.* San Francisco, CA: Jossey-Bass, 1981.

Guidelines for the Depository Library System. Washington, D.C.: Government Printing Office, 1977.

Hannigan, Jane Anne. "Vision to Purpose to Power: A Quest for Excellence in the Education of Library and Information Science Professionals," in *Libraries and the Learning Society: Papers in Response to a Nation at Risk.* Chicago, IL: American Library Association, 1984, pp. 22–62.

Hernon, Peter. "Academic Library Reference Service for the Publications of Municipal, State, and Federal Government: A Historical Perspective Spanning the Years up to 1962," *Government Publications Review,* 5 (1978): 31–50.

_____. *Use of Government Publications by Social Scientists.* Norwood, NJ: Ablex Pub. Corp., 1979.

_____ and Charles R. McClure, ed. *Microcomputers for Library Decision Making.* Norwood, NJ: Ablex Pub. Corp., 1986.

_____ and _____. *Public Access to Government Information: Issues, Trends, and Strategies.* Norwood, NJ: Ablex Pub. Corp., 1984.

_____, _____, and Gary R. Purcell. *GPO's Depository Library Program.* Norwood, NJ: Ablex Pub. Co., 1985.

Holmes, David S. "Defense Mechanisms," in *Encyclopedia of Psychology,* edited by Raymond J. Corsini. New York: John Wiley & Sons, 1984, pp. 347–350.

Jaeger, Richard M. *Statistics: A Spectator Sport.* Beverly Hills, CA: Sage, 1983.

Jick, Todd D. "Mixing Qualitative and Quantitative Methods: Triangulation in Action," in *Qualitative Methodology,* edited by John Van Maanen. Beverly Hills, CA: Sage, 1983, pp. 135–147.

Kantor, Paul. *Objective Performance Measures for Academic and Research Libraries.* Washington, D.C.: Association of Research Libraries, 1984.

Kaplan, Abraham. *The Conduct of Inquiry: Methodology for Behavior Science.* Scranton, PA: Chandler Pub. Co., 1964.

Kast, Fremont E. and James E. Rosenzweig. *Organization and Management: A Systems and Contingency Approach.* 3rd edition. New York: McGraw-Hill, 1979.

Katz, William A. *Introduction to Reference Work. Vol. II: Reference Services and Reference Process.* 4th edition. New York: McGraw-Hill, 1982.

_____ and Ruth A. Fraley, ed. *Evaluation of Reference Services.* New York: Haworth Press, 1984.

_____ and _____. *Reference Services Administration and Management.* New York: Haworth Press, 1982.

Kerlinger, Fred N. *Foundations of Behavioral Research.* 2nd ed. New York: Holt, Rinehart and Winston, 1973.

King, G. B. and L. R. Berry. "Evaluation of the University of Minnesota Libraries' Reference Department Telephone Information Service, Pilot Study." Minneapolis, MN: University of Minnesota, Library School, 1973 (ED 077 517).

Krathwohl, David R. *Social and Behavioral Science Research.* San Francisco, CA: Jossey Bass, 1985.

Lancaster, F. W. "Factors Influencing the Effectiveness of Question-Answering Services in Libraries," in *Evaluation of Reference Service,* edited by Bill Katz and Ruth A. Fraley. New York: Haworth Press, 1984, pp. 95–108.

_____. *The Measurement and Evaluation of Library Services.* Washington, D.C.: Information Resources Press, 1977.

Lynch, Mary Jo. "Reference Interviews in Public Libraries," *Library Quarterly*, 48 (April 1978): 119-141.

McClure, Charles R. "A View from the Trenches: Costing and Performance Measures for Academic Library Public Services, *College and Research Libraries*, 47 (July 1986): 323-336.

————. "Online Government Documents Data Base Searching and the Use of Microfiche Documents Online by Academic and Public Depository Librarians," *Microform Review* 10 (Fall 1981): 245-259.

————. "Output Measures, Unobtrusive Testing, and Assessing the Quality of Reference Services," *The Reference Librarian*, 11 (Fall/Winter 1984): 215-233.

———— and Peter Hernon. *Improving the Quality of Reference Service for Government Publications.* Chicago, IL: American Library Association, 1983.

————, ————, and Gary R. Purcell. *Linking the U.S. National Technical Information Service with Academic and Public Libraries.* Norwood, NJ: Ablex Pub. Corp., 1986.

———— and Betsy Reifsnyder. "Performance Measures for Corporate Information Centers," *Special Libraries*, 75 (1984): 193-204.

———— and Alan R. Samuels. "Factors Affecting the Use of Information for Academic Library Decision Making," *College and Research Libraries*, 46 (November 1985): 483-498.

Miles, Matthew B. and A. Michael Huberman. *Qualitative Data Analysis: A Sourcebook of New Methods.* Beverly Hills, CA: Sage, 1984.

Miller, William. "What's Wrong with Reference: Coping with Success and Failure at the Reference Desk," *American Libraries*, 15 (May 1984): 303-306, 321.

Mullins, Lynn S. and Richard E. Kopelman. "Unobtrusive Research," *Library Journal*, 111 (March 15, 1986): 35-38.

Myers, Marcia. "The Accuracy of Telephone Reference Services in the Southeast: A Case for Quantitative Standards," in *Library Effectiveness: A State of the Art.* Chicago, IL: Library Administration and Management Association, American Library Association, 1980.

————. "The Effectiveness of Telephone Reference/Information Services in Academic Libraries in the Southeast" Ph.D. dissertation, Florida State University, 1979.

Nachmias, David and Chava Nachmias. *Research Methods in the Social Sciences.* 2nd edition. New York: St. Martin's Press, 1981.

Nelkin, Dorothy. *Science as Intellectual Property.* New York: Macmillan, 1984.

Nunally, Jum C. *Psychometric Theory.* New York: McGraw-Hill, 1967.

Olson, Linda M. "Reference Service Evaluation in Medium-Sized Academic Libraries: A Model," *Journal of Academic Librarianship*, 9 (January 1984): 322-329.

Paisley, William J. *Behavioral Studies on Scientific Information Flow: An Appendix on Method.* New London, NH: Gordon Research Conference on Scientific Method, July 14-18, 1969 (mimeographed).

Palmour, Vernon E., Marcia C. Bellassai, and Nancy V. deWath. *A Planning Process for Public Libraries.* Chicago, IL: American Library Association, 1980.

Patton, Michael Quinn. *Practical Evaluation.* Beverly Hills, CA: Sage, 1982.

Peters, Thomas J. and Robert H. Waterman, Jr. *In Search of Excellence.* New York: Warner Books, 1982.

Plotnick, Art. "Half-Right Reference," *American Libraries*, 16 (May 1985): 227.

"Policy Statement on Continuing Library and Information Science Education," *Journal of Education for Librarianship*, 21 (Spring 1981): 351-352.

Powell, Ronald R. "Reference Effectiveness: A Review of Research," *Library and Information Science Research*, 6 (1984): 3-19.

"Requirements for Recertification of Health Sciences Librarians." Chicago, IL: Medical Library Association, n.d.

Richardson, John V., Jr., Dennis C. W. Frisch, and Catherine M. Hall. "Bibliographic Organization of U.S. Federal Depository Collections," *Government Publications Review*, 7A (1980): 463-480.

Riggs, Donald E. *Strategic Planning for Library Managers.* Phoenix, AZ: Oryx Press, 1984.

Roscoe, John T. *Fundamental Research Statistics for the Behavioral Sciences* (2nd ed.). New York: Holt, Rinehart, Winston, 1975.

Rossi, Peter H. and Howard E. Freeman. *Evaluation: A Systematic Approach.* 3rd edition. Beverly Hills, CA: Sage, 1985.

Rothstein, Samuel. "The Measurement and Evaluation of Reference Service," *Library Trends*, 12 (1964): 456-472.

Rutman, Leonard. *Evaluation Research Methods.* 2nd edition. Beverly Hills, CA: Sage, 1984.

Samuels, Alan R. "Microcomputers in Public Library Reference Work: A Rationale and Some Suggestions," in *Microcomputers for Library Decision Making,* edited by Peter Hernon and Charles R. McClure. Norwood, NJ: Ablex Pub. Corp., 1986, pp. 169–182.

―――――. "Organizational Climate and Change," in *Stategies for Library Administration,* edited by Charles R. McClure and Alan R. Samuels. Littleton, CO: Libraries Unlimited, 1982, pp. 421–431.

―――――― and Charles R. McClure. "Utilization of Information for Decision Making under Varying Organizational Climate Conditions in Public Libraries," *Journal of Library Administration,* 4 (1983): 1–20.

"Scholarly Associations Take New Interest in Writing Codes of Professional Ethics," *The Chronicle of Higher Education* (February 6, 1985), pp. 1, 8.

Schrader, Alvin M. "Performance Standards for Accuracy in Reference and Information Services: The Impact of Unobtrusive Measurement Methodology," *The Reference Librarian,* 11 (Fall/Winter 1984): 197–214.

Schwartz, Diane G. and Dottie Eakin. "Reference Service Standards Performance Criteria, and Evaluation," *Journal of Academic Librarianship,* 12 (March 1986): 4–8.

Siegel, Sidney. *Nonparametric Statistics for the Behavioral Sciences.* New York: McGraw-Hill, 1956.

Spector, Paul E. *Research Designs.* Beverly Hills, CA: Sage, 1981.

Statistical Abstract of the United States. Washington D.C.: Government Printing Office, 1984.

StatPac — Statistical Analysis Package Manual. Minneapolis, MN: Walonick Associates, 1985.

Staw, Barry M., Lance E. Sandelands, and Jane E. Dutton. "Threat-Rigidity Effects in Organizational Behavior: A Multilevel Analysis," *Administrative Quarterly,* 26 (December 1981): 501–524.

Stone, Elizabeth W., Ruth J. Patrick, and Barbara Conroy. *Continuing Library and Information Science Education: Final Report to the National Commission on Libraries and Information Science.* Washington, D.C.: Government Printing Office, 1974.

Stueart, Robert D. "Education for Librarianship: The Way It is," in *The ALA Yearbook of Library and Information Services,* vol. 9, edited by Robert Wedgeworth. Chicago, IL: American Library Association, 1984, pp. 1–8.

Swisher, Robert and Charles R. McClure. *Research for Decision Making: Methods for Librarians.* Chicago, IL: American Library Association, 1984.

Tagiuri, R. and G. H. Litwin. *Organizational Climate: Explorations of a Concept.* Boston, MA: Division of Research, Graduate School of Business Administration, Harvard University, 1968.

Tolle, John E. *Current Utilization of Online Catalogs: Transaction Log Analysis.* Dublin, OH: OCLC Online Computer Library Center, Inc., 1983 [report number OCLC/OPR/RR-83/2].

Trueswell, Richard W. "Some Behavioral Patterns of Library Users: the 80/20 Rule," *Wilson Library Bulletin,* 43 (1969): 458–461.

Tuckman, Bruce W. *Conducting Educational Research.* 2nd edition. New York: Harcourt Brace Jovanovich, 1978.

Vavrek, Bernard. "The Accreditation of Reference Services," in *Evaluation of Reference Services,* edited by Bill Katz and Ruth Fraley. New York: Haworth Press, 1984, pp. 147–156.

Vertrees, Robert L. and Marjorie E. Murfin. "Teaching the Legislative Process: An Evaluation of Classroom and Library Instruction and a Legislative History Exercise," *Government Publications Review,* 7A (1980): 505–515.

Walton, Richard E. "Strategies with Dual Difference," in *Doing Research That Is Useful for Theory and Practice,* edited by Edward E. Lawler III, Allan M. Mohrman, Jr., Susan A. Mohrman, Gerald E. Ledford, Jr., Thomas G. Cummings, and Associates. San Francisco, CA: Jossey Bass, 1985, pp. 176–203.

Webb, Eugene J., Donald T. Campbell, Richard D. Schwartz, and Lee Sechrest. *Unobtrusive Measures: Nonreactive Research in the Social Sciences,* Chicago, IL: Rand McNally, 1966.

Weech, Terry L. "Evaluation of Adult Reference Service," *Library Trends,* 22 (1974): 315–335.

Weick, Karl E. "Small Wins: Redefining the Scale of Social Problems," *American Psychologist,* 39 (January 1984): 40–49.

Weiss, Carol H. *Evaluation Research: Methods of Assessing Program Effectiveness.* Englewood Cliffs, NJ: Prentice Hall, 1972.

Whitbeck, George W. and Peter Hernon. "The Attitudes of Librarians toward the Servicing and Use of Government Publications: A Survey of Federal Depositories in Four Midwestern States," *Government Publications Review,* 4 (1977a): 183–199.

————, and ——————. "Bibliographic Instruction in Government Publications: Lecture Programs and Their Evaluation in American Academic Depository Libraries," *Government Publications Review,* 4 (1977b): 1-11.

Willet, Holly G. "Certification and Education for Library and Information Science," *Journal of Education for Library and Information Science,* 25 (Summer, 1984): 13-23.

Williams, Saundra and Eric Wedig. "Improving Government Information and Documents Reference Skills through a Staff Development Program," *RQ,* 24 (Winter 1984): 143-145.

Winkler, Karen J. "Brouhaha over Historian's Use of Sources Renews Scholars' Interest in Ethics Codes," *The Chronicle of Higher Education* (February 6, 1985), pp. 1, 8, and 9.

Witka, D. K. *Handbook of Measurement and Assessment in Behavior Sciences,* 2nd ed. Reading, MA: Addison-Wesley, 1968.

Yin, Robert K. *Case Study Research: Design and Methods.* Beverly Hills, CA: Sage, 1984.

Young, William F. "Methods for Evaluating Reference Desk Performance," *RQ,* 25 (Fall 1985): 69-75.

Zaltman, Gerald and Robert Duncan. *Strategies for Planned Change.* New York: Wiley, 1977.

Zweizig, Douglas and Eleanor Jo Rodger. *Output Measures for Public Libraries.* Chicago, IL: American Library Association, 1982.

NAME/SUBJECT/TITLE INDEX